Arm Action, Arm Path, and the Perfect Pitch: Building a Million-Dollar Arm

A Science-Based Guide to Pitching Health and Performance

Tom House
Doug Thorburn

COACHES CHOICE™

ISBN: 978-1-60679-042-7
Library of Congress Control Number: 2008943774
Cover design: Roger W. Rybkowski
Book layout: Roger W. Rybkowski
Front cover photo: G Fiume/Getty Images

Coaches Choice
P.O. Box 1828
Monterey, CA 93942
www.coacheschoice.com

This book is written for those pitchers, parents, and coaches who are looking for information and instruction that can have a positive impact on their baseball lives.

Dedication

Acknowledgments

We would like to thank everyone who helped with this project, directly and indirectly, including: Jim Peterson, Matthew Richards, Karl Meinhardt, Ryan Sienko, Eric Andrews, Marie House, Adam Meinhardt, Cole Hamels, Dan Giese, Chad Wolff, Jackson Crowther, Billy Beane, Gary Arthur, Alan Ledford, Mike Gazda, John Bava, Kevin Hilton, Perry Husband, Vilayanur Ramachandran, Lee Flippin, Dudley Tabakin, Alan Blitzblau, Doug Bird, Joe Donohue, Garrett Boetzer, Mike Swor, Eric Young, Tim Denevi, and Victoria Thorburn.

Contents

Foreword

The pages in this remarkable resource, *Arm Action, Arm Path, and the Perfect Pitch* offer a perfect blend of medical science, exercise science, and coaching science. It's a book that clarifies conventional wisdom about pitching and quantifies three-dimensional motion-analysis research on the mechanics of a pitcher's delivery.

Currently, I am a Major League pitcher with the Philadelphia Phillies. I am also a walking, talking, pitching example of how sports medicine and sports science can successfully work together.

On July 10, 2000, I broke my arm pitching a baseball and had corrective surgery one week later. At any other time before 2000, it probably would have been the end of my baseball career and my dreams of pitching in the Major Leagues. As bad as my injury was and as frustrated and scared as I was, all factors considered, it was the right time to get hurt. As luck would have it, the medical and surgical expertise of Dr. Jan Froenick repaired my arm. Subsequently, the hard work and the rehabilitation expertise of the Scripps Clinic and the National Pitching Association helped me recover and rebuild my arm and body with functional strength, flexibility, endurance, and stamina. The final piece involved helping me to understand the three-dimensional motion analysis of my delivery. This step helped me master the mechanics of an efficient delivery so I could continue to compete and perform with a healthy arm. It also gave me the confidence that I would not reinjure myself.

Obviously, a lot of things came together for me at the right time and place. That's what this book is designed to do for you as a coach, a parent, or a player. Tom House and Doug Thorburn have put together a great manuscript. It's a must read for anyone involved in the game of baseball, especially pitchers and pitching coaches. Good luck and good reading!

—Cole Hamels

It has been over two years since the publication of our last book on pitching. During this period, a lot has happened, and a lot has changed.

Looking at the baseball landscape, we can be certain of at least one thing—the integration of medical science, exercise science, and coaching science has affected the paradigm on how pitchers should prepare, compete, and repair. Obviously, we feel these changes are significant enough to warrant writing a new book.

The National Pitching Association (NPA) has combined forces with the Rod Dedeaux Research and Baseball Institute (RDRBI) at Dedeaux Field on the campus at the University of Southern California. It has also added another ML pitcher, two orthopedic surgeons, an exercise physiologist from Australia, and an NFL quarterback to its Board of Advisors. We firmly believe that these changes have enhanced our ability to develop a science-based approach to efficient, effective pitching, one that is complemented by sports-science protocols that are designed to help prevent injury.

The NPA also moved its human performance motion-analysis lab to USC. Our research efforts, along with outside advancements in sports science, have helped facilitate the evolution of information, insights, and instructional techniques concerning pitching health and performance. In that regard, the ongoing interaction with our Board of Advisors, combined with our increased R&D capacity (especially with Greg Rose at the Titleist Performance Institute) is providing us a better understanding of what constitutes efficient pitching "signatures." Being able to identify timing and kinematic-sequencing flaws in a delivery has significantly improved the quality and focus of our instruction with regard to both mechanics drills and functional strength training.

Another significant benefit of relocating our performance lab to Dedeaux Field was its impact on opening lines of communication with a number of non-baseball related professionals within the USC community, including physicians, kinesiologists, and exercise physiologists. To our knowledge, it's the first time on-the-field coaching science and in-the-lab medical science have ever co-researched and published.

Finally, we had the unique challenge of working with two young athletes from the country of India, neither of whom had ever played baseball, let alone pitched. Over a period of approximately six months, their hard work and dedication, in concert with the efforts of our staff, transformed them into legitimate professional prospects. Fittingly, they were highly scouted and showed enough skill and projectibility to sign with the

Pittsburgh Pirates. This international "first" gives us even more confidence that we are on the right path with our biomechanical, physical, nutritional, and mental/emotional coaching content, curriculum, progressions, and protocols.

In *Arm Path, Arm Action, and the Perfect Pitch,* we openly share with you everything new we've learned in the last two years. Hopefully, you will enjoy reading the text as much as we enjoyed writing it.

Yours in baseball,

Tom House
Doug Thorburn

NPA/RDRBT
NationalPitching.com/RDRBI.com
Advisory Board

Arnel Aguinaldo	Todd Durkin	Dr. Charles Preston
Dr. James Andrews	Glenn Fleisig	Mark Prior
Dusty Baker	Dr. Rick Heitsch	Anthony Reyes
Alan Blitzblau	Orel Hershiser	Dr. Greg Rose
Drew Brees	Dr. Tom House	Nolan Ryan
Jim Brogan	Randy Johnson	Bobby Valentine
Dr. Hank Chambers	Dr. Tim Kremchek	Simon Webb
Dr. John Conway	Dr. Todd Lanman	Dr. Lewis Yocum
Dave Dravecky	Robb Nen	John Young

INTRODUCTION

1

Conventional Wisdom

"Baseball is a game of failure, coached by negative people, in a misinformation environment."
                                                                —Tom House

I use the aforementioned quote in camps, clinics, and consults around the baseball world. It always gets a laugh *and* a raised eyebrow, because, unfortunately, it's true. A coach's role is to inform, instruct, and inspire athletes to be the best they can possibly be—biomechanically, physically, nutritionally, and/or, mentally/emotionally. Coaching with good intentions isn't enough, however. Never, in 40+ years of baseball, have I met a coach who intentionally tried to diminish an athlete's performance or hurt a player. On the other hand, bad information, even if it's swathed in nothing but good intentions, can impede performance and cause injury.

Given the importance of sound information, this chapter reviews a relatively extensive list of conventional wisdoms about pitching. Conventional wisdoms concerning pitching are often based on what the human eye can process at 32 frames per second (which is the maximum an eye can see). With regard to pitching, this factor can be a problem because the most crucial movements in a pitcher's delivery take place at 1/250th to 1/750th of a second. Examples of commonly held conventional wisdom concerning pitching include the following:

- Stay tall and fall
- Pitching is an unnatural movement
- Left-hander left side of the rubber
- Right-hander right side of the rubber
- Stop at the top
- Stay back for better balance
- Stay balanced over the rubber
- Don't rush
- Drop and drive
- Push off the rubber

- Don't stride across your body
- Step straight to the plate
- Don't open up your stride
- Point your toe to home plate
- Land on the ball of your foot
- Don't land on your heel
- Shorten your stride
- Break your throwing hand to second base, your glove to the plate
- Pull your glove to your hip
- Figure-8 your arms
- Captains-wheel your arms
- Get on top of the ball to create a downward angle
- Thumb to the thigh—ball to the sky
- Reach back
- Don't short-arm
- Don't throw sidearm
- Throwing a curveball hurts your arm
- Throwing a splitfinger hurts your arm
- Bend your back
- Reach down and grab grass/dirt

Given this list of thirty examples, it can be helpful to review what coaches typically teach their pitchers, based on the aforementioned conventional wisdoms:

- Balance:
  - ✓ The knee is up and at or behind the midline of the body
  - ✓ The hands are high and behind the midline
  - ✓ The back knee is parallel to the rubber
- Hand break:
  - ✓ The hands break before the lift knee starts down, or before the lower body goes forward
  - ✓ The fingers are on top of the ball when the hand is breaking
- Arm path:
  - ✓ The fingers are on top, with the pinky leading; get the hand outside the elbow as quickly as possible
  - ✓ Get flexion in the elbow on the way up; the hand raises the arm
  - ✓ Fluid arm in an L-shape, with the hand stacked on the elbow, and the elbow above the shoulder; the ball pointed to either the SS (RHP) or to the 2B (LHP)
- Front foot lands:
  - ✓ The throwing arm in an L-shape, with the hand above the elbow and the elbow above the shoulder

- ✓ The elbow and glove are inside the front shoulder, with the glove palm up
- ✓ The landing foot is in direct line with the pivot foot
- Upper-body finish:
  - ✓ The shoulders rotate
  - ✓ The lead elbow is down and past the hip pocket
  - ✓ The fingers stay behind the ball
  - ✓ The ball is released in front of the chin; the shoulder, elbow, and wrist are hinge joints
  - ✓ The throwing hand should finish below and outside the knee
- Lower-body finish:
  - ✓ The backside foot has pivoted; the weight is on the ball of the foot; the shoelaces are down
  - ✓ The frontside leg is flexed
  - ✓ The backside knee points to home plate; the knee drives forward

It is safe to say everyone (me included) has taught, or are teaching, some of the points on these two lists. Truth be known, I am both proud and embarrassed to admit that a few of them are mine. The fact of the matter is, however, *nothing* on either of these lists can be supported as a legitimate "teach" by current research. Welcome to the "how can this be" world of science-based information and instruction. On the other hand, for the game of baseball to evolve to where it should be, relying on the misinformation that is inherent in conventional wisdoms must end.

Typically, conventional wisdom has been defined as an opinion that has been repeated so often by so many people for so long that it has subsequently become accepted as *fact.* In turn, baseball coaches tended to teach based on what they (think) they see. This disconnect is the primary source of the underlying problem. Not only are coaches faced with a mountain of misinformation, they also don't actually see everything that they feel that they see.

As was discussed previously, the human eye can interpret movements at approximately 32 frames per second. As such, anything faster, and the brain is actually *processing a guess.* Because of this factor, contemporary video, DVD, television, and motion picture imagery are only projected at 32 frames per second, even though technology can provide exponentially more in the same timeframe. This concept can be illustrated, to a point, by considering a car commercial on TV. While the car is traveling at 60 mph, the wheels/tires look like they are slow, stopped, or going backward. This visual illusion occurs because the camera is only picking up the movement at 32 frames per second—exactly what a coach's eyes do when they watch a pitcher throw a baseball.

The disconnect? Three-dimensional motion-analysis technology reveals that the critical movements in a delivery take place at 1/250–1/750 of a second.

The data, however, is being processed by the brain with a visual of 32 frames per second. It's safe to say that the hand is quicker than the eye, but 1000 frames per second don't lie.

The bottom line is straightforward. If pitching coaches are to fulfill their rightful responsibilities, they must take advantage of the technology that is available and use science-based information to validate their instruction protocols. In reality, no one way exists to teach a perfect delivery. On the other hand, with the right information, instruction, and inspiration, every pitcher has a delivery that can be individualized to be perfect for him.

Doug and I have written this manuscript, *Arm Action, Arm Path, and the Perfect Pitch,* in the hope that it will become the science-based guide to pitching health and performance for baseball coaches, parents, and athletes at all competitive levels. The primary format of the book is a dialogue (between Doug and myself) in which we correlate information from three-dimensional, high-speed, motion-analysis research that has been conducted (by both the NPA and the RDRBI) on the biomechanics of a delivery with cross-specifically valid, on-the-field instruction. As such, one of our main goals is to systematically invalidate those conventional wisdoms that are without merit.

Pitcher Evaluation—On and Off the Field

☛ *Doug:* When talking to a scout or a pitching coach about mechanics, you are likely to hear that a particular player either has a "clean, smooth" delivery, or that the pitcher has "violent" mechanics. You might learn that an athlete has "great arm action," a "deceptive delivery," or creates a lot of "downward plane." All of these terms have meaning to scouts and coaches, but their definitions may differ, depending on whom you ask.

To many individuals who study the game of baseball from off the field, these terms are part of the accepted vernacular when describing pitchers, yet these expressions don't contribute to the understanding of how a pitcher succeeds on the mound. This situation can be frustrating and baffling to those individuals who are trying to learn the mechanical aspects of playing the game. What makes up a "smooth" delivery? What is "violent" about a particular player's mechanics? What constitutes "great arm action?" What makes a delivery "deceptive?" How does a pitcher create "downward plane," and why is it an advantage?

In fact, the standard lingo that is typically used to describe pitching mechanics creates a vague representation of how a pitcher accomplishes his craft. The terms that encompass this jargon are passed down without any kind of standard definition. Furthermore, their meaning is left to the interpretation of each individual talent evaluator. One scout's impression of a "violent" delivery might match another scout's opinion of "deception." One coach could define "great arm action" as following a "smooth" arm path, while another coach's definition of "good arm action" could be construed as "violent" by his colleagues.

An excellent example of the inconsistency of how different descriptive terms are applied to baseball can be seen with the use of the words "command" and "control." These two words are used by almost everybody to describe a pitcher's ability to locate the baseball. However, many people conceptualize these two terms in a vastly different way, while some individuals employ these words interchangeably in order to describe the ability of a pitcher who throws strikes and therefore doesn't walk many hitters.

At the NPA, command is detailed as the best weapon in a pitcher's arsenal (i.e., a "command pitch" that he can consistently locate whenever it is necessary). To pitch effectively in the Major Leagues, a player ideally needs to have great command of three different pitches. In contrast, control refers to those weapons in a pitcher's arsenal that are effective on any given day, given that a pitcher's "stuff" will often vary widely from one outing to another. For example, he may have control of his curveball on one particular day, but can't seem to harness his changeup. And yet, when this pitcher gets behind in the count with runners on the corners, he may need to go to his command pitch, which is—in his case—a fastball. These definitions, designed by Tom, may help explain the concepts of command and control from the point of view of one pitching coach, but by no means are these explanations standard nomenclature for all professional pitching coaches.

In contrast, analyst Kevin Goldstein of Baseball *Prospectus* offers the following distinction between these terms (Goldstein, 2006):

"On the most basic of levels.
  - *Control: not walking batters*
  - *Command: working effectively IN the zone (i.e., using all four quadrants, painting the corner, not throwing 93 mph fastballs down the pipe)."*

Goldstein is a widely respected expert on performance analysis, who skillfully combines the tools of performance stats and scouting reports to evaluate Minor League players and draft prospects. Goldstein also speaks to countless scouts through his quest for information (in addition to the aforementioned tools). All factors considered, it can reasonably be concluded that these terms were not pulled out of thin air. Kevin's descriptions provide a logical way to define command vs. control. It also details two truly different skills, given that strike percentage is not always the best indicator of how well a player spots his pitches. It is much more informative to watch the catcher's glove—from ball release until the catch—to see how far the catcher has to move his mitt from its original spot at setup. All factors considered, this step clearly shows how far the pitcher missed the intended target, which is a far better indicator of pitch command than just charting balls and strikes.

Both the NPA definition and the definition outlined by Goldstein are useful when studying pitchers. As such, neither is necessarily superior to the other. Ideally, these ideas can be incorporated together into a consistent language, which would then be used by the baseball community to communicate more effectively. In fact, applying Goldstein's definition of "command" and charting those pitches that consistently hit or miss the glove can help easily identify a player's "command pitch." It can also help determine which pitches a pitcher can "control" on a particular day. As such, the interplay of these ideas can help coaches and athletes alike learn even more about a pitcher's ability.

In reality, the currently accepted terminology with regard to pitching (especially mechanics) is inconsistent at best, and contradictive at worst. Most of the standard scouting and coaching language is simply subjective, creating a situation in which interpretation is left to the mind of the beholder.

In a similar vein, dozens of coaching theories exist with respect to ideal pitching mechanics. Like most folk tales, these theories have been accepted over time due to their repeated use over generations of pitching coaches. Much of this conventional wisdom has never been tested. Frankly, it seems to have survived largely because the resources necessary to truly analyze its validity and the resolute will to undertake the process to verify (or refute) it have been sorely lacking. This conventional wisdom has been perpetuated, based on theories that are unproven. Over time, this wisdom has become accepted truth, despite the lack of validation. In fact, this misinformation and mythology have become so rampant that even Little League coaches and dads can be heard repeating and teaching methodology to young pitchers that is grounded in conventional wisdom that was absorbed through the baseball grapevine. The good news is that the technology and the knowledge necessary to objectively study these myths now exists—a situation that opened up an entirely new realm of baseball research.

2

Motion Analysis

Tom's History with Motion-Analysis Technology

☛ *Tom:* We thought it would be appropriate, at this point, to give a brief personal and professional history with the evolution of three-dimensional motion-analysis technology and the development of a science-based pitching model. In essence, the situation involved the following timeline:

1970–1986 San Diego School of Baseball:

- First biomechanical model

1987 Arial Systems:

- Objective: Identifying a three-dimensional motion-analysis model of hitters and pitchers
- Methodology: To study the best, determine what they have in common, and then use a regression analysis to identify critical variables
- Early observations: Nolan 1988 vs. Nolan 1989 and the importance of balance and posture

1988–2000 Biokinetics and Biokinetics West:

- Validating the model with more data capture and three-dimensional analyses

2002–Present National Pitching Association:

- Testing existing theories about pitching
- Quantifying four legs of the health and performance table:
  - ✓ Biomechanics and 3-D motion analysis
  - ✓ Functional strength, flexibility, testing, and training

- ✓ Nutrition and metabolic management to prepare, compete, and repair (recover)
- ✓ Mental/emotional approach to hitters, a method for dealing with competition, adversity management, motivation to learn, and work toward success

2005–Present   Titleist Performance Institute:

- Collaboration on efforts to define the signature of rotational athletes

2007–Present   Rod Dedeaux Research and Baseball Institute:

- Integration of coaching science, exercise science, and medical science
- Screening, testing, assessing, and training for performance and health

Other Assessment Tools and Measurement Systems:

- S.T.A.T. (screening weak links, testing athleticism, assessing movement efficiencies for functional strength, and flexibility training)
- S.T.A.R. profile (mental/emotional management for stress and anxiety)
- Nutrition scanning (metabolic management for blood and brain chemistry)

I was still pitching with the Braves in the early 1970s, when I started off-season work with the San Diego School of Baseball. The group and its guest faculty formed one of the original baseball schools. More than that, its ownership included a great group of baseball minds: Roger Craig, Bob Skinner, Bob Cluck, Reggie Waller, Brent Strom, Glenn Ezell, and eventually Tim Flannery, Tony Gywnn, Alan Trammel, and Dave Smith. All of us were Major League players and/or coaches, who were continually searching for ever more information and instruction to help ourselves and our athletes stay healthy and perform better.

Our initial motion analysis employed standard, 6mm film, which we would either slow-mo or stop by hand, oftentimes burning holes in the film. At the time, the situation involved lots of great discussions and a lot of new thinking. One paradigm shift that sticks out in my mind was the night we noticed that all pitchers created movement on the ball with a straight, but angled, wrist into the release point and then pronated their palm, wrist, and forearm after the release point on all pitches, even a curveball. In response, we started teaching using a karate chop, rather than bending the wrist or snapping the fingers, on breaking balls. We also widened or split the fingers on the baseball so that our Little Leaguers could throw an off-speed pitch with the same motion as their fastballs. Roger Craig actually took that "teach" to the Major Leagues, as the Detroit Tigers' pitching coach, with great success. During his tenure in Detroit, the Tigers won the World Series in 1984. Subsequently, the split-fingered fastball has become an off-speed staple for pitchers at all levels of the game. For those of us involved in new ways to enhance performance, it was an exciting time, given that video/computer technology and exercise science were beginning to influence all sports.

In the winter of 1986-'87 a buddy of mine, Coop DeRenne, who was the pitching coach and an exercise physiology professor at the University of Hawaii, told me about a new technology in which I might be interested—high speed, three-dimensional motion analysis. He was convinced that it would be the next-level coaching tool. We looked at a Kodak system in Arlington, Texas (where I was the pitching coach with the Rangers) and an Ariel System at Vic Braden's Tennis Center in Cota De Caza, California. Ultimately, we bought the Ariel System, and by season's end (1987), Coop, myself, Dr. Tony Stellar, and a newly titled biomechanist, Alan Blitzblau, founded BioKinetics, Inc., a motion-analysis company in Irvine, California.

We started filming, digitizing, and analyzing pitchers and hitters from all over baseball. By the spring of 1988, we had captured a large enough sample of Major Leaguers in the computer to quantify an objective multivariable delivery model and an objective multivariable swing model. The epiphany for us was the realization that we had been teaching with flawed data. Up to this time, our eyes (which process visually at 32 frames per second) had been lying to us. In the process, we were unintentionally instructing with bad information. Seeing stick figures of elite athletes move in three dimensions at 1,000 frames per second was humbling. As such, we became aware that the human eye, two-dimensional standard video, television, and movie visuals had substantial limitations to the data they were providing.

Because what we had been teaching our players over the years wasn't necessarily correct, it became obvious to us that we had to let go of any conventional wisdoms that were adversely affecting the performance and health level of our athletes. During this time, we began matching our eight variable research model with cross-specific teaching protocols…matching information with instruction. Note: this undertaking will be discussed and demonstrated, in depth, throughout all of the Chapters in this book.

In the early to mid-1990s, BioKinetics moved its lab to Salt Lake City and added a new partner, Bob Keyes, who owned and operated the Utah Baseball Academy. This move enabled us to complement our professional data-capture with a steady stream of amateur athletes, in an academy environment, with pitching mounds and hitting cages. We could actually test science-based, hands-on, instructional protocols. It was a huge paradigm shift for both us and baseball. Not surprisingly, the information and instruction were met with (at best) lukewarm acceptance, as we tried to spread the word around the country in coach's clinics, camps, and consults.

In the late 1990s, we opened a satellite office, BioKinetics West, in San Diego. We continued to plug away, debugging computer hardware and software problems, and improving the efficacy of our models and the efficiency of our objective, instructional protocols. By 2002, I had teamed up with two new partners, Gary Heil, (a business guru) and Karl Meinhardt (a computer wizard) to form an organization, the National Pitching Association. During this time, we had also begun collaboration with Dr. Greg Rose, who directs the Titleist Performance Institute (TPI) in Carlsbad, California. Using a Vicon Motion System and other motion capture technology, we found parallels between baseball biomechanics and golf biomechanics.

The NPA/TPI relationship really took things to another level, which enabled our learning curve to expand exponentially. Most importantly, we identified a "signature" in rotational athletes which proved that the timing, kinematic sequencing, and mechanics of throwing/striking were virtually the same. Doug Thorburn then came on board as an intern in the fall of 2005 to help facilitate the growth in sports science and computer technology. By 2006, Doug was running the NPA lab as our resident biomechanics/ pitching coach. Doug was instrumental in the development of our motion-analysis software, as well as the statistical validation and trademarking of our pitching and hitting models. In reality, the advances that have occurred in our integration of sports science, computer technology, and coaching science is one of the main reasons for writing *Arm Action, Arm Path, and the Perfect Pitch: Building the Million-Dollar Arm.*

The aforementioned is a "cliff-note" version of how we matched baseball and motion analysis over the last 30 years. Hopefully, the synopsis has not only provided some insight about the process, it has also reinforced the fact that our efforts to improve the validated integration of science-based information, objective instruction, and player-coach inspiration continue. It is important to note that we are also making research-grounded, science-based inroads into the information and instruction of functional strength and flexibility; sports nutrition and metabolic management; and mental/emotional evaluation and preparation concerning the ability/capacity of athletes to both compete and recover. While our primary focus remains on the three-dimensional quantifications of efficient and effective biomechanics, we will touch on the other three legs of the performance and health paradigm throughout the book.

Motion Analysis and Pitching Biomechanics

☞ ***Doug:*** At the National Pitching Association, we have been studying the biomechanical aspects of the pitching delivery, using our software with a Vicon high-speed motion capture system. Our efforts have concentrated on analyzing pitchers of varying skill levels and on determining the integral components of a successful delivery. A key aspect of this analysis has been the study of some of the greatest Major League pitchers of our generation, including Nolan Ryan and Randy Johnson. This analysis of these Hall of Fame-caliber players has enabled us to learn which aspects of pitching mechanics are consistently seen across the best players in baseball. By studying what these athletes have in common and understanding how these similarities contribute to their success on the mound, this information can be used to teach pitchers of all ages how to achieve their maximum thresholds, with regard to mechanical efficiency, consistency, pitch velocity, and command.

Throughout our research, we have emphatically stressed the use of the scientific method: to form a hypothesis about pitching, to test that hypothesis by collecting and evaluating motion-analysis data, and then to form a conclusion based on the results. Many of the hypotheses that we examined were based on conventional wisdoms that have been ingrained over time among pitching coaches. Sometimes, our conclusions matched the hypothesis we were testing. In those instances, our efforts helped to validate that the particular concept has merit. A number of times, our conclusions were null, and indicated two points: that a measurable effect may not exist and/or that further research may be necessary in order to gather a larger sample of data. All factors considered, however, the most exciting experiments have been those that either completely defy our expectations or reveal a surprising trend. In these situations, we are forced to take a step back and look at the whole pitching delivery, in addition to whatever variable in which we may be interested. This step often leads to more research, which, in turn, increases our level of awareness and raises new questions that steer us to pursue other investigative efforts.

Every conclusion is best supported by more research, whether it is accepted, rejected, or found null. Sometimes we have to be wrong before we can learn what is right, and the best way to prove or disprove an idea is to form a falsifiable hypothesis, test it with the best tools available, and then analyze the results. Any conclusion that reveals a relationship or trend has value, if for no other reason, because it advances our current model of understanding.

Research is fueled by hypotheses, and we have found that real pitchers and coaches are the best at forming the educated guesses for experiments on baseball. You could ask a scientist to hypothesize about pitching, but he might unintentionally neglect something that is otherwise obvious to a player. At the NPA, we encounter dozens of new gadgets and proposed studies every year that have baseball-related applications. Some have obvious flaws. For example, one recurring mistake is that investigators involved in conducting baseball-related research tend to assume that a pitcher has a release point of 60' 6" (the distance from the rubber to home plate). In reality, we have never seen a pitcher who releases the baseball from right on top of the rubber. Most pitchers have a release point that is five to six feet in front of the stripe, or about 55 feet from the plate. While these are the types of details that tend to be obvious for those individuals who are on the field every day, they are not so apparent to those who spend most of their time in a lab. At the NPA and RDRBI, we play dual roles as both coaches and researchers. Our studies are guided by our observations on the field, as well as the considerable feedback we receive from the players with whom we work. This latter factor represents a tremendous advantage, given that players of all skill levels ask questions that help facilitate our baseball-related research.

The most powerful research advantage that we have is the tool of high-speed motion capture and analysis. 3-D motion analysis can be used to study the difference between a "smooth" delivery and a "violent" one, and to better define those terms, based on actual pitching biomechanics. The data generated from motion analysis can be utilized to break down the pitch sequence—both visually and numerically, and to compare the mechanical results for different deliveries. This information can be useful to a wide array of baseball minds, from scouts and coaches on the field to front-office personnel in player development and baseball operations. This data can also be extremely informative for players and parents, as well as other enthusiasts of baseball research.

Typically, analysis of physical on-field characteristics is left to professional scouts and coaches. On the other hand, that information can become one of the most effective tools in the toolbox for performance-evaluators of all levels. Comparing physical attributes to standard performance stats can help paint a more complete picture of a player's ability. It can also provide more information from which to make important draft-day decisions, from Major League front offices on down to fantasy baseball leagues.

Basically, motion-analysis data provide athletic performance stats for scouts and coaches. The primary advantage of motion-analysis stats is that they are much more objective than the information gleaned from a 20-80 scouting scale. Motion-analysis stats are also a very useful tool which can be used to help compare pitchers and learn more about the details of their unique skills and abilities. In addition, motion analysis can help to answer the "how" question when it comes to athletic performance, such as "how does Randy Johnson use his height as an advantage?"

One final benefit of motion analysis is the fact that pitchers can learn more about their own mechanics by undergoing an analysis and studying the results. As such, a number of people feel that our approach to mechanics is pretty complicated. However, we have found that players of all ages have the capacity to understand the material if they are intrinsically motivated to play baseball, and they are truly interested in improving. By using motion analysis, young players feel like they are playing a video game of their own pitching motion, an attitude that encourages them to learn about their mechanics from a coaching standpoint, which, in turn, facilitates the learning process. This situation helps players self-coach their pitching delivery, including recognizing their relative strengths and weaknesses, as well as appropriate techniques for improvement. In essence, a pitcher can become his own best pitching coach by evaluating his delivery through a lens that is made possible through motion capture and analysis.

Baseball has historically lagged far behind other sports, with regard to the use of motion analysis and other objective tools to measure sport-specific athletic ability. The golf industry, for example, has been utilizing motion analysis for decades to break down swing mechanics and the dynamics of club travel and impact. The information provided by these efforts has led to the development of cutting-edge golf balls, clubs, and mechanical swing techniques. As such, we have learned a lot from the exceptional work being done at Titleist Golf, which has helped pave the way for us to study the pitching delivery, using motion-capture technology. In comparison to golf, we have a lot more to learn about the mechanical aspects of playing baseball.

In football, coaches have been obsessed with watching video and reviewing game film since at least the 1960s. It took baseball another 20 years for teams to come around to adopting the same approach. Talent evaluators in football have also been using objective measurements for years to assess players' physical aptitude for playing the game. Every year, draft-eligible players flock to Indianapolis for the NFL Combine, where they attempt to best each other at a variety of objective athletic tests, such as the 40-yard dash, vertical leap, shuttle, and bench reps. They also compete in position-specific skills tests in order to demonstrate to pro scouts their unique physical gifts (e.g., arm strength, throwing accuracy, backpedaling speed, receiving hands, etc.).

Meanwhile, the scouts in charge of evaluating baseball talent rely on a subjective system, known as the 20-80 scouting scale. In this system, a position player is given a score from 20 to 80 on each of five categories of "tools," including: hitting for contact, hitting for power, fielding ability ("glove"), throwing arm, and baserunning skill ("speed"). A score of 50 is considered Major League average, while perfect scores of 80 are extremely rare, and reserved for those players with a truly elite tool.

While professional baseball scouts are trained to recognize a 70 arm or 60 power with 40 speed, outsiders usually find it difficult to understand the difference between a 50 and a 60 score. In turn, scouts sometimes will use different criteria to make their grades. When it comes to pitchers, a scout will grade a perfect "80" fastball if the athlete consistently pumps "gas" at 99 mph, with outstanding movement and location. As a rule, most everyone will agree with that assessment. On the other hand, a pitcher might get his curveball graded with a 45 by one evaluator because of lack of break ("it's flat") and a low-arm slot, while another scout might notice that there's a 15 mph difference from that player's fastball, that the pitcher's curveball consistently has the same mechanics and release point as his fastball, and that the player knows how to locate it without hanging one, and decide the same pitch is a 55.

The scouts grade will undoubtedly impact decisions about that player down the road. However, no objective standard exists on which to base the scoring scale value of 20-80, and each scout's evaluation may be based on different requirements. As such, outside evaluators do not have the trained eyes necessary to judge 20-80 with any kind of reliability, and the vague definitions surrounding 20-80 make it almost impossible to learn how to do so properly without scout training. To those individuals who study the game from the outside, the 20-80 scale is merely the code of the Secret Society of Scouts, and understanding the code's unique features and applications depends on acceptance into that fraternity.

When scouts are assessing pitchers, the 20-80 scale is typically used to grade individual pitches, while overall mechanics are described as "violent" or "smooth." There are, however, two numerical measurements that scouts employ with athletes on the mound. In reality, these computations—fastball velocity and player height—are the largest determinates of strong scouting grades. Any pitcher who is taller than 6'4" or who can hit 95 mph on a radar gun will be held in the highest regard by most scouts, and will typically be given several extra chances to succeed or fail throughout their career. On the flip side, "shorter" pitchers (i.e., those athletes under 6'1") typically are perceived to have lower expectations. Furthermore, they will also be allowed fewer opportunities to prove themselves, particularly if they can't hit the magic 90 mph on the gun.

While velocity and player height are both useful tools that have a degree of merit, it's not a coincidence that the two most reliable tools for a scout when evaluating a pitcher are also the only two objective measurements that are readily available. As such, we have attempted to identify new methods for objectively measuring performance and pitching ability. This search has led to the extensive use of motion capture and analysis.

Motion-Analysis Components

We have conducted motion analysis at the NPA Performance Lab in San Diego, California, using a configuration of 10 high-speed cameras in a U-shape pattern, surrounding an artificial pitching mound. The mound was built to MLB code for height and slope. In our investigative efforts, the pitchers throw at a distance appropriate to their age and level of play. The cameras capture data at 250 to 1,000 frames per second, which is critical when assessing an event, such as the pitching delivery, in which the entire sequence lasts less than two seconds. As previously noted, the human eye sees the world at approximately 32 frames per second, which is the same as a standard video camera. The cameras in our facility are the same as used by software companies to create realistic-looking video games, and by film studios to enhance computer-generated effects in movies.

Figure 2-1. Inside the NPA performance lab—the motion-analysis mound is on the left

The motion-analysis cameras are light sensitive, and detect light-reflective markers that are placed directly onto the pitcher's body. While suits are often used in motion capture in order to keep the dots on the athlete, we have found that the suits tend to slip, relative to the surface of the player's skin during the high intensity action of the pitching delivery. As a solution to this problem, we attach the markers directly to rigid points on the body to help ensure that we get accurate data. All told, we use 48 markers, including 14 that are attached to gear, such as a headband and wristbands (it should be noted that eight of the markers are removed prior to dynamic capture). The cameras are connected to a control box, which is responsible for providing power to and receiving data from the cameras, before sending the information to the motion-analysis computer.

Figure 2-2. MX control box

Figure 2-3. Vicon MX40 camera

We use our NPA market set and proprietary software to complement computer programs provided by Vicon to coordinate the camera setup, capture the data, and process the results of each session. The Vicon paradigms software interprets the information sent by the MX control box, and allows the motion-analysis operator to physically control the visual capture of each pitch. Each pitch that is recorded with the high-speed cameras is reconstructed to a 3-D representation, which is then processed and run through the NPA model. The NPA/RDRBI reports that are used for evaluating motion-analysis results are generated in the Vicon Polygon computer program. Throughout this book, pictures of the 3-D skeletons that are created in Polygon are included in the text—images that are also used in our reports.

Motion Analysis-Data Capture Setup and Strategy

The first step undertaken for a motion analysis is to calibrate the cameras, in order to optimize the quality of data capture. Next, player measurements are taken, such as height, weight, and leg length. Then, the pitcher is dotted up with reflective markers. The athlete stands on the mound in a T-position, at which point, about three seconds of data are captured so that the software can develop a personal calibration unique to the pitcher. These measurements allow the computer to form a more accurate model of the athlete. The player then goes through a warm-up and plays some catch before the motion-capture session. The pitcher then takes a few throws off the mound to get used to the slope. Subsequently, the pitcher lets the motion-analysis camera operator know when he is ready to start filming his pitches.

Figure 2-4. A pitcher undergoing a motion analysis at the NPA lab

Each athlete then throws 10 each of three different pitch types: fastballs (2-seam or 4-seam), breaking balls (curveball or slider), and off-speed (changeup or split-finger fastball). Every pitch is conducted from the stretch, and capture occurs when the pitcher receives a cue to begin from the motion-analysis operator. Capture ends after the pitcher's follow-through, as the ball crosses the plate. Players are instructed to not throw too many breaking balls or off-speed pitches in a row. As a result, they will mix in a fastball for every three curves, sliders, changeups, or splits.

After the full session of approximately 30 pitches, the data can be processed for a report. In the processing stage, the dots are turned into a moving stick figure for each pitch. The statistical calculations are then computed. Finally, a visual skeleton is overlaid on top of the stick figure, which is based on the physical dimensions of the player taken during the player-calibration phase.

Motion-Analysis Reports (Visual and Statistical)

The key feature of motion analysis is the data generated from each session. A few different types of reports have been designed to display the results of each motion analysis, with the goal of learning from both a visual and a statistical standpoint. The more interactive report is the multimedia CD, which shows the results of each pitch as a three-dimensional skeleton overlay. This information can be manipulated to see the delivery from any angle or point in space. The multimedia report contains videos and stills, which can be tracked frame-by-frame and at multiple speeds.

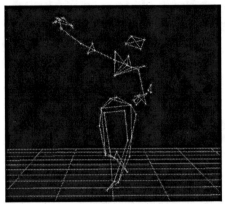

Figure 2-5. Dotted stick figure of a pitcher at release point (front view)

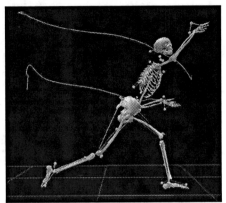

Figure 2-6. Multimedia skeleton of a pitcher at release point (side view)

The use of 10 cameras to produce a three-dimensional representation of the pitch enables every frame to be zoomed or rotated 360 degrees on any axis, in order to view the pitch delivery from any distance or angle. This feature is extremely important for coaches, because the optimal viewing angle is different when analyzing each of the critical points in the pitching delivery. For example, the best angle to see a player's leg lift and body thrust is a side view (i.e., from the third-base side for a right-hander). The best angle to see balance and posture, however, is directly behind or in front of the player. Sometimes, the optimal angle is from a point in space that is impossible with a standard video camera, such as with a bird's eye view from above the mound. A two-dimensional video camera depends on a single viewing angle. As a result, some critical points of a pitcher's delivery are difficult to observe. In fact, a coach would have to see several pitches from different angles in order to get the same information that the NPA system provides on a single pitch.

During motion analysis-data capture, a standard digital video camera (i.e., 32 frames per second) is set up to capture each pitch, while linked with the 10 high-speed cameras. The visual multimedia reports then combine the 3-D motion-analysis data with the 2-D camera video, so that the pitcher and his skeleton are synchronized throughout the delivery on the same page for each pitch. This step helps the player (and his coach) to study the skeleton delivery and see it as himself pitching, rather than some abstract cartoon pitcher.

The report is broken down into separate sections for each of three pitch types, including fastball, breaking ball, and off-speed. Each pitch type has a link to its own page, with videos and 3-D stills that are pre-set to strategic viewing angles, as well as color-specific skeletons for each. The motion-analysis multimedia reports also have a comparison page, with links that show skeletal overlays of the player's fastball on top of his breaking ball, off-speed pitch, or any combination therein. This technique is also used to show 3-D skeleton comparisons from different motion-capture sessions, so that we can track progress or changes in a pitcher's mechanics over time.

Figure 2-7. Screen-shots from a multimedia comparison report, with a pitcher's fastball from his first visit (light skeleton) overlaid with his fastball from his most recent session, at three different points in the delivery

The visual 3-D report is standard for pitchers who undergo a motion analysis. Written statistical reports that are designed for research and evaluation of professional players are also utilized. The multimedia report is typically more than sufficient for breaking down the mechanics of amateur players, whose inefficiencies are relatively dramatic. When it comes to professional athletes, however, the weak links in a pitcher's delivery can be tougher to see, even at 250 to 1000 frames per second. The stat reports are a more sensitive tool for evaluating subtle differences, and making small incremental improvements can have a relatively large impact for professional players who are trying to gain an extra edge.

The statistical results from different motion-analysis sessions over time can be compared to track a player's progress, and objectively evaluate how well a player is taking to his coaching and conditioning regimen. The written reports can also be used to objectively break down the strengths and weaknesses in a pitcher's delivery, and compare those results to typical numbers for the player's competitive skill level. For professionals, the information can show a pitcher how his mechanics stack up against his counterparts, whether he plays in the Major Leagues or is in the Minors and trying to get there. The combination of data from 3-D visual reports and written stat reports can paint a very clear picture of a pitcher's delivery, with respect to signature, timing, kinematic sequencing, and mechanical efficiency.

3

NPA/RDRBI Model

Biomechanical Signature, Timing, Kinematic Sequencing, and Mechanical Efficiency: Ideal Ranges

☞ *Doug:* The past 20 years of research have taught us a lot about the mechanics of the pitching motion. In the process, we have learned about how specific pieces of delivery work together, and have gained a better understanding of how to evaluate pitchers. In addition to the overall motion-analysis database of about 2000 pitchers, we work with thousands of pitchers every year, ranging in skill from Little League to the Major Leagues. All of this research has taught us to focus on some of the overlooked aspects of successful pitching mechanics, and has enabled us to better understand how to work with players to help them improve.

The NPA model for pitching mechanics is an ongoing project. In fact, we are continuously testing the model and updating it with new findings. Although we have studied some of the best pitchers in the game, it sometimes takes a new discovery to figure out why some players were successful in the past. In that sense, as long as there are more questions to be asked, studied, and answered about pitching, the model will never be a finished product.

This chapter highlights some of the key findings from the motion-analysis research that we have conducted over the last two decades. The information has a direct application concerning how players are evaluated throughout this book. Understanding the key aspects of timing and kinetic sequencing, mechanical efficiency versus personal signature, and ideal ranges for pitching mechanics enable us to evaluate the conventional wisdoms of pitching from a very unique and detailed perspective.

Biomechanical Timeline—Sequence of Events in the Kinetic Chain

One of the biggest innovations in our research has been the discovery that timing and kinetic sequencing are extremely critical to the pitching delivery. The pitching motion involves a complicated series of physical movements, and the end result is dependent on a player's ability to coordinate those movements in a specific order within a brief amount of time. This revelation has opened up a new perspective on pitching, and has provided us with a better understanding of how to teach proper technique to developing players.

Biomechanical timing is specific to a universal throwing/striking "signature." It is important, however, that each pitcher is able to find the optimal timing pattern or rhythm for his delivery, and is able to consistently repeat his motion with that same timing for each type of pitch. This attribute will enable the player to find a repeatable stride and release point for every pitch in his repertoire. On the other hand, a pitcher who changes his timing on different pitches may give clues to opposing hitters that telegraph the incoming pitch. Furthermore, the "timing paradox," which states that the more time a pitcher takes from first movement to ball release, the more things can go wrong with his delivery.

The related concept is the proper sequencing of the events within the kinetic chain of the pitching motion, as shown in Figure 3-1. Each of the critical events of the delivery makes up a different link in the kinetic chain. The chain link of coordinated leg lift and body thrust ("lift & thrust" in the timeline) is necessary to generate the next link of stride and momentum. In turn, both of these factors are influenced by the preceding base link of balance and posture with both the windup and stretch position. This whole sequence gets the player into foot strike, which occurs when the foot of the lift leg hits the ground on its way back down from maximum lift. Each link in the kinetic chain represents either an opportunity or a risk to take the delivery out of sync. As such, it is critical that every pitcher learns the proper timing and sequencing of these events in order to take advantage of how the body naturally performs the act of throwing a baseball (i.e., his signature).

In reality, however, some of the links in the chain are much more difficult to coordinate than others. As can be seen from looking at the time ranges within the progression illustrated in Figure 3-1, the events near the end of the chain occur in much smaller time intervals. A pitcher has approximately one full second to get from first movement into foot strike. In the process, he covers three links in the chain during that time. At that point, a pitcher has an average of just 0.30 seconds to cover the next four links in the chain. The events that should occur after foot strike are the most likely to fall out of sequence, partially as a result of this relative proximity in time, but also as a consequence of how efficient the dynamic of the kinetic chain is as the critical events play out.

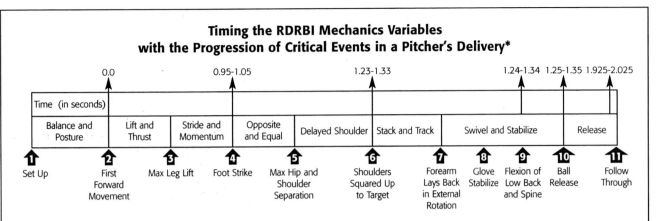

**Timing the RDRBI Mechanics Variables
with the Progression of Critical Events in a Pitcher's Delivery***

	0.0		0.95-1.05		1.23-1.33			1.24-1.34	1.25-1.35	1.925-2.025

Time (in seconds)

Balance and Posture	Lift and Thrust	Stride and Momentum	Opposite and Equal	Delayed Shoulder	Stack and Track	Swivel and Stabilize	Release

1 Set Up — 2 First Forward Movement — 3 Max Leg Lift — 4 Foot Strike — 5 Max Hip and Shoulder Separation — 6 Shoulders Squared Up to Target — 7 Forearm Lays Back in External Rotation — 8 Glove Stabilize — 9 Flexion of Low Back and Spine — 10 Ball Release — 11 Follow Through

1 Set Up from windup or stretch, set correct posting foot location on rubber with proper heal angle

2 First forward movement of total body

3 Maximum leg lift, knee lift, and/or foot flick

4 Foot Strike with stride length at 90-100 percent of body height, spine on centerline

5 Max Hip and Shoulder Separation at 40-60 degrees

6 Shoulders Squared Up to Target with torso upright, low back and spine in hyperextension

7 Forearm Lays Back in External Rotation

8 Glove Stabilizes over landing foot

9 Torso, low back, and spine go into flexion

10 Arm snaps into Ball Release 8"-12" in front of landing foot

11 Follow Through—arm pronates in deceleration, shoulders continue to rotate, torso continues to lean forward head up/eyes up, as back leg pops up through the same path as throwing arm

*The optimal kinematic/kenetic efficiency in a pitcher's delivery is a function of:
  A. Timing
  B. The RDRBI Bio-mechanical Variables with
  C. The proper sequencing of critical events

Figure 3-1. Timeline of critical events

The chain metaphor is appropriate, given the fact that the pitcher's body transfers energy through specific movements to deliver the baseball. The timing and sequencing of these movements creates a kinetic chain that follows the progression of critical events. In other words, each link in the chain has a direct effect on the links that follow. As a result, more time and opportunity exists for a player to disrupt the chain and subsequently affect later parts of the delivery.

This realization has had a big impact on the techniques we employ for coaching. As such, it has become absolutely necessary to work with mechanical efficiency in the proper sequence, beginning with the set-up position. If we attempt to fix a pitcher's mechanics out of sequence, it will greatly hinder that player's development. For example, we may be working with a pitcher with a balance problem at leg lift, as well as a subsequent issue with his glove near the release point. If an attempt is made to correct the mechanical flaw near the release point, and then go back and work with the pitcher's balance, the athlete will often find that the "corrected" glove side is a problem again. This situation will occur because the pitcher had wired his mechanics to follow a sequence that started with a balance problem, and then corrected his glove to compensate for that down the kinematic sequence chain. On the other hand, when the balance problem was corrected, the player's brain and body programmed a new sequence, one to which the glove correction was not connected. This factor can result in a loop of constant mechanical alterations, which is frustrating for both the player and his coach.

The more efficient method for players and coaches is to adjust the pitcher's mechanics according to the proper sequence of the kinetic chain. In other words, it is necessary to first fix the athlete's balance and posture in order to begin programming the chain for this pitcher's ideal delivery. In particular, balance and posture are two elements that are extremely critical throughout the delivery, from setup to release point. Once the pitcher has achieved consistent balance, he can begin to correct any mechanical flaws that occur later in the progression. Furthermore, fixing an athlete's early problems will often result in a correction of the later issues. For example, getting the aforementioned pitcher's balance straightened out may lead to having his glove position close to ideal, without his receiving any further instruction.

When we were conducting our early studies on pitching mechanics, we discovered through statistical regression analysis that having strong balance and posture was the most common ingredient to success for the best pitchers in the game. In fact, the regression also indicated that the importance of each critical event in the progression decreases as you move along the kinetic chain. We now understand that this result was a precursor for the development of the timeline, since it revealed that the regression was sequence-dependent, with the best players having the most basic and earliest elements of the delivery in common. As a result, these athletes are set up to have more consistency in the following links in the chain, which has a ripple effect on pitching mechanics as the athlete moves through the progression.

Signature vs. Timing, Sequencing, and Mechanics

☛ **Doug:** A pitcher must be at the right place at the right time with the right sequence of events to be efficient and, ultimately, healthy and effective. One big distinction exists between timing and sequencing with respect to mechanics: proper sequencing is an important element of mechanical efficiency, but timing is what initiates the progression and is partially dependent upon an athlete's personal signature. The sequence of critical events will be the same for each pitcher who achieves a high degree of mechanical efficiency. On the other hand, more potential problems exist with the variability of timing from one pitcher to another.

In the progression of critical events, the timeline is marked by suggested time ranges, representing the typical timing patterns for athletes with strong mechanical efficiency. Each pitcher has a "natural vs. taught" timing pattern to "line up" his delivery for ideal results. While this timing pattern can change over time, the best pitchers typically fall into these suggested ranges. As such, timing can be influenced by a combination of his genetic signature and his instructed mechanical efficiency. Once a pitcher has found his own personal ideal timing, he can move into the next phase of skill mastery—coordinating functional strength and flexibility in order to acquire biomechanical consistency.

It should be noted that one of the key aspects of the NPA–RDRBI model is that a pitcher's ideal delivery is shaped by his genetic personal signature, as well as his level of learned mechanical efficiency. In that regard, key factors, such as style of leg kick, method of achieving hip-shoulder separation, and elbow angles at foot strike, are dictated by what feels most natural to the athlete, which can vary widely across the player population. These factors are considered signature-specific to each individual pitcher. From a coaching perspective, we try not to alter that unique signature. Signature-specific components of the delivery need to be isolated from mechanical efficiency, and players tend to have a particularly difficult time with coaching solutions that disrupt their own personal signature.

For example, over time, we have found that a strong link exists between how much torque, or load, a player can generate (as measured by the maximum angle of separation from the athlete's front hip and back shoulder) and how much velocity that player can get on his fastball. Roger Clemens and C.C. Sabathia are two athletes who have had successful MLB careers who can each throw upwards of 96 mph. Research has shown that each player creates a hip-shoulder separation angle of 55 degrees or more (which is on the high end of the spectrum) when he pitches. Each of these players, however, uses very different methods to create that torque, as will be discussed later.

The fact that a pitcher has an individual signature helps explain why some of the best players of all-time have had similar mechanical efficiency, even though they had deliveries that looked vastly different. The distinction between efficiency and signature is especially significant from a coaching perspective. Mechanical efficiency can be improved with proper instruction, but signature-specific elements of the pitching delivery are unique to the player and a relative non-teach for coaches.

Figure 3-2 provides images of Jake Peavy and Trevor Hoffman, both of the San Diego Padres. It can be seen that each pitcher uses a very different method for leg lift. Peavy brings his lift knee straight up to his left shoulder, with his toe pointing toward third base. In contrast, Hoffman gets a higher lift than his teammate, while bringing his lift knee up toward his right shoulder and pointing his toe toward the sky. The direction of lift and point of the toe are purely signature-specific, while the height of the leg lift is influenced by both mechanical efficiency and personal signature.

Figure 3-2. Jake Peavy and Trevor Hoffman, two teammates with very different styles of leg lift, each unique to his own personal signature

Throughout this book, we use and refer to measurements made from motion-analysis as we study the conventional wisdoms for pitching mechanics. Many of these stats will be new, and may need some explanation. Some of the values represent an element of player signature, while others are controlled, with regard to the fact that they isolate mechanical efficiency. In addition, some measurements are also indicative of both signature and mechanical efficiency. When these variables are considered, it is important to keep in mind that while mechanical efficiency can be improved with training, the degree of improvement might be limited by the influence of the athlete's personal signature. If a coach tries too hard to improve efficiency in these areas, the pitcher may struggle to find his proper mechanical consistency or to exhibit the timing and sequencing that are ideal to his signature. With regard to timing, for example, we have found that many young pitchers often take too long to get into foot strike. In turn, most of these players show marked improvement when they can get from first forward movement to foot strike in about 0.95 to 1.05 seconds. Faster, however, is not always better. A player can go overboard, getting into foot strike so fast that it has a negative impact on the rest of his delivery.

Whenever we're asked to show someone a 3-D skeleton of the "perfect delivery," we have always responded with the same answer: "Sorry, but one doesn't exist." The perfect delivery is itself a myth, since the influence of signature prevents a single solution that can be considered industry-standard. We would first need to classify dozens of different prototypes, based on the typical characteristics of signature. Then, we would have to run an ideal mechanical efficiency model for each prototype in order to create enough "perfect delivery" skeletons to cover the possible variations in player signature. This task creates a challenge for coaching and player evaluation, which is where the "art" lies in the "art and science of coaching."

What we can do is point to examples of successful MLB pitchers who have close to ideal mechanics, given their signature. "Ideal" is defined as the upper echelon of values that we have come across, while accounting for the occasional outlier or genetic freak. The best pitchers of all time can generate up to 60 degrees of hip-shoulder separation, a benchmark that represents the ideal value and goal for developing players. While there are occasionally pitchers who will exceed the ideal levels that have been established by the greats of the game, these incidences are incredibly rare. The best example of one of these "freaks" is actually Nolan Ryan, whose mechanics are so incredibly efficient that no one reasonably expects other pitchers to achieve his levels of ability. Greg Maddux is another pitcher who is a bit of a freak. For the most part, however, his mechanics are close to 100% efficient, and are a great example of what "ideal" mechanics should look like. Not surprisingly, a very strong link exists between mechanical efficiency and performance on the field. In fact, most of the best pitchers in the game tend to have very strong mechanical efficiency. For the pitchers who are still honing their delivery, we try to anchor them on the best values and help them to reach the ideal ranges.

Ideal Ranges

The database that has been accumulated through motion-analysis research has covered athletes of all ages and skill levels over the last 20 years, including some of the most talented pitchers to have ever played the game. Along the way, we have learned that the best players of all time typically have the best mechanical efficiency. For example, Nolan Ryan is not only the all-time strikeout king, but he also set the NPA/RDRBI record for stride-length efficiency, which is a statistic that describes how far a pitcher strides relative to his height. Over time, we have come to understand the value of using ideal ranges for motion-analysis stats that describe pitching mechanics. Ideal ranges represent the optimum values for these stats, based on the best results that we have come across through our research. We can also compare a player's numbers to ideal ranges and typical values for other skill levels, in order to understand how a pitcher's mechanics stack up against his peers.

The aforementioned data also enables us to develop a mechanical efficiency rating for a particular pitcher. Mechanical efficiency ratings put a pitcher's motion-analysis results on a comparative scale with the other pitchers in our database. Specifically, we measure 10 distinct variables that reflect mechanical efficiency, and assign each measure a score out of 10, with 10/10 representing the ideal range.

The scores are relative. For example, a high school player could score 60 points out of a possible 100, but he would not necessarily flunk the test, since 60 is a fairly average score for a high-school athlete. We would look at the individual values to see if he scores any 8s or 9s on the mechanical efficiency ratings, in order to recognize his relative strengths compared to his peer group, and then do the same for the 3s and 4s to analyze his weaknesses. On the other hand, a professional athlete can use the mechanical efficiency ratings system to gauge his mechanical efficiency compared to other professional pitchers. He can also utilize the system to determine the efficiency levels he needs to achieve in order to be on par with his competition. For example, he may be at a 74% level of efficiency, a measure that he could boost to 78% with an improved hip-shoulder separation and a longer release point. This information provides both the player and the coach with a guideline concerning the work that can be done to improve the athlete's efficiency.

4

Challenging Conventional Wisdom

The Pitching Delivery Broken Down

☛ **Tom:** In the book's introduction a number of opinion-based conventional wisdoms that baseball coaches ascribe to were listed. (In fairness, it should be noted that quite a few of them were mine.) In this chapter, our focus is specifically narrowed as part of our ongoing effort to dispel those conventional wisdoms that adversely affect the information and instruction delivered to pitchers concerning timing, kinematic sequencing, and/or delivery biomechanics. Doug refers to this effort as a "timing-based approach for analysis of conventional wisdom." The first step is to define the following eight regressed pitching variables from a coaching perspective:

- Balance/posture—Balance, with the head over the belly button between the balls of the feet, with the feet armpit-width apart, the big toe of back foot in the arch of front foot, and the knees bent equally. Assume a posture that involves a spine-to-hip angle that will stabilize the pitcher's head throughout the delivery.
- Lift/thrust—Lift the front leg naturally, while simultaneously thrusting the front hip/butt toward the target, keeping the head/spine over the navel.
- Stride/momentum—Stride in a natural direction as far and as fast as possible, with the stride foot landing naturally, six-to-seven feet from the rubber.
- Opposite/equal arms—Mirror the glove side arm to the throwing arm into, at, and just after the foot strike.
- Hip/shoulder separation/late shoulder rotation—Find 40° to 60° of separation between the front hip and the back shoulder into foot strike and delay shoulder rotation until the head and spine move forward to 80%+ of stride length.
- Stack/track—Keep the head and spine vertical, with the low back in extension until the shoulders square up to the target; then, go into flexion of the low back just before the throwing arm accelerates to release point.

- Swivel/stabilize—Keep the glove over the landing foot and move the torso to the glove.
- Release point/follow-through—Release the baseball 8″ to 12″ in front of the landing foot and let follow-through happen.

The next step is to compare and kinematically sequence these variables, from feet to fingertips, correlate and time them from the body's first initial forward movement into its final post-delivery deceleration.

Before Doug begins his step-by-step analysis of a player's pitching mechanics, it would be beneficial for you to refresh your memory about the coach's conventional wisdoms by going over the list of conventional wisdoms that were detailed in the first chapter. You should pay particular attention to all those conventional wisdoms that involve the instruction of: position and stance on the rubber; timing and movements of the extremities and torso; timing, length, and direction of the stride, and position and angle of the foot strike; timing and arm actions, arm slots, and arm positions; timing and body positions, postures, and hip/shoulder angles; and timing and torso/extremity position/movements into the release point/follow-through.

As you review the coach's conventional wisdoms, you shouldn't be concerned if you teach or have taught any of them. Don't forget, many of them are mine, and I've actually taught most of them. I continually remind myself it's more about where you are going than where you've been. Everyone learns from the past; the process is called experience. One of the hardest steps in coaching is to let go of something marginal that has been part of your teach, for something that will make your teach better.

Analysis of Conventional Wisdom With a Timing-Based Approach

☞ *Doug:* Having covered the basics, the next step is to dig into some conventional wisdoms concerning pitching mechanics. Our book features about a dozen examples of conventional wisdom that we look into in detail, each of which is expressed in the form of a phrase that a pitching coach might use during the course of instruction. A few of the examples include multiple quotes that address the same pitching myth. Each concept is broken down and interpreted. Then a sophisticated set of tools is utilized to look for numerical trends, correlations, and visual evidence that will support or refute the claim.

The process of analyzing a pitcher's mechanics begins by examining a pitcher's setup from the stretch position, moving from the chronological beginning of the pitching delivery forward along the kinetic chain of events (shown in the timeline), until we get to ball release and follow-through. This strategy is consistent with the emphasis on mechanical timing and sequencing, and helps us to understand how each part of the pitching delivery can influence other aspects down the line. In that regard, the following four different sections of the delivery are critiqued:

- The set-up position from the stretch
- First movement to maximum leg lift
- Maximum leg lift to foot strike
- Foot strike to ball release

The analysis undertakes a Sherlock Holmes-type of approach to analyze conventional wisdom, since we look for clues to solve some of the mysteries of pitching mechanics. Our tools for investigation go beyond a magnifying glass, however, and include:

- Screen-grabs of 3-D skeletons from NPA/RDRBI motion-analysis sessions
- Numerical data generated through NPA/RDRBI motion analysis
- Game-time photographs of MLB pitchers, courtesy of Getty Images

The photos of MLB pitchers are used to visually compare and contrast the mechanics of the best baseball players on the planet. These images help us to identify those aspects of pitching that are essential attributes for elite athletes. Other pictures, taken from motion-analysis data, show skeletons for specific pitchers to analyze their delivery from strategic angles and points in time (e.g., Figure 4-1).

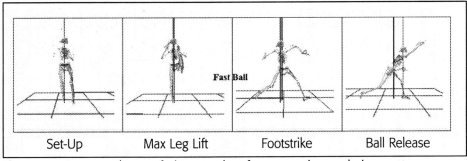

| Set-Up | Max Leg Lift | Footstrike | Ball Release |

Figure 4-1. An example set of pictures taken from a motion-analysis report

Finally, the statistical data from motion analysis is used to objectively break down the mechanical components of the pitching delivery. We have worked with players and used the NPA/RDRBI database to set up relatively small studies to test many of the conventional wisdoms that are reviewed in this book. Some investigative efforts are more like case studies, since they are designed for individual pitchers. In these case studies, a player is asked to make an alteration in his delivery, based on a conventional wisdom, just as many coaches would do with a new pitcher on their staff. We then record three-to-four pitches with the alteration, compare the results to his previously recorded fastballs as a control, and then measure the differences. As a result, it can be determined whether making the mechanical change had a direct effect on the functional results achieved by the pitcher.

Because some of the studies require a larger sample of pitchers, we used a randomly selected sample from the NPA/RDRBI database. While the full database contains over 2000 pitchers and has been compiled over 20 years, we normally utilize the most recent players as a sample in our studies, since we have gone through multiple motion-capture systems over the last two decades. Over time, the visual representation has changed dramatically as the technology has improved. Concurrently, our ability to make physical measurements has improved as well. As a result, we try to choose a sample of players who were captured on the same system, on the same mound, and in the same building with the newer technology.

The sample used throughout this book features 33 of our most recent pitchers, in order to get a relevant sample of athletes for analysis and to take advantage of the newest toys. The majority of pitchers in this particular group were new to the instructional methods of the NPA/RDRBI at the time of the analysis. Most of the players in this group were either captured in their first week of the NPA/RDRBI summer prep program or went through a peak performance package. In the latter instance, these athletes came to San Diego from out of town for a full pitching assessment. This approach provided a more representative sample of mechanical tendencies for pitchers of these age ranges and skill levels, as opposed to using players who have been regularly exposed to NPA/RDRBI methodology. The rest of the data set is comprised of professional players at varying levels of organized ball who came to San Diego for an assessment. The detailed breakdown of the 33 pitchers in this sample is described in Toolbox 1.1, which is included in the appendix at the end of the book.

The data set also features a preponderance of college players, since most of the pitchers who come into the NPA/RDRBI performance lab for a motion analysis are college-level performers. As such, random selection has produced these ratios. All factors considered, this factor should be advantageous for our purposes, given that the best players for analysis are typically about college age. Why? Because college tends to be a breaking point for serious athletes, who are likely to show much more consistency from pitch to pitch than younger players who are still physically developing. In addition, most college players still have a lot of room for improvement, with regard to their level of mechanical efficiency.

Professional players are excellent for analysis, but if we used only pros in this sample, then the results would not necessarily be applicable to those pitchers who are still trying to advance to that elevated level of competition. The majority of pitchers who seek our help as coaches are those who are looking for an edge to jump to the next level, whether that's from high school to college or from the Minors to the Majors. As a result, we have created a database that features committed, established pitchers who still have room for improvement.

All factors considered, the sample of athletes that we studied offers a strong indication of the tendencies for the critical group of pitchers who are on the cusp of "the next level," whether that be youth, college, or professional. These players are those who have the most to gain from utilizing motion analysis to learn more about their own delivery. As such, the sample does not provide a large representation of younger players, who tend to have poorer measurement numbers than the figures in this book, and tend to exhibit a greater level of inconsistency from day to day and pitch to pitch. It does, however, give these younger athletes a delivery for which to strive. The sample only includes a small representation of MLB pitchers, athletes who are obviously a stronger group when it comes to mechanical efficiency and consistency. It does, however, reflect those players who have reached a physical and psychological maturity level for self-maintenance with respect to mechanics, conditioning, nutrition, and the appropriate mental approach to competition and learning the game.

The professional athletes won't be neglected in the book, of course. One of the special features of the book involves looking at pictures of some of the best pitchers in the Major Leagues in order to compare and contrast their mechanical tendencies. It is not a coincidence that the best pitchers of our generation also have some of the best mechanics in the game. These players not only exemplify how an ideal delivery can look, but also help coaches to better understand which aspects of mechanics are consistent with successful performance on the field.

We utilized the data from our motion-analysis studies involving 33 pitchers to conduct research to test the conventional wisdom of pitching mechanics and coaching. Some of the studies required that we divide the 33 players into groups, based on a specific measurement. Other investigative efforts entailed smaller case studies that involved looking at just one or two individual pitchers, in which case we altered a single mechanical variable to measure the effect of that specific factor on a particular player. Overall, the experiments provided a method to study specific aspects of conventional wisdom. The reliability level of these efforts was aided by our ability to establish experimental controls within our performance centers in both San Diego and Los Angeles (refer to Toolbox 1.2).

As the results from our 33-pitcher sample were analyzed, we looked for correlations in the data to see if any trends could be identified. The relationship between different variables was evaluated, using the correlation coefficient, r^2, which is described in more detail in Toolbox 1.3. The values for r^2 fall within the range of $-1.00 \rightarrow +1.00$, with positive numbers indicating that the variables increase and decrease in a tandem relationship to one another, and negative values indicating an inverse relationship. The relative strengths of the correlations were evaluated, using the standards outlined in Toolbox 1.3. As the axiom goes, "correlation does not prove causation." On the other hand, the computed r^2 values contribute to our understanding of how mechanical links in the chain of the pitching delivery are interrelated. The relative strength of the correlations provide further indication of the reliability of those relationships, as well as help us to account for the presence of confounding variables.

THE SETUP

Section 2

5

Breaking Down the Setup Position

Coaches' Conventional Wisdom for the Setup Position

- "Wide stance from the stretch, straight front leg, weight shifted onto the back leg"
- "Left-handers pitch from the left side of the rubber; right-handers pitch from the right side"

Breakdown: The Setup Position

The setup is a very critical component of a pitcher's delivery, since it provides the base for the kinetic chain of events. As the physical starting point of the pitch sequence, the setup position has an impact on the end points of ball release and follow-through. In many ways, a pitcher's setup determines how the rest of the delivery will be executed. It affects factors such as balance, posture, momentum, stride length, and ultimately pitch command and velocity. Consistently starting out with a setup that is the ideal complement to a player's signature will have a positive effect on every phase that follows in the delivery.

The chapters in this section address the setup, specifically from the pitcher's stretch position. Throughout Major League baseball, pitchers throw approximately 2/3 of all pitches from the stretch, including those crucial pitches that occur with men on base. Every starting pitcher in baseball has to pitch from the stretch frequently throughout the game, often going back and forth with the windup, from inning to inning. Focusing on the stretch position as the pitcher's setup is studied enables us to generalize the results of our efforts to a larger population of players.

As such, a number of pitchers are not as consistent with either their stretch or their windup, compared to the other. Some pitchers throw exclusively from the stretch, because they can't find a windup that gets them into the proper position. Other pitchers, those who tend to rely on their windup for rhythm, typically have a hard time finding consistent timing from the stretch. With many pitchers, the windup is relatively simple, and is just a step into the stretch-setup position. For others, the windup is more complicated and takes much more time. In this respect, pitching from the windup has more potential for problems than pitching from the stretch, since it involves additional movements to coordinate and entails more time to throw the delivery out of sync.

6

"Wide Stance From the Stretch"

"Wide stance from the stretch, straight front leg, weight shifted onto the back leg"

Many pitchers are taught to set up their delivery by adhering to the rules detailed in this particular piece of conventional wisdom. In fact, examples of this type of setup are common in the Major Leagues. Players using this setup begin with a wide stance, their feet set up further than shoulder-width apart, their front leg straight (with no bend in the knee), while the back (posting) leg has some bend to it, which effectively shifts a player's weight over the posting leg. The logic of having a different degree of bend in the knees seems to be grounded in the reasoning that balance can be aligned with flat ground, rather than the slope of the mound, and that the bend in the posting leg is enough to compensate for that slope. The wider the stance, the more the player will have to bend the posting knee to compensate for the slope. Overall, this technique gives the pitcher a line of sight that is parallel to flat ground, and favors a momentum shift along a flatter plane.

A pitcher's task, however, involves directing his momentum down the slope of the mound, rather than parallel to flat ground. Attaining optimal mechanical efficiency requires that a pitcher take advantage of his environment, such that his center of mass follows a trajectory that is parallel to the slope. With optimal balance, the player's head will also follow a path that is parallel to the slope, while staying directly above the center of mass of the body (COMB), such as illustrated by the skeleton in Figure 6-2. This step is easier to accomplish when the athlete sets up with a stretch position that is balanced relative to the mound. The setup with a wide stance and different knee bend creates an obstacle for the pitcher to overcome before he can take advantage of the mound to generate momentum down the slope and into foot strike.

Figure 6-1. Pedro Martinez (2004) illustrates a good example of a wide stance at setup, with different bend in his knees and weight shifted toward the back foot

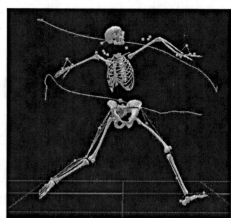

Figure 6-2. A motion-analysis pitcher with exceptional balance throughout the delivery, with parallel trajectory lines for his COMB and COMH (center of mass of the head), following the slope of the mound

Each leg weighs approximately 20% of body weight. Accordingly, a 200 lb. pitcher who sets up with a wide stance must move backward to lift 40 lbs. of leg off the ground. This factor can make timing and momentum less efficient and can have an effect on later phases in the pitcher's delivery. In addition, the pitcher who starts with a bent back leg stays over that leg when he lifts his front leg, which also creates an obstacle for generating early momentum. The picture of Pedro Martinez is a good example of how the conventional wisdom setup looks on a Major League pitcher. The natural response for a player with this setup is to bring the lift leg and COMB up and back toward second base to find a balanced position at maximum leg lift. Martinez is actually an exception to the rule, because he is able to overcome these obstacles to initiate momentum directly toward the target from setup. Typically, players with a wide, imbalanced setup will delay their first forward movement toward the plate until after reaching maximum leg lift.

In reality, a player is at a disadvantage if he waits until maximum leg lift to initiate movement toward the plate. Furthermore, standing over the rubber on one leg is not an ideal position for generating forward momentum. Significant benefits exist for those pitchers who start forward movement as soon as their front foot lifts off the ground, one of which is the ability to generate momentum from an athletic power position on both feet. This step is easier to accomplish by starting with a more balanced position, with the COMH directly over the COMB and between the balls of the feet, with the feet spread armpit-width apart. This positioning is very similar to a basketball player taking a free throw, with the knees bent as far as necessary to find the player's natural balance height.

The balanced angle of knee bend can also be found by having the pitcher get into his natural hitting stance. Most athletes will quickly find a strong balance point, which can be directly applied to their stance for pitching from the stretch. It's interesting that even most beginning-level basketball players can find a strong balance point at the free-throw line, and just about every pitcher can find a balanced hitting stance when asked to swing the lumber. Yet, when it comes to the hill, balance is often tossed out the window so that a pitcher can "stand tall" or "shift weight to the back leg." Figure 6-3 illustrates an example of a balanced setup from the stretch.

Figure 6-3. Johan Santana displays a great example of a balanced posture, with the head over the navel, in between the balls of the feet, the feet close to shoulder-width apart, and equal bend in both knees

Because of different body heights and levels of body composition, every player's optimal balance point at setup will be different, especially with respect to the degree of knee bend and the resulting head height. Ideal balance is a factor of functional strength and what feels comfortable to the athlete. In this regard, the goal for each pitcher is to keep the head stable with respect to his center of mass throughout the entire delivery. A good indicator for an ideal starting balance point is the height of the player's head from maximum leg lift into foot strike, since most pitchers will find their natural balance height during this phase of the delivery, regardless of their starting balance. However, the more a player has to adjust to find that optimal balance point, the tougher it will be for him to find consistent balance throughout the delivery for every pitch. With developing players, the ideal balance point for a pitcher will change as the athlete grows taller, gains weight, or has a significant change in his level of functional strength and flexibility.

Many individuals believe that overhand throwing is an unnatural act, and that pitchers are bound to get hurt as a result. In reality, however, humans have been throwing objects overhand for thousands of years. As such, the human body can withstand the rigors of pitching as long as it is supported by an appropriate level of functional strength and flexibility, manageable workloads, and proper mechanics.

The one factor that is unnatural about pitching is the mound itself. Accordingly, it is not shocking that many coaches have attempted to circumvent the obstacle presented by the slope. When the pitching mound was raised in the 1960s, the result was a much steeper slope, which may have had an even larger impact on pitching performance than the increase in height. It should be noted that baseball's problems associated with a slope are not restricted to the pitching mound. Minute Maid Park in Houston for example, has an elevated slope in centerfield which affects the mechanics and accuracy of throws to both cut off men and/or bases.

The difficulties produced by the slope of a pitching mound help explain why some coaches still adhere to the aforementioned conventional wisdom. On the other hand, we have also seen how a pitcher can achieve a balanced setup, while working *with* the mound. He safely takes advantage of the slope, by maintaining his balance, gaining forward momentum from first movement to leg lift, stride, and into foot strike. When instructing a pitcher, it is important to realize that a player's optimal balance can change over time. As such, the player may need help to find his own ideal balance. In that regard, a coach can help a pitcher choose a setup that adjusts his natural balance and posture to the environment of the mound. In other words, a setup that is conducive to using the slope to help generate early momentum from a stable position on two feet.

Tom's Wrap-Up

The following coaching tips can help a pitcher find his optimal stance or setup, from the windup and/or stretch position. On the rubber, the pitcher should line up the ball of his posting foot with the arch of the landing foot, his feet armpit-width (or slightly less) apart and his knees bent equally. This setup facilitates the foot pivot (in the windup) and the leg lift (in both the windup and stretch), which, in turn, minimizes posture change and any negative affect it might otherwise have on a pitcher's level of balance/posture. This factor occurs because the big toe-to-arch positioning puts the lift leg slightly in front of the belly button (COMB). Standing with the feet armpit-width apart puts the lift leg inside the width of the torso. In this setup, lifting the front leg (20% of body weight) does not adversely affect balance or posture, which is our first critical biomechanical variable. It also facilitates the timing of the body's first forward movement, because of the following factors:

- When the feet are even, or the front foot is open, the pitcher's upper body has a tendency to lean back at leg lift to facilitate the lift, which results in an unwanted change in his level of balance/posture.
- When the feet are spread wider than a pitcher's shoulders/torso, his total body will shift toward second base to accommodate leg lift, which also causes an unwanted balance/posture change.
- When both knees are bent equally (at an angle that keeps the head level with the leg lift and forward body movement), no up/down posture change occurs to negatively affect the athlete's balance or timing.

Furthermore, any combination of the aforementioned three factors can adversely affect a pitcher's *timing* (a point that will be expanded upon later in this text).

7

"Lefty to the Left Side, Righty to the Right Side"

"Left-handers pitch from the left side of the rubber; right-handers from the right side"

One of the most common conventional wisdoms held by pitching coaches is, "left-hander left side, right-hander right side." The concept states that a left-handed pitcher should set up from the left side of the rubber (the first-base side) to create a better angle at release point on the hitter, and that the third-base side is the best positioning for a right-hander. It is designed to be especially effective for like-sided batters, such that a left-handed pitcher throwing from the extreme left side of the rubber will create a difficult angle of trajectory for a left-handed hitter. Consequently, this technique would tend to make things easier on opposite-sided hitters. As such, it's puzzling that a coach would teach this approach, especially to a starting pitcher. A starter has to be able to get out hitters of all types, multiple times throughout the game, and has to be prepared for a team that stacks its lineup with opposite-handed batters to exploit platoon splits. Perhaps, the strategy is more appropriate for use by situational relievers, rather than the starting pitchers who face a variety of hitters.

Tactically, the "left-hander left side" rule doesn't work as well as perceived for most pitchers, as long as there is the related negative side effect against right-handed hitters. When it involves the pitcher's setup and its influence on the rest of the delivery, however, the practice of moving to the extreme side of the rubber can have other consequences. In that regard, the spot on the rubber from which the pitcher begins his delivery also dictates where he will finish it, and helps determine the position of the pitcher's upper and lower body at release point.

As the pitcher goes from lift and thrust to stride and momentum (refer to the timeline), the athlete's back foot stays very close to the rubber. Just after foot strike, however, the back foot drags down the dirt of the mound, as the body tracks from foot strike to release point. The pitcher's back foot will drag down the mound in a path until that foot comes off the ground. This typically occurs just after release point in a balanced, efficient delivery. However, some players lift their drag foot off the ground prior to release point. This typically occurs as a result of improper balance that involves the head getting out in front of their center of gravity.

The trail that is traced by the back foot is referred to as the "dragline," and can take many shapes. It may be straight, crooked, curved, or look like the "Z" from Zorro. To date, our research indicates that the shape of the dragline is a signature-specific element of the delivery, and doesn't have much of an effect on the end result. On the other hand, we have found that the finishing position of the drag line at release point is a critical indicator in the pitching sequence.

At release point, the ankle of the drag foot typically lines up with the position of the player's head and spine. Ideally, every pitcher should have his spine lined up on the middle of the rubber to the middle of home plate, as his shoulders square up perpendicular to the target at release point. In order to measure this factor, we needed a reference point. Our solution was an imaginary line that runs from the center of the rubber to the middle of home plate, approximating the average catcher's target, a reference point we refer to as the center line. In this regard, we measure the distance from the ankle of the pitcher's drag foot and drag line to the center line to indicate how far his head and the spine are off-center at release point.

Figure 7-1. Roger Clemens at maximum external rotation (MER), with his drag foot lining up with his spine position, and his trunk rotated square to the plate

We can also measure the angle of rotation for the pitcher's trunk and shoulders, to determine if he will have to compensate his upper-body mechanics in order to hit the intended target when his body is off the center line. This angle is measured relative to a position perpendicular to the center line, which equates to having the shoulders square to the catcher's glove. This measurement is also taken at the point at which the pitcher reaches maximum external rotation (MER) of the throwing shoulder and forearm, which happens when the throwing arm lays back just before starting forward into internal rotation (refer to Figure 7-1). This element occurs within 0.02 seconds of ball release, and it is a critical time for a pitcher to be square to the target.

The effects of being off the center line can be studied by reviewing the motion-analysis data from our 33-pitcher sample. For example, for the entire population of our study, the correlation between drag-foot distance from the center line and angle of trunk rotation (relative to perpendicular) was $r^2 = +0.445$, with $n = 87$ ($N = 29$). This correlation suggests that a positive relationship exists between ankle distance and drag line from center line and trunk rotation angle. This finding indicates that pitchers have to compensate for being off center line by overrotating the trunk and shoulders prior to release point (at MER).

This effect can be better understood by digging a bit deeper to examine how a change in distance from the drag foot line to the center line is related to trunk rotation at the individual-player level. Running the same correlation for each of the 29 pitchers for which we had data (correlating the three different pitch types), we found that the average within-player correlation was even stronger than that for the whole group, with a value of $r^2 = +0.616$. Table 7-1 details the distribution of this data, which helps to explain the increase.

14 players at $r^2 = +0.95 \rightarrow +1.00$	
6 players from $+0.80 \rightarrow +0.94$	
3 players from $+0.45 \rightarrow +0.79$	
0 players from $0.00 \rightarrow +0.44$	
4 players from $-0.44 \rightarrow 0.00$	
1 player at $-0.79 \rightarrow -0.45$	
0 players at $-0.94 \rightarrow -0.80$	
1 player at $-1.00 \rightarrow -0.95$	
Summary: 23 players positive (3 medium, 6 strong, 14 very strong)	
6 players negative (4 weak, 1 medium, 1 very strong)	

Table 7-1. Within-player correlations, ankle distance from center line compared to trunk rotation angle at MER

Overall, 23 out of the 29 pitchers (79.3%) showed a positive correlation, none of which qualified as a weak relationship (note: a detailed explanation of the r^2 values is available in Toolbox 1.3). When evaluating this data, it should be noted that just three data points per player were correlated. As a result, only the most extreme correlations can be considered an indicator of a possible trend. In other words, the four players who fall between −0.45 and +0.45 can essentially be tossed out, since those values are pretty unreliable when dealing with a sample size of n = 3 for each correlation.

It is interesting to note that there were 20 players (69.0%) who showed a strong within-subject correlation of +0.80 → +1.00, with 14 of those falling above +0.95—eight of which exceeded +0.98. However, only one player showed a significant negative correlation between the dragline distance from the center line and the angle of trunk rotation. This finding is further evidence to suggest that a strong link exists between these two variables at the player level. In other words, the trunk rotation angle increases as the pitcher's drag foot moves further from the center line at release point.

The direct effect of moving a pitcher to the extreme side of the rubber is easy to demonstrate by looking at a specific player example. We conducted a study that involved a couple of the pitchers from an NPA Summer Prep Program in an attempt to determine what actually happens when this particular bit of conventional wisdom is put into action. The players began by pitching from the spot on the rubber that felt most comfortable to them. They were then instructed to throw three-to-four pitches from the appropriate extreme side of the rubber, based on the conventional wisdom, just as many coaches would instruct the pitchers on their staff to do. Table 7-2 illustrates the results of those two case studies, which involved one right-handed pitcher and one lefty:

Pitcher A (LHP)		
	Regular fastball	*Left side of the rubber*
Distance, drag ankle-center line, RP	3.09 inches	17.4 inches
Angle of trunk rotation from the center line at MER	12.7 degrees	20.1 degrees
Pitcher B (RHP)		
	Regular fastball	*Right side of the rubber*
Distance, drag ankle-center line, RP	0.80 inches	21.0 inches
Angle of trunk rotation from the center line at MER	0.55 degrees	10.1 degrees

Table 7-2. The effects of moving a pitcher to the extreme side of the rubber

As Table 7-2 shows, when the left-handed pitcher A starts his delivery on the left side of the rubber, he finishes with his drag ankle far to the left of the center line, 17.4 inches away from center. In this case, the player's spine is also to the far left of the center line at release point. As a result, pitcher A must overrotate his trunk and shoulders 20.1 degrees in order to compensate for being offline of the intended target. The same scenario is true for pitcher B, relative to the right side of the rubber. The conventional wisdom throws him off the center line by 21.0 inches, which causes an overrotation of 10.1 degrees. This factor can have even further repercussions, since a pitcher will usually alter his posture with late head movement in an attempt to adjust his spine from the off-center position.

The results of our data suggest that the position of a pitcher's spine (relative to the center line) will impact the angular position of the player's trunk and shoulders at release point. If the pitcher finishes with his drag ankle and spine lined up with the center line, he will be able to get his shoulders square to home plate at MER, which is the most mechanically-efficient position. For comparison, consider a bowler or a dart-thrower who fails to square their shoulders to the target, but instead begins the throw from an off-center angle. It would be very difficult to hit a small target precisely, such as a specific bowling pin or a bull's eye on the dartboard, if the athlete's shoulders are not square with the object at which he is aiming. Similarly, when a pitcher misses the center line on the same side as his throwing arm, the mechanical result is that the player needs to overrotate his trunk in order to compensate for the off-line positioning, which can create havoc on a pitcher's release-point consistency. Perhaps more importantly, NPA/RDRBI research suggests that this overrotation can even increase the risk of the player incurring an arm injury. If a player misses the center line on his glove side, the typical result is that he will not be able to complete full trunk rotation before ball release (underrotation). While this situation is less common, it will, however, prevent the pitcher from taking full advantage of the kinetic energy that has been generated. As a result, he will usually release the ball before reaching maximum angular trunk rotation, which limits the resulting pitch velocity.

A confounding variable exists with respect to the angle of trunk rotation, given that the position of the drag foot and spine, relative to the center line, is not the only thing that can have an impact. Another factor involving trunk rotation is the overall timing of the whole delivery, from first movement to release point. The ideal upper-body position is achieved in concert with a level of timing that is perfect for that pitcher. If a player takes too long to get into foot strike, he will often experience overrotation at MER and release point. The result is usually a pitch that is low and away from the intended target (to a like-sided hitter). It is likely that this effect has something to do with the 12.7 degrees of overrotation that pitcher A registered on his regular fastball, in addition to his finishing 3.09 inches off the center line for that pitch. On the other hand, if a player gets into foot strike too soon, he will not have enough time to execute full trunk rotation before ball release. As a consequence, the resulting pitch will travel up and inside to a like-sided hitter.

The conventional wisdom of "lefty to the left side of the rubber, righty to the right side" is a less than ideal fix for most pitchers. Furthermore, it can have a negative impact on functional results. A pitcher's position on the rubber at setup has a direct effect on the position of the body at release point. As such, the setup position should not be dictated by a hard rule like "right-handers right side, left-handers left side." From a coaching perspective, this point brings up a very important consideration: it is advantageous to let a player show how he naturally throws a baseball, and then adjust his positioning to line him up with the target. This approach works better than arbitrarily dictating a position to which the athlete must artificially adjust his release point. In effect, every pitcher should find a template for his personal signature. Then, both the player and the coach can work to craft mechanical efficiency.

The coaching fix for the dragline problem is relatively simple. The first step is to have the pitcher draw a straight line in the dirt from the middle of the rubber down the center of the mound toward the middle of the plate, (i.e., the center line). The pitcher is then asked to go through a full delivery from any spot on the rubber that feels most comfortable, while noting where that position is. The coach watches the finish of a pitcher's dragline through his release point. The release point should finish on the center line. The next step is to measure the distance that the dragline is off the center line. The pitcher's setup on the rubber is adjusted accordingly. In other words, the pitcher should move on the rubber to a position where the dragline will finish right on the drawn center line. For example, if the pitcher's first delivery results in a dragline that is three inches to the right of the center line at release point, the player should then adjust his setup position by three inches to the left of that "most comfortable" setup position. This positioning should get the athlete to a spot that will have the pitcher's head and spine on line when his shoulders are square to the target (just prior to the release point).

Tom's Wrap-Up

"Lefty left side, righty right side." This piece of conventional wisdom is simply inappropriate. Any position on the rubber that ends up causing a pitcher's head and spine to be off the center line when his shoulders square up to the catcher's target will cause a late posture change, an inconsistent release point, and excess stress on the throwing arm, shoulder/elbow complex. Not one of the aforementioned is good for a pitcher's level of performance or health.

In reality, the best pitchers in the game find that their most efficient and effective starting position on the rubber is that position which results in a dragline (no matter what it's configuration) that finishes on the center line between the middle of the rubber and the middle of home plate.

LIFT-OFF

Section 3

8

Breaking Down First Movement to Leg Lift

Coaches' Conventional Wisdom, First Movement to Leg Lift:

- "Stay back."
- "Stop at the top."
- "Find a balance point."
- "Stay over the rubber."
- "Use a slide step from the stretch."

Breakdown: First Movement to Maximum Leg Lift

Once a pitcher is positioned on the rubber with a setup that is optimal to his level of balance and strength, he can begin the kinetic sequence of delivering the ball to the catcher's target. The first movement in the kinetic chain of events for a pitcher is lifting his front leg off of the mound. Skilled baserunners who steal on a pitcher's "first movement" will take off as soon as that front heel lifts off the ground. For the purpose of our analysis, this marks the beginning of the "pitch cycle", which is completed with ball release.

We have seen how a pitcher's setup position has a strong influence on the other phases in the delivery and how it can have an effect on first movement. Likewise, we can observe how a player gets from first movement to maximum leg lift can have an effect on timing, sequencing, and mechanics for the events that follow in the kinetic chain. This section examines the conventional wisdom that involves the critical event of "leg lift and body thrust," the latter of which describes the direction and magnitude of a player's weight shift from first movement into maximum leg lift.

9

"Stay Back"

"Stay back."
"Stop at the top."
"Find a balance point."
"Stay over the rubber."

Some pitching coaches hold specific opinions concerning what a pitcher should do with his balance and center of mass (COMB), from first movement to maximum leg lift. The four examples of conventional wisdom at the beginning of this chapter are often used to describe the same general concept underlying these opinions. Many coaches ask the pitchers on their staff to shift their weight back toward second base after first movement, while also making sure to "stay over the rubber." These players are instructed to "stay back" and "stop at the top" of their delivery (a.k.a. maximum leg lift), in order to "find a balance point" on the posting leg. Pitchers are expected to do this before they start their momentum toward the plate, which these coaches like to see occur after maximum leg lift. This aforementioned method is extremely popular among pitching coaches in Japan. In Japan, pitchers, such as Hideo Nomo and Daisuke Matsuzaka, seem to exaggerate how long they stay back and stop at the top, particularly from the windup. This chapter, however, primarily addresses the issue of players who stay back or stop at the top when pitching from the stretch position.

The approach that contrasts with stay back and stop at the top is to have the pitcher initiate momentum toward home plate, rather than shifting his weight toward second base. In this instance, a pitcher does not wait until maximum leg lift to get moving down the mound, and, instead, he thrusts his weight toward the target immediately upon first movement. Players who direct their energy straight toward the plate will not stay over the rubber. Instead, they will be moving forward as they reach maximum leg lift, and will be leading with their front hip toward the target, rather than stopping at the top of maximum leg lift.

At the NPA/RDRBI, we have created a measure that indicates how a pitcher directs his energy from first movement to maximum leg lift. This statistic has been appropriately named the "energy angle." It is an instantaneous measurement, taken at maximum leg lift, which describes how far the pitcher's center of mass has traveled toward the plate, relative to his posting leg. The closer the pitcher is to home plate at maximum leg lift, the higher his energy angle. Pitchers who stay back will tend to have lower values for their energy angle, compared to players who direct their momentum toward the target immediately upon leg lift.

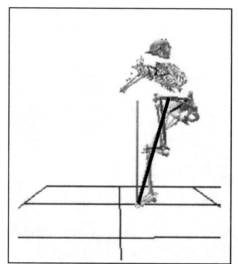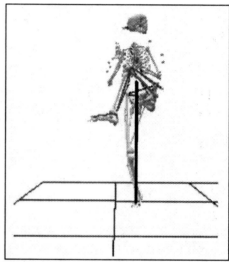

Figure 9-1. Two pitchers from the NPA/RDRBI database—one with exceptional energy angle (9-1a), compared to a pitcher who "stops at the top" (9-1b)

The player skeletons in Figures 9-1(a-b) that were captured via motion analysis can help further clarify the importance of the energy angle. Both players are from our 33-pitcher experimental database, including one with an especially strong energy angle, averaging 13.3 degrees (Figure 9-1a), and another who "stops at the top," with an average energy angle of 1.14 degrees (Figure 9-1b). The vertical line in Figure 9-1a is a vector running upward from the pitcher's toe on his posting foot, perpendicular to the plane of the rubber. The diagonal line represents the length from the posting toe to the pitcher's center of mass of his body (COMB). Accordingly, energy angle is defined as the angle created between the two lines at the time-point of maximum leg lift.

Historically, many of the great all-time pitchers have taken advantage of early momentum to generate a strong energy angle, including Bob Feller, Sandy Koufax, and Bob Gibson. This factor holds true for the current generation of elite pitchers as well. Figure 9-2 shows five of the greatest pitchers in Major League baseball, at the point of maximum leg lift, before their hands have started to break. As a general rule, great pitchers have great mechanics. All factors considered, most observers, both inside and outside the game, would conclude that the five players illustrated in Figure 9-2 have "clean, smooth" deliveries. However, we later learn that these five aces also share some common mechanical traits that most scouts and coaches consider violent in other pitchers.

Figure 9-2. The five Aces at maximum leg lift: Pedro Martinez, Roy Oswalt, Greg Maddux, Randy Johnson, and Johan Santana

These five pitchers, who are the active MLB leaders for career ERA (through the 2007 season, minimum 1200 innings pitched, on active roster for 2008) are:

- Pedro Martinez   2.80
- Roy Oswalt   3.07
- Greg Maddux   3.11
- Randy Johnson   3.22
- Johan Santana   3.22

Collectively, Martinez, Maddux, and Johnson have defined an entire generation of pitching excellence. Each already owns a closet full of awards, while the other two pitchers on the list—Oswalt and Santana—are well on their way to Hall of Fame careers. This list features three of the top four active pitchers in strikeouts, Ks per nine innings and hits per nine innings; four of the top five in WHIP, and five of the top 10 in K/BB, as well as the top three active pitchers in wins and W-L percentage. Not surprisingly, these five pitchers also have incredible mechanics, despite the fact that they have different physical makeups and don't appear to have similar deliveries at first glance. In that regard, we will be referring to images of the five aces throughout our examination of conventional wisdom, in order to determine how they compare at critical points in their deliveries.

As a group, these five players do an exceptional job of creating a strong energy angle through their early initiation of forward momentum. None of the pitchers look as if he is staying back through leg lift, and they were all clearly moving forward prior to this point in their delivery. In fact, at maximum leg lift, most of these players look very similar with respect to energy angle. Pedro Martinez and Roy Oswalt look nearly identical, and the same could be said for Randy Johnson and Johan Santana from the left side. Greg Maddux generates a similar energy angle, but with a lower leg lift.

Two factors should be considered when examining the thrust sequence of the delivery. The first aspect to take into account is the timing of the initiation of forward movement toward the target. In that regard energy angle serves as a good indicator of how early a pitcher gets it going. Those players who stay back and stop at the top have a delayed initiation of forward movement, and don't direct their energy toward home plate until the lift leg is in the air, usually not until after maximum leg lift. Typically, these players have a wide setup stance, and must shift their weight backward to "find a balance point." In other words, their forward movement is then initiated from standing on one leg, which is an inefficient position for generating maximum momentum. Most of the best pitchers in the history of the game consistently start their movement toward home plate from the moment the front foot lifts off the ground, while simultaneously coordinating their leg lift and body thrust from a balanced position.

The second factor involved with lift and thrust is the velocity component of the pitcher's forward momentum. Some pitchers move slowly down the mound, while others appear to "rush" their delivery because they are moving so fast. As such, the velocity of the pitcher's COMB can have an effect on their energy angle measurement. For some pitchers, their level of velocity will change, depending on the timing and sequencing of their delivery. This factor will be covered in more detail in the next progressive link of the chain of pitching mechanics.

Table 9-1 illustrates the average energy angle for the pitchers who were studied in the NPA/RDRBI investigations, with statistics from our 33-pitcher sample. Because critical data was missing for three of these players, the sample size for energy angle in the data set is n = 90, N = 30. (Note: N refers to the number of subjects, while n refers to the total number of measurements taken in the data set).

The average energy angle in the entire sample population is 6.67 degrees. The data breakdown shown in Table 9-1 details the averages for the professional, college, and high school pitchers, respectively. On average, the high school players seem to have a much lower energy angle than either the

All pitchers	6.67 degrees, +/- 0.29 degrees, n = 90
Pro	6.93 degrees, +/- 0.30 degrees, n = 21
College	7.04 degrees, +/- 0.41 degrees, n = 51
High school	5.31 degrees, +/- 0.72 degrees, n = 18

Table 9-1. Average energy angle for the NPA/RDRBI study sample

Pro–college	$t = 1.16$	Insignificant
College–high school	$t = 12.46$	Significant ($p < 0.005$)
Pro–high school	$t = 9.42$	Significant ($p < 0.005$)

Table 9-2. Unpaired t-tests for each sample group

college players or the professional athletes. In that regard, table 9-2 shows the results of an unpaired t-test that was conducted to see if the difference among these groups is statistically significant.

As Table 9-2 indicates, the average energy angle for the high school players was significantly lower than either the college pitchers or the pro athletes. This factor indicates that it is probably an advantage for a pitcher to have a larger energy angle, given that college and professional players are widely perceived as the most talented groups in baseball, with respect to experience, performance, and mechanics. On the other hand, the difference in energy angle between the pro and college players in our data set was insignificant. It is interesting to note, however, that the professional athletes had a much tighter distribution of data, with a smaller standard deviation—despite a much smaller sample size.

In general, the trend of having higher standard deviations for players with less experience (while accounting for sample size) can be expected, a factor which reflects the relative consistency of the data for players within that group. Younger players typically are more inconsistent with their mechanics between different types of pitches, as much more variation is inherent in the pool of younger players. In contrast to professional pitchers who obviously represent the top end of the skill/talent curve, the skills and mechanics of high school players are all over the map. While examples of young pitchers who do one or two things exceptionally well with respect to mechanics can often be found, they tend to have a very difficult time with other parts of the pitching sequence, as well as exhibiting consistency in repeating their delivery.

As has been seen, a strong energy angle is an attribute that the best pitchers have in common. From Pedro Martinez and Roy Oswalt to the top pros in our data set, successful pitchers initiate forward momentum directly from setup, and are moving toward the plate as they get into maximum leg lift. A key question that must be answered, however, is how does a good energy angle impact the rest of a pitcher's delivery?

To address this issue, we grouped the data according to the strength of energy angle, in an attempt to determine if any trends emerged within those groups of pitchers. The energy angle data presented in Table 9-3 involves three different groups, with eight pitchers in each group (each group has n = 24, N = 8). The strong energy-angle group is comprised of the eight pitchers with the highest average energy-angle ratings in our 33-pitcher data set, while the weak energy-angle group includes the eight pitchers with the lowest average values. We then created a third group by randomly selecting eight pitchers from those remaining in the middle of the energy-angle charts to serve as a baseline group of players who were close to the population average for energy angle.

Group	Average energy-angle	SD (+/-)
Strong energy-angle	9.67 degrees	0.39 degrees
Weak energy-angle	3.44 degrees	0.29 degrees
Baseline	6.04 degrees	0.23 degrees

Table 9-3. The energy angle of the groups in the NPA/RDRBI sample

The strong energy-angle group included five pitchers from the college level, two players from high school, and one professional athlete. The weak group contained four college players, three athletes from high school, and one professional. The baseline group had four college players as well, along with one pitcher from high school and three professional athletes. As such, the composition of the groups was sufficiently similar so that the skill level of the players should not have an undue influence on the results of our study.

One of the key advantages of initiating early forward movement to create a strong energy angle is that the pitcher should theoretically be able to generate more momentum from a power position with both of his feet on the ground, rather than waiting until maximum leg lift to begin moving toward the target. Using motion analysis, we tracked momentum as the average velocity of the pitcher's COMB—from first movement to foot strike. The velocity of COMB measurement allows us to measure the effect, since physics dictate that momentum is equal to mass times velocity (p = m x v), and the pitcher's mass is a constant in the equation. As such, if a pitcher's energy angle helps to generate more momentum, then our experimental groups should reflect that relationship with the velocity of COMB.

Group	Average energy-angle	SD (+/-)
Strong energy-angle	8.88 feet/second	0.24 ft/s
Weak energy-angle	8.48 feet/second	0.11 ft/s
Baseline	8.78 feet/second	0.15 ft/s

Table 9-4. The average velocity of COMB by group

As Table 9-4 shows, the differences between these groups appear to be pretty small at first glance, with just a 0.40 feet/second gap between the strong energy-angle group and the weak energy-angle group. However, the tests for significance, as detailed in Table 9-4, tell a slightly different story.

Strong vs. weak:	$t = 7.42$ for $n = 24$	Significant ($p < 0.005$)
	$t = 4.28$ for $N = 8$	Significant ($p < 0.005$)
Strong vs. baseline:	$t = 1.74$ for $n = 24$	Insignificant
	$t = 1.00$ for $N = 8$	Insignificant
Weak vs. baseline:	$t = 7.99$ for $n = 24$	Significant ($p < 0.005$)
	$t = 4.60$ for $N = 8$	Significant ($p < 0.005$)

Table 9-5. Velocity COMB into foot strike

The difference between the strong energy-angle pitchers and the baseline group was found to be statistically insignificant, while the players in the weak energy-angle group were determined to be measurably worse at generating momentum than the rest of the pitchers in the experiment. The significance of this difference holds up, compared to both the strong group and the baseline sample, even if the player sample size of $N = 8$ is used to compensate for clustering effects in the 3-pitch data. The results shown in Table 9-5 help to demonstrate that late initiation of forward movement creates an obstacle for a pitcher to achieve maximum momentum into foot strike.

Pitchers who have a good energy angle with strong momentum should have the ingredients necessary to generate a relatively long stride, since they are using that momentum to get further faster than players who have a weak energy angle. When calculating stride length, we controlled the confounding signature-related variable of a pitcher's height by simply dividing stride length by height, in a measure we refer to stride-length efficiency, which is reflected as a percentage of body height. Table 9-6 provides a breakdown of the stride-length efficiency ratings of our experimental groups.

Group	Average stride-length efficiency	SD (+/-)
Strong energy-angle	93.68 %	0.93 %
Weak energy-angle	90.47 %	0.75 %
Baseline	92.39 %	1.22 %

Table 9-6. A breakdown of stride-length efficiency ratings of the NPA/RDRBI sample set

Once again, the strong energy-angle group fared better than either the weak group or the baseline group when it came to creating a longer stride, as measured by the front of the rubber to the ankle of the landing foot. The weak energy-angle group achieved the smallest average stride length in the study, as compared to player height. Table 9-7 details the unpaired t-tests that reveal the strength of the differences between the various groups in our investigation.

Groups	t-test results	Significance
Strong vs. weak:	t = 13.19 for n = 24	Significant (p<0.005)
	t = 7.60 for N = 8	Significant (p<0.005)
Strong vs. baseline:	t = 4.13 for n = 24	Significant (p<0.005)
	t = 2.38 for N = 8	Significant (p< 0.050)
Weak vs. baseline:	t = 6.58 for n = 24	Significant (p<0.005)
	t = 3.79 for N = 8	Significant (p<0.005)

Table 9-7. Stride-length efficiency between groups (t-tests)

As Table 9-7 indicates, the differences in stride-length efficiency were significant for every between-group assessment, with the difference between strong and weak energy-angle players particularly strong. The results show that the strong energy-angle group had the best stride-length efficiency by a significant margin, which is another point that supports the argument that staying back is an inefficient method for moving into maximum leg lift.

The significant advantage for the strong energy-angle group is that these players are getting "further faster" than the weak energy-angle pitchers. As can be seen, the body is traveling faster for the strong energy-angle players. In addition, they clearly get further from the rubber with a longer relative stride. When thinking about how to determine if a pitcher has a fast delivery, however, we immediately reach for a stopwatch, in order to see how long it takes the player to get from first movement into foot strike, and then into ball release. In this regard, the key issue that arises is whether having a strong energy angle helps an athlete to get into foot strike in less time.

Group	Average time into foot strike	SD (+/-)
Strong energy-angle	0.94 seconds	0.02 seconds
Weak energy-angle	1.23 seconds	0.04 seconds
Baseline	1.09 seconds	0.03 seconds

Table 9-8. Average time into foot strike for the NPA/RDRBI sample groups

Sure enough, the pitchers in the weak energy-angle group take an incredible 30.8% more time to get into foot strike than the players who have a strong energy-angle. While this factor only amounts to a difference of 0.29 seconds, such a disparity is a large amount of time with respect to the whole pitch cycle. Consider that 0.29 seconds is approximately how much time many players take to complete the next four links in the kinetic chain that follow foot strike. By the time the average weak energy-angle pitcher gets into foot strike, the average pitcher in the strong energy-angle group has already completed ball release! Meanwhile, the baseline group falls appropriately right in the middle, between the weak and strong groups, taking an average of 16.0% more time than the strong energy-angle group to get from first movement to foot strike.

Groups	t-test results	Significance
Strong vs. weak:	t = 33.46 for n = 24	Significant (p<0.005)
	t = 19.28 for N = 8	Significant (p<0.005)
Strong vs. baseline:	t = 20.83 for n = 24	Significant (p<0.005)
	t = 12.00 for N = 8	Significant (p<0.005)
Weak vs. baseline:	t = 13.79 for n = 24	Significant (p<0.005)
	t = 7.95 for N = 8	Significant (p<0.005)

Table 9-9. Time into foot strike (seconds)

As Table 9-9 indicates, the measurement of foot-strike timing has yielded the largest measurable difference between our strong and weak energy-angle groups. In fact, the correlation for the entire data set between energy angle and foot-strike timing is $r^2 = -0.794$ (n = 90, N = 30), which indicates a very strong inverse relationship between the two variables. The correlation shows that players with a low energy angle take relatively longer to get into foot strike across the board. Collectively, the results of the last three measurements suggest the following sequence: those pitchers who initiate momentum directly from first movement, resulting in a strong energy-angle, are able to generate a fast velocity of COMB, which, in turn, helps to create a longer stride length in relatively little time.

While a well-functioning kinetic chain can be beautiful, getting into foot strike is only half the battle. As such, these results don't tell the whole story as to why these factors are an advantage. Gaining a longer stride with more momentum in less time may sound like a good idea, but how does this impact the final result? As we dig deeper into this issue and continue our way down the kinetic chain, we'll see how the numbers compare to conventional wisdom. The first step is to take a quick look at how these groups compare with respect to the dragline. Measuring the dragline allows us to study how all of these events contribute to links in the chain that follow foot strike. In this regard, the primary point of concern is the dragline distance from the front of the rubber to the ankle of the drag foot at release point.

The length of the dragline is affected by stride and momentum, as well as how far forward a pitcher can stack and track his upper body after foot strike. This distance also serves as an indicator of how far the pitcher has traveled from the rubber at release point. Tables 9-10 and 9-11 show that the players with a strong energy-angle continue the ongoing trend and get further with their dragline than the other pitchers in our study.

Group	Average dragline distance	SD (+/-)
Strong energy-angle	23.30 inches	0.75 inches
Weak energy-angle	19.44 inches	0.63 inches
Baseline	21.58 inches	0.50 inches

Table 9-10. Dragline distance from the rubber (inches)

Groups	t-test results	Significance
Strong vs. weak:	t = 19.34 for n = 24	Significant (p<0.005)
	t = 11.14 for N = 8	Significant (p<0.005)
Strong vs. baseline:	t = 9.37 for n = 24	Significant (p<0.005)
	t = 5.40 for N = 8	Significant (p<0.005)
Weak vs. baseline:	t = 13.07 for n = 24	Significant (p<0.005)
	t = 7.53 for N = 8	Significant (p<0.005)

Table 9-11. Dragline distance between groups (t-tests)

As expected, the strong energy-angle pitchers achieve a longer dragline than the baseline pitchers, who, in turn, have a significantly longer dragline than the players with a weak energy-angle. As such, the timeline of critical events has helped to predict and establish these relationships, and to better understand the value of these numbers so that we can apply the results when working with pitchers on the mound.

The conventional wisdom that says pitchers should stay back and stop at the top is one of the most widely accepted concepts with respect to pitching mechanics. In fact, a number of Major League organizations teach this idea throughout their development system. Furthermore, numerous pitching coaches all over the country adhere to this conventional wisdom at every level of baseball competition. At the NPA/RDRBI, we have learned to recognize the value of achieving a large energy angle. Successful pitchers in our extensive database have shown the same measurable trends that have been quantified in this chapter. In fact, any individual who ever gets the chance to watch rare video of the elite pitchers of the early 20th century will see that the best pitchers have never stayed back or stopped at the top. Among the *elite* pitchers who have generated an exceptional energy angle over the years are Sandy Koufax, Bob Feller, Bob Gibson, Walter Johnson, and Lefty Grove.

The popularity of "stay back" is so widespread that the idea of "lift and thrust" is often met with great amounts of criticism. In contrast, every piece of evidence suggests that a strong energy angle is a beneficial, if not integral, component of ideal pitching mechanics. It is a common link among the greatest pitchers in Major League history, including the best players in the game today, as well as the great athletes of years past. Unfortunately, bringing up the teach of initiating forward momentum immediately upon first movement is heresy in many coaching circles... *unless* the slide step is being discussed (a factor that will be addressed in the next chapter).

Tom's Wrap-Up

Before the "slide step" (in reality, "lift and thrust") is covered, it is helpful to put a "ribbon" on "stay back" and "stop at the top." Quite simply, both directives are invalid conventional wisdom teaches. Each causes inefficient timing, sequencing, and biomechanics, which singularly or collectively can have a negative impact on an athlete's level of performance and/or injury.

10

"The Slide Step"

"Use a Slide Step from the Stretch"

Using the slide step with men on base has become the accepted method for pitchers in the game today. In fact, the practice is encouraged by coaches at all competitive levels—from the Major Leagues on down to Little League. Conventional wisdom states that using a slide step from the stretch, rather than a normal leg kick, will get the pitcher to his release point in less time. The underlying objective of the slide step is to get the ball into the catcher's hands more quickly, in order to give him a better chance to throw out a runner who might be attempting to steal on the pitcher's first movement.

One of the interesting points about the slide step is that it is advocated by some of the same coaches who adhere to the precepts of "stay back" and "stop at the top." However, a key ingredient of the slide step is the initiation of forward momentum directly from first movement. In other words, these coaches are effectively telling their players to stay back when pitching from the windup, but do the opposite and move straight toward the target with runners on base. This message can be confusing, to say the least.

To this point in the book, one of the ongoing themes has been the importance of mechanical consistency, especially with respect to timing and sequencing. In effect, if a player is instructed to stay back from the windup, but get it going from the stretch, he has to master two completely different deliveries to be consistently effective.

When it comes to developing very young players, using the slide step is a lot to ask of someone who hasn't yet mastered the windup or the stretch, and whose body is growing so fast that its level of functional strength and flexibility is changing constantly. As such, we ask many of the young pitchers whom we see to pitch exclusively from the stretch until they have gained some mechanical consistency and functional strength.

Parents come to the NPA/RDRBI with Little Leaguers who have "a great arm from shortstop but can't throw hard or throw strikes from the mound." Why does this situation exist? One problem is the mound itself, which presents a new throwing and timing obstacle for Little League pitchers. Compounding this problem is the fact that many Little League mounds are not kept in proper condition. A young player may pitch from a mound with an appropriate slope in one game, and then pitch the following week from a steeper or flatter mound that has a relatively deep hole in front of the rubber and an even deeper hole in the landing area.

The second reason many Little League players have the problem with the transition from infield to the mound is the windup. When playing shortstop, even a young player will usually get his momentum going toward the target as soon as he starts to throw. Normally, he will display some degree of fluid timing from catch to release. On the other hand, when these same pitchers toe the rubber, they begin to imitate what they see on television. A kid will elaborately raise his hands over his head and try to challenge Dontrelle Willis for the biggest leg kick in baseball (non-Nolan division), all before even looking at his target to make the pitch. This approach gets in the way of what the player does naturally to throw any object, not just a baseball. Obviously, assuming a simple stretch position, with a comfortable leg kick and body thrust, offers the easiest solution for developing the basic elements involved in the timing and sequencing of efficient mechanics.

Clearly the slide step was designed to save delivery time from the stretch. The important point, however, is to know how much time it saves, versus a regular delivery, in order to study the tactical validity of the conventional wisdom. At the NPA/RDRBI, we ran a small experiment with a couple of pitchers to conduct a case study on the subject. Both players had been taught a slide step in the past, but were currently using a regular leg kick from the stretch position. This study captured a few of their fastballs using a slide step during their motion-analysis sessions, and compared them to their fastballs from the regular stretch. Table 10-1 presents the results of this study.

Pitcher C	Regular fastball	Slide-step fastball	Difference
Time of pitch cycle	1.12 seconds	0.97 seconds	0.15 seconds
Time to foot strike	0.97 seconds	0.83 seconds	0.14 seconds
Max leg height	54.7 %	43.6 %	11.1 %
Pitcher D	Regular fastball	Slide-step fastball	Difference
Time of pitch cycle	1.08 seconds	0.96 seconds	0.12 seconds
Time to toot strike	0.90 seconds	0.80 seconds	0.10 seconds
Max leg height	54.1 %	43.4 %	10.7 %
Energy angle	5.50 degrees	7.94 degrees	2.44 degrees

Table 10-1. Comparative case study of the impact of using a slide step vs. a regular stretch when throwing a fastball

Pitcher C had a pitch cycle of 0.15 seconds less for the slide step pitch, compared to his regular delivery from the stretch. Furthermore, he got into foot strike 0.14 seconds quicker. Pitcher D, on the other hand, got rid of the baseball 0.12 seconds faster with the slide step, including 0.10 seconds faster from first movement to foot strike. It should be noted, however, that both of these pitchers already had a relatively fast time into foot strike and ball release with a regular fastball from the stretch. Accordingly, it could reasonably be expected that players who are slower than average could see larger differences in release-point timing if they tried to use a slide step. Those same players will also have a tougher time adjusting to the difference in timing, the larger it gets from natural leg kick to slide step. It is also important to note that both pitchers lifted their front leg to about 54% of body height with a regular leg kick, but that number was down to approximately 43% for the slide-step fastball. This factor indicates the degree to which these pitchers altered their leg lift for the slide step, and it is interesting to observe that both of these pitchers made a similar adjustment.

Table 10-1 also included the energy angles for Pitcher D in order to make a specific point: many players can see a benefit from using the slide step, because it gets them to initiate forward momentum much sooner than they would with a regular leg kick. For example, pitcher D went from a relatively average energy angle of 5.50 degrees on his regular fastball to a strong 7.94-degree angle with a slide step. This marked change typically indicates that the pitcher has room for improvement with his regular stretch, by starting forward momentum sooner in his delivery. Many "stop-at-the-top" pitchers only show a good energy angle when they pitch with a slide step. The challenge that these players face, however, is that they typically have big problems with consistency, because the timing involved is so different.

To provide a baseline study of the functional costs and benefits of the slide step, an assumption can be made that the average pitcher releases the ball about 0.15 seconds quicker with a slide step than with a regular motion. This assumption should be appropriate, given the data for pitchers C and D and their relatively quick deliveries. As such, the question becomes, "What is the effect of delivering the ball 0.15 seconds faster?" The most obvious effect is that the catcher has about 0.15 seconds longer to try to throw out a stealing baserunner than he would with a regular delivery. The not-so-obvious effect is what the slide step does to a pitcher's mechanics.

As has been noted, the slide step can help initiate forward momentum. In fact, some "stop-at-the-top" pitchers do better with their timing from the slide step as a result of early momentum. On the other hand, the positive effect that energy angle has on timing and stride length can be negated by the low leg kick. A pitcher's style of leg kick is an aspect of his personal signature. In reality, some pitchers have a tougher time with the transition to employing a slide step than others. Using early momentum with an unnaturally small leg lift will cause many pitchers to get into foot strike too soon, before their upper body is ready to deliver the baseball. This can throw off the timing and sequencing of the events that occur in that short period of time between foot strike and ball release. The resulting pitch will often end up poorly located, with diminished velocity.

Detailing the benefits and costs of utilizing a slide step can help define its net usefulness. The benefits of a slide step are that it reduces the time from first movement to ball release by 0.15 second and that it offers a higher energy angle for many pitchers. In contrast, the main costs of using a slide step include the loss of natural leg kick, the loss of ideal timing, the need to adapt to a new delivery (particularly for young players), the potential for mislocated pitches, and the potential loss of velocity.

The relative impact of these pros and cons can be influenced by a pitcher's mechanical consistency. Without consistency, a pitcher might not receive much of a benefit in pitch-cycle time or his energy angle. Meanwhile, a pitcher can minimize many of the costs by achieving consistency in timing and mechanics with the slide step. The question then becomes: how do these effects translate to the tactical use of the slide step in a baseball game?

To answer this question correctly, it is necessary to travel back to the time when the slide step was popularized. Therefore, it is essential to take a look at the run-scoring environment that produced the perceived need for the slide step in the mid-1980s. Table 10-2 presents the stolen-base and selected offensive production totals for the 15-year period from 1977–1991, detailed in five-year increments (stats via www.baseball-reference.com).

Time period	SB attempts/game	Runs/game	HR/game
1977–1981	1.123	4.276	0.756
1982–1986	1.123	4.320	0.824
1987–1991	1.135	4.312	0.828

Table 10-2. Stolen base and selected offensive production totals for the period 1977–1991

From 1977 to 1991, Major League players, such as Rickey Henderson, Tim Raines, and Vince Coleman, were tearing up the base paths, routinely stealing more than 70 bases in a season. In fact, Henderson stole 70 or more bases five times between 1980 and 1986, while Raines did it every year from 1981–1986. Coleman was only 24 years old in 1986, but already had two consecutive years of 100+ steals under his belt, and would top the century mark again in 1987, followed by 81 stolen bases in 1988. In the 1980s, speed was perceived as one of the biggest assets a player could bring to the field, and it is relatively easy to see why Major League teams felt the need to do something to stop the opposing team's running game. As Table 10-3 indicates, things started to change in the 1990's.

Time period	SB attempts/game	Runs/game	HR/game
1992–1996	1.065	4.696	0.946
1997–2001	0.975	4.913	1.101
2002–2006	0.780	4.722	1.075

Table 10-3. Stolen base and selected offensive production totals for the period 1992–2006.

The rate of stolen-base attempts per game has been decreasing steadily for the last 20 years. With it, the 70-steal season has just about vanished. In fact, the 78-steal performance that Jose Reyes accomplished in 2007 is tied (with Marquis Grissom, 1992) for the highest number of stolen bases in a season since Vince Coleman's '88 performance. The only other player to break the 70-steal barrier since 2000 is Scott Podsednik, who swiped exactly 70 with the Milwaukee Brewers in 2004. While there were 15 player-seasons with 80+ stolen bases between 1980 and 1988, no player in Major League baseball has surpassed that mark since then. Overall, the number of stolen-base attempts per game has decreased almost 17% from the time period of 1977–1991 to 1992–2006.

It is also interesting to note that run-scoring and home-run rates in the Major Leagues began escalating sharply in the early 1990s, and then peaked later in the decade. The last five years saw less run scoring and fewer home runs per game than the previous five-year period, although levels are still higher than they were at the beginning of the offensive explosion. Comparing the two 15-year time periods of 1977–1991 and 1992–2006, the number of runs per game increased by almost nine percent, while ratios of home runs per game increased by close to 30%.

The increase in run scoring has created a different offensive environment in the game today. The strategy of playing "small ball" to manufacture a single run has diminished utility as long as league-wide, run-scoring increases. Meanwhile, stealing bases is a key component to the "small-ball" strategy. Successfully stealing a base also loses all marginal value if the baserunner later scores on a home run, since a home run would have plated the runner from any base. As the statistics show, the odds of that occurrence happening have greatly increased since the days when the slide step became popular.

The on-field dynamic of Major League baseball fluctuates over time. Not surprisingly, the usefulness of the stolen base is sensitive to this ever-changing dynamic. As such, a manager is less inclined to call for a steal attempt if his team is down by more than two runs late in the game. The odds of a two-run spread increases with general run-scoring rates. For example, in an environment of low run-scoring, a manager has more incentive to play for one run in the early innings, because that lone run might be enough to win the ball game. In the high-octane offensive environment that exists in baseball today, however, it becomes more important for a team to put together a big inning. As a result, the risk of generating an out on the base paths as a consequence of a failed stolen-base attempt becomes much more valuable than the prospect of gaining an extra base.

To the proponents of the slide step, the decrease in the number of stolen-base attempts over the last two decades can be construed as evidence that the strategy is working. It can also be argued, however, that steal attempts are down because of the change in baseball's offensive environment. In reality, there are so many factors in play in this situation that it is impossible to isolate one particular reason for the decrease in the number of stolen-base attempts. The important point to take from this discussion, however, is that preventing stolen bases does not have the same relative benefit that it had in the 1980s. Stolen-base attempts have become increasingly rare. Meanwhile, the marginal value per stolen-base attempt at the Major League level has decreased at the same time.

The offensive pressures that brought about the popularization of the slide step no longer exist in the game today. Given this changing situation, the question must be asked, "Is the benefit of the slide step still worth the cost tradeoff?" It is important to note that the key issue is not whether the slide step was a good idea in the first place. Instead, the fundamental concern is whether it is a practical method for Major League pitchers in baseball's current environment.

In reality, at any competitive baseball level below professional players, the variation in receiving ability, "pop" times, arm strength, and accuracy among amateur catchers is large enough that the 0.15 second advantage afforded by using a slide step can't reasonably be expected to make a consistent difference with respect to success in throwing out attempted basestealers. Only at the elite levels are catchers reliable enough to consider this type of mechanical change. After all, a slide step has zero benefit if the catcher's throw is off the mark. As a result, amateur coaches have little incentive to alter a pitcher's mechanics in order to provide their catchers with an "advantage" on a stolen-base attempt.

In an average baseball game, a pitcher will make about two-thirds of his pitches from the stretch position. The most crucial pitches of each game are made from the stretch, with runners on base threatening to score. A pitcher gets to start every inning fresh from the windup. About one-third of the time, however, the first hitter of the inning will get on base and put the pitcher into the stretch with zero outs. Once he's in that spot, he will be pitching from the stretch until the bases clear (e.g., pickoff, a double play, runs scoring, failed stolen base, etc.).

From 2002 to 2006, Major League teams averaged 0.780 stolen-base attempts per game. In effect, a pitcher can have a 110-pitch outing, throwing approximately 70 of those pitches from the stretch. The odds are that maybe one of those 70 pitches will actually involve a stolen-base attempt. Think about that; a pitcher is asked to completely alter his mechanics for 70 pitches, so that the catcher might have a better chance to throw out a runner on just one of those pitches. Compounding the issue is the fact that there will be many games during the season in which no runner will attempt to steal a base. In those situations, all of those pitches with a slide step will be wasted. If this same pitcher hangs just one of those 70 pitches as a result of being too quick with his slide step, it could end up in the right field bleachers, plating at least two runs in the process. This begs the question: how many runners will that pitcher have to help get caught stealing just to make up for the runs that scored on the slide step-induced home run?

The biggest problem with the continued use of the slide step is that it ignores the importance of the single-most meaningful aspect of every play on the baseball diamond: the pitch itself. As has previously been discussed, conventional wisdom has led some coaches to teach their pitchers to alter their mechanics in order to create an enhanced angle on hitters. All factors considered, these coaches should understand the importance of pitch execution. Scouts who evaluate pitching talent study what the ball does from release point until it hits the catcher's glove, sometimes at the expense of evaluating mechanical efficiency. Grades for pitches are doled out based on movement, and some coaches approach mechanics based around the type of trajectory that the pitcher creates at release point. Therefore, it seems odd that many coaches appear so eager to sacrifice a pitcher's mechanical signature, efficiency, consistency, velocity, command, and pitch trajectory just to keep a baserunner hugging first base.

The fact is that a pitcher has one job: to deliver the pitch that was called to the catcher's target. He is asked to do this job repeatedly, up to 100 or more times per game. Because a pitcher's job is the most important on the diamond, a coach better have a pretty good reason to make a change to how the pitcher gets his job done. In the case of preventing stolen bases, the responsibility falls on not just the pitcher, but also the catcher, the infielders, and the baserunner himself. If the catcher can't make the transfer from glove to hand, or makes a poor throw, or the infielder bobbles that throw, then the outcome of the stolen-base attempt is literally out of the pitcher's hands, regardless of how quickly he delivered the baseball. In reality, sometimes a baserunner has lots of speed and gets a good jump, and is going to steal a base no matter who was on the mound or behind the plate.

This situation does not absolve the pitcher of all responsibility for baserunners. He has the ability to contribute to preventing stolen bases without throwing a pitch to the hitter. Most baseball people refer to this ability as a pitcher's "pick-off move." At the NPA/RDRBI, however, we teach every pitcher a "hold-'em-close" move. We renamed the pick-off because the real objective for a throw-over to first base is to keep the runner close, and prevent him from getting a good lead. A pitcher with a good "hold-'em-close" move does not need as quick of a delivery to have the same impact on preventing stolen bases. However, once the pitcher initiates movement toward home plate, everything he does should be triggered toward the single goal of executing a perfect pitch. For most players, a slide step is not ideally conducive with this goal.

Another benefit to the slide step—one that hasn't been addressed to this point—is the potential psychological impact that it can have on opposing players and managers. If an opposing coach sees a pitcher with a high leg kick from the stretch, he will often assume that the pitcher is very slow to the plate. In response, he'll have every player with speed try to steal second base, especially at the amateur levels. Pitchers who use a slide step discourage the strategy of running rampant, even if they are not particularly quick to the plate. By the same token, pitchers who employ a strong lift and thrust to generate momentum will get into ball release very quickly, compared to pitchers who stay back. As such, a coach whose team attempts to run on these pitchers will quickly find out that they don't need to use a slide step to give their catcher ample time to show off his arm and make a throw.

The slide step was put into practice in a different time in baseball, and it was designed for a different brand of Major League baseball than currently exists. While it may have been appropriate for a game built on speed, today's game is fueled by power. The initial days when the slide step evolved entailed a time before motion analysis, when baseball was still coming to grips with this factor called "pitching mechanics," and how they influence the result of every pitch. The books written by Tom in the 1980s and early 1990s show how much his perspective has changed in the last 20 years thanks to motion-capture technology. In fact, many of the conventional wisdoms that are being challenged in this book are based on Tom's past teachings.

Despite this evolution, Major League baseball teams continue to employ the slide step with their pitchers in an effort to quell the running game. We have discussed all of these concepts with individual scouts from different Major League organizations, and they have literally laughed at the idea of big league teams ditching the slide step. Interesting enough, each of these scouts agreed with the logic of not employing the slide step, and none of these scouts have offered any reasonable counterarguments that would sway our analysis. While we may have convinced the scouts themselves (or maybe not), not one of these individuals thought that their organization would be willing to buck such an established convention, regardless of the science or the logic behind it.

The bottom line is that the slide step is being used to prevent an occurrence that has become increasingly rare in an offensive environment—in which preventing the stolen base should take a back seat to focusing on preventing the long ball. As has been seen, however, these conditions are not mutually exclusive. A coach still has the choice to have his pitcher use a slide step to prevent steals, though it puts his pitcher at greater risk for giving up home runs. Even more importantly, using the slide step can create inefficiency by forcing a player to learn new mechanics that can go against the grain of personal signature and timing. As such, the best reason to avoid teaching the slide step to younger players is because it can hinder development. Accordingly, it is essential that coaches shift their focus away from altering the mechanics of their pitchers in an attempt to prevent stolen bases, and back toward finding the delivery for each pitcher that results in ideal pitch execution while minimizing injury risk.

Tom's Wrap-Up

Why not teach slide-step *timing* with a normal leg lift from both stretch and windup? A final note: When timing a pitcher from the windup, do not start the clock until the pivot foot is posted, and the total body initiates the first forward movement toward the target.

This section has addressed a number of conventional wisdoms, including "don't rush," "stay back," "stop at the top," "stay over the rubber," and "find a balance point." Each of these precepts involves teaching a mechanic that can adversely affect timing, momentum, and the natural kinematic sequencing of a pitcher's delivery. These teaches make even less sense when coaches tell a pitcher to "slide" or "glide step" with men on base to help him be quicker to the plate. How would you process being told "don't rush," "stay back," but "slide step" to "be quick and release the ball out front?" Convoluted? Absolutely! Yet, believe it or not, pitchers can get skilled at these inefficiencies, even though it's more efficient and effective to initiate forward movement simultaneously with leg lift. The best instruction would be this simple: in one second or less, start to fall, lift to tolerance, and stride as far and as fast as possible without losing your balance or posture. As such, for both coaches and players alike, the statistical evidence that supports the importance of first forward movement, dynamic balance, stride distance, and time is quite clear.

STRIDE & MOMENTUM

Section 4

11

Breaking Down Leg Lift to Foot Strike

Coaches' Conventional Wisdom, Leg Lift to Foot Strike

- "Don't rush:"
  - ✓ "Drop and drive"
  - ✓ "Tall and fall"
- "Break your hands toward second base, your glove toward the plate:"
  - ✓ "Reach back"
  - ✓ "Break your hands early"
  - ✓ "Thumbs to thigh, ball to sky"
- "Stride straight at the plate:"
  - ✓ "Don't stride across your body"
  - ✓ "Don't open your stride"
- "Don't land on your heel:"
  - ✓ "Land on the ball of the foot"
  - ✓ "Point your toe toward the plate"
- "Shorten your stride"

Breakdown: Leg Lift to Foot Strike

This section describes, discusses, and debunks a bunch of conventional wisdoms involving a pitcher's movement toward home plate. The laws of inertia and the physics of biomechanics reveal that pitching is a simple concept with a complex series of adaptations. An object at rest wants to stay at rest, while an object in motion wants to stay in motion. Energy into the baseball is maximized when total-body mass is directed and delivered as far and as fast as physically possible without adversely affecting kinetic energy, timing, kinematic sequencing, and mechanical efficiency. In contrast, each of the coach's conventional wisdoms that are listed at the beginning of this chapter can adversely affect a pitcher's natural delivery or what we call his *genetic signature.*

Maximum leg lift is a critical point as a pitcher moves from setup to foot strike. Timing also plays an important role during this phase of the delivery. While the ideal amount of time from first movement to foot strike may vary from pitcher to pitcher, the numbers fall within a narrow range. Despite this small variance, attaining ideal timing into foot strike is one of the toughest tasks for a pitcher to accomplish. Why? Because functional strength and flexibility are also part of the balance and posture that are necessary for a pitcher to find timing consistency through leg lift and body thrust into foot strike.

Weak links, muscle failure from overuse, and lack of recovery are examples of reasons why young pitchers from Little League baseball to Major League baseball can struggle to find their ideal timing from setup to foot strike (particularly when pitching from the stretch). Many players are unaware that timing and sequencing are critical to repeatable mechanics, health, and performance. Surprisingly, there are pitchers at the MLB level who 1) don't know their own ideal timing signature, and/or 2) who lack the functional strength necessary to maintain it. This factor is an area where the established greats really distinguish themselves on the mound. The previously discussed "five aces" do an outstanding job of getting into foot strike from the same position at the same time with the same sequence, whether it is a fastball in April or a curveball in September. Nolan Ryan, for example, was known to land in the same *cleat mark* on every pitch for a whole game.

It is important to remember that "ideal" timing is both relative and specific to each pitcher. One pitcher might find his ideal delivery by getting into foot strike 0.90 seconds after first movement, while such a timing sequence would be too fast for some other players. Regrettably, a number of baseball coaches and athletes exist who don't realize the importance of timing. In fact, most pitchers don't know what *their* ideal timing signature is or feels like. Making matters worse, there are several ungrounded nuggets of conventional wisdom that dictate how a pitcher should get from first movement into foot strike, covering timing, speed, and the physical movements necessary to striding far and fast. As such, these are just the tip of the conventional wisdom iceberg.

12

"Don't Rush"

"Don't rush."
"Drop and drive."
"Tall and fall."

Many pitchers are told not to "rush" through their delivery, but rather to take their time with a nice "smooth" pace. In turn, those players who generate a lot of momentum right out of the box are often derided for having "violent" mechanics. Pitchers who have earned the "violent" tag are assumed to be at an increased risk for injury, while the pitchers with smooth mechanics are projected to be safe in comparison. If a delivery is too violent, the pitcher will get sent to the bullpen, with the intention of limiting the wear and tear on his arm. From a pitching standpoint, however, the definition of "violent" has not been established. As such, many baseball scouts and coaches disagree on what constitutes a violent delivery. As you've already read and will read many times in this book, coaches tend to only teach what they can see. Slowing a pitcher down ("don't rush") is a well-intentioned coaching tip that allows an instructor to "see" a perfect delivery, at the expense of what may already be dynamically efficient mechanics for a pitcher at higher speeds.

Those players who have a strong energy angle (a by-product of initiating movement toward the target as soon as the front leg lifts off of the ground) often seem to rush from first movement into foot strike. As was pointed out previously, these players will often have a lot of speed and momentum as they get into foot strike, which increases their stride length and kinetic energy. The evidence so far has suggested that all of these factors are integral aspects of strong mechanical efficiency. On the other hand, many coaches discourage a high degree of momentum. For these coaches, it's difficult to accept the fact that what is otherwise pleasant to the eye may not be functional on the mound when the athlete is competing.

To investigate this matter further, it is helpful to take a closer look at the momentum measure previously discussed—the velocity of the center of mass of the body (COMB), from first movement to foot strike. This variable is not an instantaneous measure of velocity, but rather the average velocity for the early links in the chain. Accordingly, if a player's body covers 7.00 feet of ground in 1.00 second from first movement to foot strike, his velocity of COMB is 7.00 feet/second.

All pitchers	8.61 feet/sec, +/- 0.10 feet/sec	n = 92
Pro	8.71 feet/sec, +/- 0.14 feet/sec	n = 24
College	8.60 feet/sec, +/- 0.15 feet/sec	n = 52
High school	8.45 feet/sec, +/- 0.15 feet/sec	n = 16

Table 12-1. Average velocity of COMB into foot strike

As Table 12-1 shows, the professional pitchers in our data set generate the most momentum, on average. Furthermore, the velocity levels decrease with skill level. While this finding would seem to be further evidence that generating momentum is a good thing, the numbers appear to be pretty close together, with the pros generating just 3.1% more velocity than the high school players, on average.

Pro-college	t = 3.08	Significant at $p < 0.005$
College-HS	t = 3.50	Significant at $p < 0.005$
Pro-HS	t = 5.60	Significant at $p < 0.005$

Table 12-2. Unpaired t-tests for each average velocity of COMB into foot strike sample

Similar to the energy-angle groups, Table 12-2 indicates that the difference in momentum between each of these skill groups is significant, despite the small difference in numerical magnitude. The small standard deviations indicate that the data points are tightly distributed, and that a player with a value of 8.70 feet/second is significantly better at generating momentum than a pitcher who travels an average of just 0.10 feet/second slower. It's likely that a much greater disparity in magnitude would be observed if instantaneous velocity of COMB at foot strike were calculated, rather than the average. By taking the average measurement, we fail to determine whether momentum is consistent (linear) or changing over time (curved). If players generally increase their level of momentum as they get close to foot strike, then the pitchers with a high average velocity of COMB would likely show even higher instantaneous velocities in comparison.

In fact, many pitchers show a distinctly non-linear pattern with respect to velocity of COMB from first movement to foot strike. These players display one speed from first movement into maximum leg lift, and then find a "second gear" to get from leg lift into foot contact. Pitchers who stay back and stop at the top will not only have a slow speed, but also a negative velocity of COMB if they move backward to get into leg lift, before moving forward. Rather than a second gear, these players look more like they are shifting from reverse into first gear, once they get going toward the plate. This effect is impossible to detect using the average velocity of COMB measurement, but it could be measured by utilizing instantaneous velocities at different points in the delivery.

Nolan Ryan is a great example of a pitcher who found a "second gear." During his playing career, Nolan would initiate his forward momentum as soon as his heel lifted off the ground, but he drifted toward the plate very slowly as he got into maximum leg lift. Ryan had an extremely high leg kick, and after reaching maximum lift, he would suddenly burst from that position into foot strike. When you overlay Ryan's delivery on top of just about any other elite pitcher, he will lag behind the other player until leg lift, after which, he will surge past his counterpart, getting into foot strike in less time and with a longer stride. The presence of the "second gear" illustrates how energy angle and average velocity of COMB can be misleading, with respect to describing the momentum of certain players. It should be noted, however, that Nolan Ryan is a biomechanical exception to many rules, and his shift from first gear into essentially third gear is extremely unique. Very few players have an obvious forward "gear change," and we have personally never seen one that's as dramatic as Ryan's.

When evaluating energy angle, an apparent connection between COMB velocity and stride length efficiency was observed. For example, the players in the good energy-angle group showed significant improvement in both of these measurements as well. As such, it makes intuitive sense that generating more momentum leads to a longer stride. Looking at the whole sample, a correlation of $r^2 = +0.702$ (n = 92) exists between velocity of COMB and stride-length efficiency, which is a strong, positive indicator that confirms this relationship for the athletes in our data set.

Accordingly, it would appear that "rushing" isn't such a bad idea after all, unless generating more kinetic energy and gaining a longer stride length are considered a negative. The question of whether a longer stride is truly a benefit will be addressed later in this book, as some coaches think that a shorter stride is an advantage. To this point, all indications support the premise that the aforementioned variables are positively correlated with performance, given that the best players have the highest values for all of these mechanical stats.

There are many more examples of players who go too slow with their delivery than players who go too fast. The NPA/RDRBI has studied how going too slow into foot strike can have an effect on the links that follow in the kinetic chain. One of the more popular sayings at the NPA/RDRBI to describe one typical result states that "it's not a spinning out problem, it's a going too slow problem." The "spin-out problem" will be covered in more detail in the next section. At this point, the focus is on addressing other aspects of the "going too slow problem."

Coaches who tell their players not to rush their delivery usually prefer that their pitchers take their time by staying back. Once the pitcher has stopped at the top, however, these coaches then ask their players to follow yet another conventional wisdom to get from maximum leg lift into foot strike. In this case, the conventional coach has two choices: "drop and drive" or "tall and fall." Both of these proposed solutions involve the pitcher staying tall at maximum lift. One of them suggests that the player "drop" by lowering his center of mass, while the other concept tells him to "stay tall" and "fall" down the slope of the mound.

These conventional wisdoms are intertwined in a similar line of thinking—both of the conventional solutions for what to do after maximum leg lift involve inefficient dynamic balance. Dynamic balance is a term that describes how well a pitcher keeps his head over his center of mass throughout the entire delivery. As such, any movement that veers from a trajectory that is on the target line and parallel to the slope of the mound is inefficient. A pitcher who fails to have balance going into foot strike will have a very difficult time coordinating the links that follow in the kinetic chain. In the process, he will place himself at an increased risk of injury, while diminishing his level of performance.

Taking it further, any solution that asks a pitcher to stay tall above his natural balance height will fail to take advantage of optimal balance. In turn, it will create obstacles to achieving mechanical efficiency into foot strike. Likewise, "drop and drive" results in the pitcher undergoing a forced change in balance, from leg lift to foot strike. Both of these conventional instructions deter a pitcher from the goal of sustaining optimal dynamic balance, an attribute that requires minimal head movement relative to the player's center of mass, while maintaining a height that is suitable for his level of functional strength.

While this section has presented a discussion of how favorable it is for pitchers to generate a great deal of momentum, deliveries that involve such momentum can also appear to be "max effort," which is a warning sign for many coaches and scouts. Pitchers who have a max-effort delivery are perceived to be at a higher risk of fatigue and/or injury, even though no consensus opinion exists as to what constitutes "max effort." To some, the term is equivalent to rushing from leg lift into foot strike, and is used interchangeably with the "violent" tag. To others, a max-effort delivery is one with high angular velocities of the pelvis, trunk, or throwing arm. These attributes are commonly described as violent by some evaluators, and yet there are others who would disagree and call it "great arm action."

The key is to let the pitcher show the coach his ideal timing, rather than have the coach tell the pitcher what the player's ideal timing should be. Every player can tell when he executes a good pitch. The key fundamental for a coach is to help a pitcher identify and anchor on the timing that will provide him with a high degree of mechanical efficiency. In this regard, most coaches have found that the best method is to let the pitcher find his ideal timing, naturally, in the bullpen. If an athlete starts out too slow, then the coach can have the player work on initiating momentum sooner, until he finds a pitch where he "lines everything up" and throws a great pitch with good mechanics. With a stopwatch in his hand, the coach can then tell his pitcher that he got into foot strike in "X.XX" seconds on that pitch, and that he should try to find that timing again. When he hits that timing again later in the bullpen session, it's the coach's job to point it out and anchor on that timing signature for future instruction. It's best to personalize a pitcher's delivery. Telling the pitcher that the anchored pitch is his timing, and nobody else's, entitles a timing ownership that is unique and becomes an integral part of the player's personal signature.

If timing into foot strike is so important, the issue arises as to why is it yet equally underappreciated by many pitching coaches. It's common to see even Major League pitchers, who have inconsistent timing, miss their target badly on a pitch and then curse in frustration, without knowing why they missed. Conversely, we have worked with players as young as 10 or 11 years old who have been able to find their own personal ideal timing. The combination of timing awareness and regular practice enables them to find mechanical consistency and throw strikes. Even these young players can identify why a pitch missed the target, once they understand the fact that going faster or slower can affect their command of pitch execution.

This factor is a major area of pitcher development that apparently gets overlooked by some professional teams, judging by the relative age of the big leaguers who struggle with timing consistency. This problem simply doesn't exist with the five aces, or most of the other pitchers who have found prolonged success at the highest competitive level.

In our opinion, having the ability to repeat the personal ideal timing is the single most critical aspect of the pitching delivery. In fact, it would even make sense for organizations to require that the developing pitchers in their respective systems achieve a level of consistency with respect to mechanical timing and efficiency before ascending to the highest level. In that regard, every pitcher in the organization should have a personal benchmark for his ideal timing signature, with the knowledge that these benchmarks are not necessarily static and evolve over time. The big leagues are not the ideal platform for a rookie to make timing, sequencing, and/or mechanical adjustments. Every pitcher should quantify and know his own delivery better than anyone else on the planet, including his pitching coach.

Tom's Wrap-Up

Our response to the conventional wisdoms of "don't rush," "drop and drive" is "please do rush your delivery." When shifting your weight initially, go as far and as fast as your total body will physically allow. Then, stay (dynamically) balanced with minimum head movement or posture change, because one inch of inappropriate head movement can cause up to two inches at release point. Finally, land into foot strike between .95–1.05 seconds to optimize kinetic energy, kinematic sequencing, and efficient mechanics.

13

"Reach Back"

"Break your throwing hand toward second base, and your glove to the plate."
"Reach back."
"Break your hands early."
"Thumbs to sky, ball to thigh."

The throwing arm is often the first thing that people notice about a pitcher, including most hitters, coaches, scouts, and fans. This observation is natural, since most individuals who watch the game pay attention to the baseball right out of the pitcher's hand. Obviously, the throwing arm has a strong influence on delivering the ball to home plate. Terms such as "arm path" and "arm action" are used to describe how a pitcher gets his pitching hand from out of the glove to the point of ball release. As such, many coaches have strict advice for this sequence.

The pitching hand typically breaks from the glove hand soon after maximum leg lift. In that regard, many pitchers are instructed to "break their throwing hand toward second base, and their glove to the plate" during this phase. Many of these players are taught to "reach back" with the pitching hand as they get from leg lift into foot strike, such that the throwing arm fully extends to a straight position. Some coaches believe that this step will help to generate more velocity, and since radar-gun readings are the bread and butter for most pitching evaluators, throwing-arm extension has become a teaching staple. That being said, Figures 13-1 and 13-2 show how the five aces break their hands and get into foot strike.

Martinez and Oswalt both seem to follow the conventional wisdom to a T. They are each clearly bringing the throwing arm toward second base, with the glove to the plate. Both pitchers are "reaching back," with a throwing arm that is close to full extension. Greg Maddux brings his arm back toward second and his glove to the plate, but is not reaching back to the extent of either Oswalt or Martinez. Maddux, instead, has a bit of slack or bend in his throwing arm as he gets into foot strike.

Figure 13-1. Martinez, Maddux, and Oswalt breaking the hands as they get into foot strike

Figure 13-2. Johnson and Santana display a different approach

Figure 13-2 shows Randy Johnson and Johan Santana, both of whom bend their elbows more than the preceding other three aces. Both players also get some additional upper-body twist to create hip-shoulder separation. The result is that their throwing hand points beyond second base, as each gets into foot strike. The glove is pointing closer to the left-handed batter's box than straight at the plate.

Although it doesn't perfectly apply to all of these elite pitchers, it seems that the conventional wisdom addressed in this chapter does have some merit. In particular, the "reach-back" concept does not appear to be as prevalent as the "hand toward second, glove to home" rule with these pitchers. The conventional wisdom, however, doesn't stand up if we look just a bit further down the active ERA leader board at the next pair of elite pitchers. Brandon Webb is actually tied at #4 with Johnson and Santana with a 3.22 ERA for his career (through 2007), although Brandon's performance involves fewer innings. The #7 pitcher on the active ERA leader board is longtime Atlanta Brave John Smoltz. Figure 13-3 illustrates Webb and Smoltz as they get into foot strike.

Figure 13-3. Webb and Smoltz have a more unique method of breaking the hands

Neither of these players is reaching back toward second base after breaking his hands. In fact, Webb is already bringing his pitching hand upward into a "cocked" position, before he has begun to rotate his trunk and shoulders. Meanwhile, Smoltz brings his elbows up higher than his shoulders, while leaving his hand and glove pointing downward as he gets into foot strike. The mechanical tendencies deviate further from the conventional wisdom as we move through these pairs of elite pitchers, and lead us to question whether "reach back" is an optimal solution for all players.

One factor that all seven of these players have in common at this point in the delivery is each of these pitchers shows an "opposite-and-equal" upper body as he gets into foot strike. Opposite and equal refers to a pitcher's elbow angles, and implies that the player should have the same angle of bend for both the pitching arm and the glove-side arm, and that those arms should appear opposite, such that they mirror each other. A closer look at the images in Figures 13-1, 13-2, and 13-3 shows that all of these pitchers achieve opposite-and-equal elbow angles, whether they bring their hands straight back like Roy Oswalt, with a bend like Randy Johnson, or pointed vertically like Webb or Smoltz. It's actually the angle of the shoulders, relative to the hips, at foot strike that determines the direction of the arms as the hands break.

The glove-side arm "mirrors" the elbow angle of the throwing arm for each of these elite players, a factor that serves as another strategic point for preserving dynamic balance throughout the delivery. The equal-and-opposite arms help to keep a pitcher balanced in the same way that it does for a tightrope walker. One factor that the best pitchers in the game consistently display is opposite and equal as they get into foot strike. Achieving this positioning isn't as easy as it looks, however. Young players have an especially tough time with opposite and equal. A baseball weighs five ounces, while the average Little League glove weighs about one-and-a-half pounds. Such an imbalance can be difficult to overcome on every pitch, especially if a pitcher lacks sufficient functional strength.

As has been seen, the "break the hands toward second base" rule works pretty well for some pitchers, but opposite and equal does a better job of describing what the best players do on the mound. Like many conventional wisdoms, "reach back" is an attempt by some coaches to get every pitcher on

Figure 13-4. Cole Hamels of the Philadelphia Phillies displays a classic example of opposite-and-equal arm angles that most coaches look for, with his throwing hand breaking toward second base, and his glove mirroring that action toward the plate

their staff to look the same during this phase of the delivery. In reality, the method that a pitcher uses to break his hands and get the upper body prepared for foot strike is largely based on his personal signature. The conventional wisdom is perhaps too specific, since the pitchers who follow such rules will usually result in an opposite and equal. On the other hand, there are many pitchers with a good opposite and equal who do not adhere to the conventional wisdom.

Another example of conventional wisdom involves the concept of breaking the throwing hand from the glove. In this regard, some coaches tell a pitcher to "break your hands early," such that the pitching hand separates from the glove close to maximum leg lift. The theory underlying this advice is that pitchers who break their hands early will have more time to reach back as far as possible with the pitching hand, and reap the perceived velocity benefits of further reach. This conventional wisdom is a rare example of coaches trying to dictate kinematic sequencing in the delivery. As has been discussed, timing is an element of both sequencing and mechanical efficiency. Some players will naturally find it difficult to adjust their timing to the concept of "break your hands early." The more dramatic result of following such advice is the ripple effect it can have on the kinetic chain and the disruption of a pitcher's kinematic sequencing.

When a pitcher breaks his hands, it essentially begins the upper-body portion of the delivery. After the arms have reached opposite and equal, the pitcher initiates the angular rotation of his trunk, such that the chest and shoulders rotate around the spine. For a right-handed pitcher, the trunk rotates counter-clockwise (bird's eye view) from a position facing toward third base, while a left-handed pitcher rotates clockwise from a starting position facing first base. Timing and sequencing the trunk rotation is a critical aspect of mechanical efficiency, and these conventional wisdoms can disrupt that timing by artificially starting the upper-body sequence too early.

The pitching delivery coordinates a combination of linear and rotational movements into a precise sequence that takes place within a very narrow range of time. The three rotational elements that are necessary to throw a baseball occur in the following order:
- Angular rotation of the pelvis (hips) around the spine
- Angular rotation of the trunk (shoulders) around the spine
- Angular rotation of the throwing arm (at shoulder and elbow)

The angular rotation of a pitcher's pelvis starts soon after maximum leg lift, and continues during stride and momentum, as measured by tracking the line that represents the player's hips in degrees of rotation. With this in mind, the terms "pelvis rotation" and "hip rotation" will be used interchangeably in this book. Neither term should be confused with external hip rotation, which describes the movement at individual joints, such as when the front leg "opens up" to get into foot strike. Likewise, the term "rotation of the shoulders" will sometimes be used to describe trunk rotation around the spine, as the degrees of rotation are tracked as the left and right shoulders move through the motion. External and internal rotation of the throwing shoulder/elbow at the joint is the third type of angular rotation involved in the pitching sequence. Internal rotation of the throwing arm (at the shoulder/elbow) occurs just after the pitcher's forearm lays back and reaches maximum external rotation (MER). MER ideally coincides with the time that the trunk and shoulders rotate square to the plate. Internal rotation of the throwing shoulder/elbow coincides with low back and trunk flexion, with the forearm moving forward and snapping straight into the release point and follow-through.

Figure 13-5. Cole Hamels at maximum external rotation (MER) of the throwing arm (at the shoulder), just before the forearm starts forward into internal rotation and ball release

The difference in timing between pelvis rotation and trunk rotation creates a separation between the front hip and the throwing shoulder. The axis lines through the hips and shoulders can be tracked to study the angle of separation that is created due to this timing difference. The result is that a pitcher appears to "load" his upper body by delaying trunk rotation, while the hips are rotating to prepare the lower body for foot strike, which increases hip-shoulder separation until trunk rotation begins. This load is actually very similar to that of a hitter, which is also based on hip-shoulder separation and timing of upper-body rotation.

Some pitchers display a very large load with their upper body, and appear to "show the numbers" (on the back of their jersey) to the hitter. This factor has been seen already with Randy Johnson and Johan Santana. Another great example of this situation is 2007 A.L. Cy Young Award winner, C.C. Sabathia. These players all use their upper body to create separation between their hips and shoulders. Compared to the average pitcher, these players typically have a

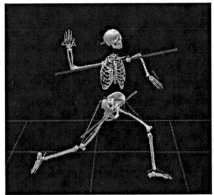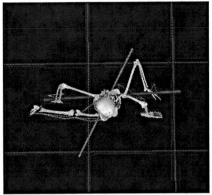

Figure 13-6. Side and top motion-analysis views of a pitcher at maximum hip-shoulder separation. The lower line is an axis through the hips, while the upper line is an axis through the shoulders, which is tracked for angular trunk velocity.

smaller degree of relative hip rotation. Examples of pitchers throughout the Majors also exist who rely on large hip rotation to generate hip-shoulder separation and torque, such as Roger Clemens. As Figure 13-7 shows, Clemens has very little upper body load when compared to Sabathia, but his extreme advantage in hip rotation is evidenced by the direction that their belt buckles are facing at this point in the delivery.

Figure 13-7. C.C. Sabathia (left) uses a big upper body load to "show the numbers" and create separation, while Roger Clemens (right) relies more on hip rotation.

Sabathia and Clemens are an interesting contrast, representing both ends of the spectrum for pelvis-to-trunk rotation ratio. Most pitchers fall somewhere in-between these two extremes. In reality, very few players generate as much total hip-shoulder separation as either Sabathia or Clemens. Such a rotational load has a large impact on pitch velocity, and it's not a coincidence that both of these pitchers have been known to consistently throw fastballs at speeds over 95 mph.

It's this hip/shoulder separation that comes into play with "break the hands early." This teach can promote a premature start to other links in the chain, thereby encouraging a pitcher to begin trunk rotation too early. Some pitchers even get their shoulders going prior to foot strike. This factor can have a number of consequences, ranging from mechanical inefficiency to an enhanced risk of injury. This limitation is similar to the risk of going too slow into foot strike. Both teaches, going slower and breaking the hands early, can cause a pitcher to overrotate his upper body into MER and release point, resulting in a "spin-out problem." A pitcher who breaks his hands too early and goes too slow into foot strike actually compounds timing, sequencing, and mechanics problems, which increases his chances of injury and decreases his consistency of performance.

This discussion leads us to a review of the consequences of early trunk rotation, the importance of foot strike, and how it relates to hip-shoulder separation and rotational velocity. If a pitcher begins trunk rotation prior to foot strike, the pelvis is rotating, which minimizes total degrees of hip and shoulder separation. Delaying the initiation of trunk rotation until after foot strike will ensure that the hips have rotated far enough to at least generate a fair amount of separation, regardless of whether it's a "big-shoulders pitcher" like Sabathia or a "big-hips" pitcher like Clemens. The key issue, in this regard, is determining what constitutes a fair amount of separation.

Elite Major League pitchers, such as Clemens and Sabathia, can generate close to 60 degrees of hip-shoulder separation, regardless of whether they favor hips or shoulders. The ratio of trunk rotation to pelvis rotation is based on personal signature, while the angle of separation is an indication of mechanical efficiency. Most professional pitchers create somewhere between 40 and 60 degrees of hip-shoulder separation for every pitch. In comparison, the pitchers in our 33-player data set had an average of 50.04 degrees of hip-shoulder separation, with a standard deviation of +/- 0.89 degrees (n = 99).

Foot strike is also a critical factor in angular rotation, because of the influence of ground forces, similar to the previous example of generating forward momentum from the setup position. Previously, the point was made that players who wait until maximum leg lift to direct their movement toward the plate don't generate as much momentum as those pitchers who initiate forward movement directly from setup, as measured by energy angle. The implication is that it is easier to create momentum from a balanced setup than it is when standing on one leg. In other words, it is an advantage to generate energy with both feet on the ground.

This same concept applies to angular trunk rotation. If a pitcher waits until foot strike to begin upper-body rotation, he can take advantage of ground forces to increase the angular velocity. On the other hand, if trunk rotation is initiated before foot strike, the player will not be able to maximize that power, with only the posting foot in contact with the ground.

To visualize this concept, the key is to consider how a hitter generates a load with upper-body torque before initiating his swing. Every hitter in Major League baseball waits until after his front leg has come back into contact with the ground before starting to swing with his upper body. In fact, you will struggle to find a Little Leaguer who starts his swing before batter-foot strike. In order to try it for yourself, you can imagine an incoming pitch. Next, you should start the hitting sequence by lifting your front foot off of the ground and shifting your weight. Then, you should try to start the swing before that foot comes back down. Starting the swing prior to foot strike feels very awkward, and is extremely inefficient for generating power.

The mechanical process that is involved with the hitting swing is very similar to pitching a baseball. Likewise, delayed trunk rotation shares many of the same advantages for hitters and pitchers. However, the big difference is that hitters don't seem to have a problem with early upper body rotation, while many pitchers struggle with the concept. You will even see Major League pitchers occasionally begin trunk rotation prior to foot strike on a poorly executed pitch. Meanwhile, younger pitchers have a particularly tough time coordinating the rotational elements of the delivery. Some players even fire their hips and shoulders at the same time, such that they look wired together, and fail to create any Hip-Shoulder Separation.

All pitchers	0.022 seconds, +/- 0.003 sec	n = 99
Pro	0.024 seconds, +/- 0.005 sec	n = 27
College	0.024 seconds, +/- 0.004 sec	n = 54
High school	0.012 seconds, +/- 0.008 sec	n = 18

Table 13-1. Average time difference between trunk rotation and foot strike

Table 13-1 provides a closer look at our experimental group of pitchers. In this aggregate group, the whole population had a correlation of $r^2 = +0.342$ (n = 99) between angle of hip-shoulder separation and the time difference between foot strike and the start of trunk rotation. This statistic shows that a medium-strength positive relationship exists between separation and timing of trunk rotation, relative to foot strike, for the pitchers in our data set. The data show the breakdown for these players by skill level, in which the pros and collegians averaged the same timing difference between foot strike and the start of trunk rotation. The high school pitchers, on the other hand, had an average delay of 0.012 seconds, or half of that for the more experienced pitchers. Accordingly, it can be generalized that pitchers with strong separation also tend to delay trunk rotation until after foot strike, and that these factors are advantages for highly skilled players.

At this point, it would be helpful to revisit the factor of hands and the issue of "when should pitchers break their hands?" Breaking the hands is somewhat signature-specific, with respect to timing. As such, an early break can influence a pitcher's ability to efficiently execute his delivery. Most pitchers can find an appropriate time to break their hands without focusing on when it takes place. However, some players have difficulty finding the best moment to separate hand from glove. All factors considered, "break your hands early" is not a very good rule for most pitchers, given how it impacts the rest of the kinetic chain. An interesting corollary issue involving the hands is what happens if a pitcher breaks his hands "late"?

One strong advocate of late break is Carlos Gomez, formerly of *The Hardball Times*. Gomez is a former professional ballplayer, currently a scout, and a self-described "mechanics geek." Carlos, who breaks down players' mechanics on his web page, is an astute evaluator of pitching. According to Carlos, breaking the hands later *"leads to a quicker arm circle,"* a term that refers to the path of the ball from out of the glove to opposite and equal and then into maximum external rotation (MER). (Gomez 2007)

If breaking the hands early can trigger a premature angular rotation of the shoulders, then it follows that a later break can bring about a delay in trunk rotation, relative to foot strike. Most coaches are now aware of the fact that it is critical that a pitcher gets into foot strike prior to initiating upper-body rotation, in order to maximize hip-shoulder separation and angular velocity of the trunk. Accordingly, some pitchers can benefit from a later breaking of the hands, as long as this step is associated with a similar delay with the start of trunk rotation.

Coaches, however, should be cautious when they're working with a pitcher on trunk-rotation timing. It is definitely possible for a pitcher to wait too long to break his hands or begin angular rotation, if it results in him having to hurry

Figure 13-8. Roy Oswalt of the Houston Astros delays his upper-body rotation after foot strike, helping to maximize hip-shoulder separation

through the links that follow in the chain. These players may fail to get to opposite and equal with their arms at foot strike, a point when it is most critical to have tightrope balance. On the other hand, the delay may be so long that the pitcher cannot rotate his upper body far enough by release point. Such a player will experience similar results as the slide step victim, with respect to pitch velocity and elevation.

Hip-shoulder separation is a key component of pitch velocity, and we have conducted research at the NPA/RDRBI to help quantify the impact of this factor. In 2005, a study was designed and conducted by NPA head coaches Eric Andrews and Ryan Sienko, under the guidance of Tom. "Doug the Intern" helped out in the study with data tracking and entry.

Andrews and Sienko had pitchers play catch on flat ground from their knees, allowing them to isolate the rotational aspects of the pitching delivery and to concentrate on hip-shoulder separation. Each pitcher had a unique hip angle from the two-knee position. The possible range of angles in this position varied from square to the throwing partner to "closed" 90 degrees (facing first base for LHP and third base for RHP); though no individual players were at either extreme. The pitchers were assisted in finding the appropriate angle for their hips and knees by starting off at 45 degrees (splitting the distance between the extremes), and then adjusting their position, based on the degree of trunk rotation at release point. If a pitcher was found to "open up" with his front shoulder in overrotation, he was then required to adjust his starting two-knee position to a more closed position. If the player looked like he "throws across his body," which is a symptom of under-rotation, his hips were opened up at setup to compensate. Once the pair of pitchers had found their appropriate hip angles, their pitch velocities from the knees were recorded, using a radar gun. Approximately 20 minutes later, these players had their pitch velocities recorded, using the same "JUGS" radar gun, while throwing off a bullpen on the NPA clay mounds.

The results of this study indicated that pitchers of all ages were able to generate about 80% of their mound velocity, while throwing from their knees. A comparison was made of the average velocities for 10 pitches each from the knees and from the mound. The 80% ratio held strong for players of all shapes, sizes, and skill levels, with an overall sample size of 200 pitchers. For professional players, this effect amounted to a difference of 17-19 mph, while high school players gained closer to 15 mph on the mound, compared to throwing from their knees. What this experiment showed was that only 20% of real velocity is attributed to the linear or directional factors (e.g., stride and momentum, the slope of the mound, and low-back extension/flexion). This finding was a shock to many coaches. As such, it helped to underscore the importance of hip-shoulder separation, trunk rotation, and internal rotation of the pitching shoulder, with respect to pitch velocity.

During the velocity study, the pitchers were never told how or when to break their hands, either from their knees or on the mound. We just helped them find the setup that produced a mechanically efficient release, and allowed each pitcher to do the rest naturally. When working with a player, the focus should be on helping the athlete achieve ideal timing and sequencing with his delivery. All factors considered, the best time for a player to break his hands will be dictated more by the pitcher than his coach. Many players find a good time to break their hands and maximize hip-shoulder separation without instruction, therefore, coaches don't need to fix this particular element unless it is severely broken.

The majority of pitchers can benefit from a further delay of trunk rotation. Our research efforts show that most players can also stall trunk rotation by maintaining opposite and equal arm angles until foot strike. This element is a stark contrast to pelvis rotation, since pitchers have little control over the point in their delivery that the hips fire. Accordingly, among the three options available to a player to influence hip-shoulder separation, timing of trunk rotation is the one factor that pitchers can work on to improve efficiency, while hand-break timing and pelvis-rotation timing are mostly elements of personal signature. These unique aspects offer clues to a coach as to how to work with an individual player. If a pitcher has a lot of natural hip rotation, like Roger Clemens, the coach can expect to see relatively little upper-body load, and realize that the situation works, given the player's signature. On the other hand, when confronted with a player with little natural hip rotation, the coach can help the pitcher increase hip-shoulder separation by delaying his start to trunk rotation and perhaps with a larger "twist" in the upper body, like C.C Sabathia.

Speaking of C.C. Sabathia and his big "twist," some coaches dislike pitchers who utilize the upper body like Sabathia, or produce a large scapular load like Randy Johnson, because it appears that they show the ball to the hitter from behind their back near opposite and equal. The assumption follows that the hitter can see the ball and the pitcher's grip to determine what type of pitch is coming. However, a problem exists with this theory, a dilemma that involves how most hitters mentally approach their craft. For example, the great hitters of all time, such as Ted Williams, select out a visual "window," through which the pitcher's hand and the baseball come through at release point. These hitters do this to focus visual attention from the moment they see the ball leave the pitcher's hand, at which point they have approximately 0.20 seconds to read the pitch and make a decision, before it is too late to start the swing. This decision is based on visual information, such as pitch velocity and trajectory, the position of the ball in the hitter's "window," and the result of all previous pitches thrown with similar trajectories.

A hitter would have an extremely difficult, if not impossible, time creating an extra momentary visual window to locate Sabathia's hand during the fraction of a second that it's visible behind his back, just before his shoulders square up into stack and track. Then, imagine the hitter having to make a quick saccadic eye movement back to the release point window, and readjusting his focus to that spot within the 0.30 seconds between foot strike and ball release. Any delay in his visual adjustment would prevent the hitter from reading the pitch type or location. This situation would create much more of an obstacle than an advantage for the majority of hitters at any skill level.

Coaches are naturally motivated to "fix" their pitchers. In fact, some coaches attempt to employ a fix, even if nothing seems broken. Most pitching coaches and scouts have particular pet peeves, with respect to mechanics, or certain things that they like to see in every player. Often, this mindset coincides with techniques that the coach himself utilized during his playing career. Not surprisingly, they like to "teach what got 'em there." While nothing is wrong with utilizing past experience to aid with instruction, the impact of an athlete-specific signature means that rarely does a single optimal solution exist that a coach can use to mold every pitcher.

As a group, coaches often put too much focus on the throwing arm when evaluating mechanics for pitchers, especially during the early phases in the delivery. Our research suggests that "reach back" and "break the hands toward second base" fall under the category of conventional wisdom that might work for some pitchers, but will disrupt the development of many others. In this sense, it is similar to the flaw inherent with the "left-hander setup on the left side of the rubber" dictum. As such, the coaching solution involves working with the pitcher's signature, rather than against it, in order to achieve the appropriate opposite and equal arm angles at foot strike.

When encountered with a pitcher who has trouble finding opposite-and-equal arm angles at foot strike, pitching instructors who look for such balance may be tempted to fix the throwing arm to appropriately "mirror" the glove side. In reality, however, pitchers have a much easier time by making the reverse adjustment—fix the glove-side elbow and shoulder angles to mirror what the pitcher already does naturally with his throwing arm. This way a coach can help a player achieve mechanical efficiency, while working in concert with what the athlete does naturally.

Tom's Wrap-Up

"Reaching back" has nothing to do with how far "in front" a pitch is delivered. In fact, the arms travel with the body. The closer the body gets to home plate, the closer the arms get to home plate, and the closer release point gets to home plate. After 20+ years of motion analysis, we know that hands/arms happen. They are a non-teach, if they stay opposite and equal, mirroring each other into foot strike. In other words, it isn't "reach back" or "break your hands early," it's let hands/ball/glove happen. When the hands break and how the hands break should be a non-teach for coaches. The only possible teach involved with the throwing-arm path is to leave it alone and to match the glove arm in an "opposite/equal" or "mirror image" into foot strike. Hips/shoulders separation will determine the direction of the throwing arm and glove arm after the hands break.

14

"Stride Straight"

"Stride straight at the plate."
"Don't stride across your body."
"Don't open your stride."

☛ **Doug:** The coaches' quotes detailed above reflect the overall emphasis on striding straight at the plate, and landing without opening up or closing off the front leg at foot strike. In this instance, opening up the front leg refers to the fact that the pitcher strides off-center to his glove side. Striding "across your body," on the other hand, involves landing in a position that favors the throwing-arm side, relative to the center line. The conventional wisdom states that opening up the front leg will cause the pitcher to also open up his front shoulder too early (i.e., premature trunk rotation), while striding closed will cause a pitcher to throw "across his body" (i.e., incomplete trunk rotation).

Figure 14-1. Pedro Martinez strides straight at the plate into foot strike, while Randy Johnson lands with more of a "closed" front leg

The setup section featured a review of how body position has an influence on mechanical efficiency and the end results of each pitch. The setup was shown to have a strong impact on physical positioning later in the delivery, with ideal placement on the rubber determined by a player's signature. Along these lines, the different types of stride that a player can take to get into foot strike can also be examined. Such a study can show how stride positioning relates to both personal signature and the mechanical efficiency of the remaining links in the kinetic chain.

The conventional wisdom of "stride straight at the plate" adheres to the notion that the front foot, like the drag foot, is an indicator of whether the pitcher gets his shoulders and trunk square with home plate. Foot-strike position, however, is the result of pelvis and hip rotation after maximum leg lift, in addition to positioning on the rubber at setup, all of which are heavily influenced by a pitcher's signature. In contrast, the drag foot is an indicator of spine position at release point, which is a reflection of mechanical efficiency when compared to the center line.

To test the conventional wisdom, our 33-pitcher data set from motion analysis can be evaluated to look for trends and significant differences. Table 14-1 provides a breakdown of how the pitchers in each skill level in our data set land—open, closed, or straight.

Group	Open (%)	Closed (%)	Straight (%)
All pitchers	4 (12.1%)	13 (39.4%)	16 (48.5%)
Pro	1 (11.1%)	3 (33.3%)	5 (55.6%)
College	2 (11.1%)	8 (44.4%)	8 (44.4%)
High school	1 (16.7%)	2 (33.3%)	4 (66.7%)

Table 14-1. A breakdown of pitchers' landing positions in the NPA/RDRBI data set

All factors considered, it's pretty amazing that these percentages are so stable across skill levels, especially considering the sample size. About half of the players within our population follow convention and stride straight at the plate. Meanwhile, over three-fourths of the other players' stride closed, while only four pitchers in the entire group have an open stride.

Breaking down the pitchers, based on how they stride, enables us to further study the conventional wisdom involving stride and to look at how stride type impacts the angle of trunk rotation near release point. If conventional wisdom holds true, the study should find players in the closed stride group who "throw across their body," with a significantly lower angle of trunk rotation at maximum external rotation (MER) of the throwing arm, relative to square to home plate. Similarly, the open-stride players can also be tested for overrotation. In this instance, it is very important to take a cautious approach because of the extremely limited number of pitchers in the open-stride group. Unfortunately, critical data points were unavailable for one closed- and four straight-stride pitchers. As a result, our breakdown includes 12 players for each of those two groups, rather than 13 and 16, respectively.

Closed stride	4.29 degrees, +/- 1.13 degrees	n = 36, N = 12
Straight stride	4.50 degrees, +/- 0.54 degrees	n = 36, N = 12
Open stride	4.10 degrees, +/- 1.11 degrees	n = 12, N = 4

Table 14-2. Average angle of trunk rotation at MER, by stride type

As Table 14-2 shows, the group that overrotates the most, relative to shoulders square to home plate at MER, is actually the group of straight-stride pitchers. The open-stride group, which was expected to register the highest average value of overrotation, was actually the closest to being square. In fact, this group exhibited a smaller angle of rotation than even the closed-stride pitchers. Because this finding seems incredibly counterintuitive, it is necessary to test these differences for significance.

Closed vs. straight:	t = 0.97	Insignificant
Open vs. straight:	t = 1.62	Insignificant
Closed vs. open:	t = 0.51	Insignificant

Table 14-3. Unpaired t-test comparison between groups of average angle of trunk rotation

As Table 14-3 indicates, none of these differences are significant within an acceptable level. As such, the results of our study aren't as backwards as they seemed at first glance. The data suggest that no discernable relationship exists between stride direction into foot strike and angle of trunk rotation at MER. The t values are those generated when using the sample of data points (n = 36, 36, 12). The significance decreases when substituting the subject sample size (N = 12, 12, 4). The conventional wisdom, then, appears to lack validity, based on the results of these 28 pitchers.

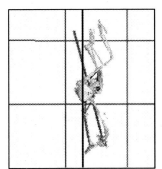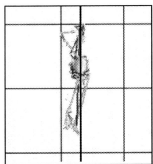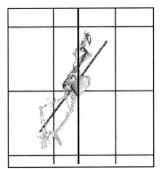

Figure 14-2. Motion-analysis examples of an open stride (LHP—left), stride straight at the plate (RHP—center), and a closed stride (RHP—right). The line that runs parallel to the center line and through the center of the head illustrates the target line, relative to a player-specific reference point.

It is understandable that coaches adhere to the conventional wisdom involving stride, given that "stride straight at the plate" is most pleasing to the eye, and it makes intuitive sense for mechanical efficiency. This factor also underscores how conventional wisdom is developed in general, with underlying ideas that are based upon subjective insight rather than objective evaluation. The real power of motion-analysis data is its ability to quantify the details of pitching mechanics. As a result, we can develop studies that yield precise measurements that provide a better understanding of those elements that are most crucial to a successful delivery. The experience of renowned pitchers and pitching coaches, such as Nolan Ryan and Tom House, enables us to create the best possible tests of mechanics theory. In turn, motion-capture technology allows us to search beyond what we can see with our own eyes.

The "stride straight at the plate" rule is a good example of the essential relationship that exists between conventional wisdom and objective analysis. The research that is conducted using motion analysis is driven by the theories and observations of players and coaches. Without this piece of conventional wisdom to produce a testing hypothesis, we wouldn't have a starting point for research. As such, someone had to say, "Stride straight at the plate," before it could be tested.

Motion analysis is used to make the proper measurements and to collect data, which, in this case, involves stride direction and angle of trunk rotation. When the resultant data is analyzed, we then bring it all back together by attempting to explain the results of the study in question, using a combination of conventional coaching wisdom and any relative knowledge gained from previous research.

Having reached the last stage of our review of "stride straight," we must try to explain why stride direction has no apparent effect, using a combination of coaching knowledge and what has been learned previously through motion analysis. The best explanation for the lack of a consistent relationship between stride type and angle of trunk rotation is that the landing position at foot strike is a function of pelvis and hip rotation, one that is influenced more by personal signature than mechanical efficiency. That's the coaching explanation. Using the knowledge that has been gained through motion analysis and the study of trunk-rotation angle, we know that the ability for a player to get his shoulders square to home plate at the right time is determined by other elements, including timing into foot strike and position on the mound, relative to the center line near release point.

The coaching explanation was in effect for the velocity study conducted by Eric Andrews and Ryan Sienko, which included measuring throws made from the knees. When the players threw from their knees, they received help finding the appropriate angle for the hips and position of the knees. As such, each pitcher was able to get his upper body square with his receiving partner at MER. Each player had a unique angle of the hips and pelvis, ranging from very open to very closed. Despite this initial variance, everyone finished with an appropriate trunk-rotation angle. While the influence of personal signature has been apparent to us for as long as we have been utilizing the knee drill with our players, it took our motion-analysis data to validate our observations.

The conventional wisdom of "stride straight at the plate" isn't necessarily wrong, since it is appropriate for about half of the pitchers whom a coach will come across, based on the results of our sample. The real problem lies with the other half of players, whose personal signatures demand that they land open or closed, in order to achieve optimum mechanical efficiency. The fact that "stride straight" helps about half of the pitchers in the general player pool might influence some coaches to use it as an all-encompassing rule. On the other hand, doing so will become a source of frustration for coach and player alike, when the other 50% struggle heavily to find consistency and efficiency by following this bit of conventional wisdom.

In reality, the conventional wisdom of "stride straight at the plate" will continue to have a following, just as long as there are players who actually do "throw across their body" with a closed stride, or "fly open" with an open stride. Some players will fall into these two categories, and in these situations, their coaches will be rewarded for fixing the problem. On the other hand, imagine a coach who has just arrived to work with a new team that has a staff of 10 pitchers, all of whom he has never seen. In turn, this coach attempts to enforce hard rules on all of his pitchers, based on conventional wisdom. Odds are that half of his staff would have no trouble with the "stride straight" rule, while the other half would actually be worse off for following the coach's instructions.

Confusing the situation even further, there are some pitchers who exhibit both signature and a mechanical inefficiency in the same direction. For example, some players have a naturally open lower-body position at foot strike, but still have a tendency to go too far and overrotate with their upper body. The best coaching solution for these players involves three choices in the setup position, which brings us back to the precept that starting in the right position helps get a pitcher to finish in the right position. In this instance, these options entail the following:

☞ **Tom:**
   ☐ *Choice #1:* When the pitcher sets up from the stretch, he can move his posting foot heel, adjusting the angle of his foot to a more closed position. If this technique sounds familiar, it is very similar to the instructions for the knee drill, while substituting the knee position with foot position as the ground anchor. Accordingly, for the open-stride pitcher who overrotates, the solution is to close the angle of the setup pelvis to compensate, until he finds a spot that gets his upper body square to the plate. While the result might still be a relatively open position, the lower body will be properly set up to prepare the upper body for ball release.

☐ *Choice #2:* Another option for a pitcher with stride inefficiencies would be to change the angle of leg lift. By taking the lift leg knee either more toward second base or less toward second base, the timing of hip/shoulder separation, and then delayed shoulder rotation, can better complement stride direction and landing foot position.

☐ *Choice #3:* Pitchers also have the option of standing at different places on the rubber when initiating their wind-up/stretch. For example, when a LH pitcher who strides closed or across his body begins too far to the left on the rubber, he will finish too far to the left, relative to the center line at ball release. On the other hand, a LH pitcher who opens up into foot strike and stands too far to the right side will land with a stride that is also too far open. If one corollary to the rule exists, it is that positioning at setup and ball release is dictated by personal signature, and thus unique to each individual athlete. Therefore, a coach can help a pitcher find an ideal position at release point by making adjustments with the setup position, which is customized to the player's signature. If there is one general rule that can be applied to what has been learned so far, it's that physical positioning at setup directly translates to positioning at ball release.

Tom's Wrap-Up

Ultimately, the coaching tool kit for stride is quite simple. Let each pitcher's drag line determine where and what his setup on the rubber should be. This step will optimize the "signature" of his stride, direction, and length. In other words, move each pitcher on the rubber until the player's drag-line configuration (no matter what it looks like) finishes on the center line between the middle of the rubber and the middle of home plate. Doing so insures that his spine and head will also be on the center line, thereby positioning his torso for the most efficient hip and shoulder separation, late shoulder rotation (80% of velocity), and low-back extension and flexion, as his shoulders square up to the target and his throwing forearm snaps from external rotation into ball release (20% of velocity).

15

"Don't Land on Your Heel"

"Don't land on your heel."
"Land on the ball of your foot."
"Point your toe toward the plate."

☛ **Doug:** As long as we're on the subject of how to stride, we might as well get into the rules that coaches typically use to tell pitchers how to land. In fact, there are very specific instructions for how a pitcher should get into foot strike. As the foot comes down from maximum leg lift, some coaches advocate that players should "point their toe toward the plate." Furthermore, when the landing approaches, conventional wisdom states that pitchers should "land on the ball of their foot," as opposed to "landing on their heel." Old-school coaches believed that heel-strikers would lock out their front knee, which could then impede an efficient follow-through.

In this instance, such instructions seem like a case of micro-managing on the part of pitching coaches, given that every pitcher gets to a flat foot position, regardless of which part of the foot comes into contact with the ground first. Whether the pitcher goes heel-first or toe-first into foot strike, he will be flat-footed within 0.02 seconds, with no affect on trunk rotation. Meanwhile, the conventional wisdom of "point your toe toward the plate" is simply an extension of "stride straight toward the plate," with the assumption that the toe point will direct the landing leg into a "straight" position. As has been discussed, the "stride straight" rule only applies to about half of all pitchers across the board. Accordingly, my initial reaction to this piece of conventional wisdom was that it was probably an aspect of personal signature, and that landing heel-first or toe-first wouldn't have a significant influence on the end result.

Because reactions and assumptions aren't sufficient enough to provide definitive answers to questions about whether to land heel-first or toe-first, a science-based justification for instructing pitchers to land on the ball of the foot needs to be found. Fortunately, we have plenty of data to analyze on the

Figure 15-1a. Pedro Martinez lands on the ball of his foot

Figure 15-1b. Roy Oswalt lands on his heel

Figure 15-1c. Greg Maddux lands on his heel

Figure 15-1d. Randy Johnson lands on a flat foot, possibly favoring the heel

Figure 15-1e. Johan Santana lands on his heel

subject. The best place to start is at the top, and the first step is to check out how each of the five aces gets into foot strike.

As Figures 15-1a through 15-1e show, three of the aces clearly violate conventional wisdom, as they get into foot strike by landing with the heel first. Another pitcher, Randy Johnson, looks as if he lands on a flat foot, but could be favoring the heel. Meanwhile, the only elite pitcher in the group who lands on the ball of his foot is Pedro Martinez.

The fact that just one of the five aces follows the convention was certainly a surprising result. It could be argued that statistical randomness can easily account for anomalies within a sample size of just five players. On the other hand, this undertaking does not involve looking at a normal distribution of pitchers. These players are arguably five of the greatest pitchers in the Major Leagues, athletes who represent the very tip of the tail on the talent curve. The lack of adherence to conventional wisdom by these players is a strong piece of evidence, despite the small sample.

Because we have a larger set of pitchers that we can study, the next step is to check out the 33 pitchers in our motion-analysis data set. In general, it might be expected that most of these pitchers would follow convention, given both the 50/50 option and the assumption that landing on the ball of the foot is an advantage over landing on the heel. If truly a mechanical advantage exists, in this regard, it would seem that pitchers would naturally tend to find the most efficient method, even without specific instruction. Furthermore, our database of relatively experienced players ought to reflect this trend, that is, if the conventional wisdom holds water.

Group	Land on ball of foot (%)	Land on heel (%)
All pitchers	10 (30.3%)	23 (69.6%)
Pro	2 (22.2%)	7 (77.8%)
College	6 (33.3%)	12 (66.7%)
High school	2 (33.3%)	4 (66.7%)

Table 15-1. Analysis of the landing patterns of pitchers in the NPA/RDRBI data set

As Table 15-1 shows, the players in our sample actually violate expectations and show the reverse trend. Every skill level has at least two-thirds of its pitchers landing on their heel, with the highest group percentage from the professionals. If we were to take a more cynical approach to the conventional wisdom of "don't land on your heel", then it would be reasonable to expect that the results would be split more evenly among the total population, with perhaps high degrees of variance between skill levels. However, the distribution is relatively uniform and clearly favoring landing on the heel, from the five aces to each of the skill groups in our motion-analysis data set. At this point, not only is this particular piece of conventional wisdom failing to describe the mechanical tendencies of successful pitchers, it also looks like this instruction might be inefficient, compared to the alternative.

Differences in mechanical efficiency in our data set were tested by dividing up the motion-analysis pitchers into two groups, and then analyzing strategic variables. The 10 players in our data set who land on their toe or ball of their foot made up the first group (the toe group), while the heel group was comprised of a randomly selected matching sample, which resulted in just 10 of the 23 heel-landing pitchers being included in the study. In reality, "random" is not the correct term, because we used alphabetical order to select the first 10 pitchers who land on their heel. This approach had at least one fortunate consequence, as it actually gave us a perfectly balanced experiment, with respect to skill level, as well as sample size. Each of the two groups included six college pitchers, two high school pitchers, and two professional pitchers (n = 30, N = 10 for each group).

In this study, we looked at a variety of measures that might be influenced by landing style at foot strike. The first factor we examined was stride-length efficiency. Chronologically, this element should be the first measurement that would be affected by landing on the heel or the toe. Accordingly, we tested to determine if either method provides an advantage toward creating a longer stride, relative to the pitcher's height.

Group	Average stride-length efficiency	SD (+/-)
Heel	92.28 %	1.03 %
Toe	92.95 %	1.12 %
Heel vs. toe: $t = 2.41$	Significant (at $p < 0.025$)	n = 30
$t = 1.39$	Insignificant	N = 10

Table 15-2. t-test analysis of stride-length efficiency in heel versus toe landing patterns

As Table 15-2 indicates, the toe group has a slight advantage with respect to stride distance, although the effect is not as strong as most of the other factors that we have studied. As such, we only have confidence in the results at the level of $p < 0.025$. Because the significance of the difference disappears if we use the group samples of N = 10, any advantage that the toe group has in this regard is slight.

Group	Average release-point efficiency	SD (+/-)
Heel	97.54 %	1.28 %
Toe	97.81 %	1.46 %
Heel vs. toe: $t = 0.76$	Insignificant	n = 30
$t = 0.44$	Insignificant	N = 10

Table 15-3. t-test analysis of release-point efficiency in heel versus toe landing patterns

Foot strike is a very critical time-point in the pitching delivery. Accordingly, we should account for the possibility that the advantages provided from landing on the heel or ball of the foot don't go into effect until after foot contact. As Table 15-3 shows, however, the results for release-point efficiency are even closer than those for stride length. As such, it can be reasonably concluded that landing on the heel or the toe has little-to-no effect on the release-point distance.

Group	Average release-point height	SD (+/-)
Heel	57.67 inches	0.84 inches
Toe	58.00 inches	1.21 inches
Heel vs. toe: t = 1.22	Insignificant	n = 30
t = 0.71	Insignificant	N = 10

Table 15-4. t-test analysis of release-point height in heel versus toe landing patterns

It could be argued that landing on the ball of the foot helps a pitcher to "stay tall" into foot strike, which many coaches teach their players in order to create a higher release point. As Table 15-4 indicates, however, these groups show no detectable difference, when compared for height of the pitching hand at ball release. The data fails to support the idea that either landing on the heel or ball of the foot has an effect on a pitcher's height when the ball leaves the pitcher's hand.

Group	Average balance at foot strike	SD (+/-)
Heel	1.95 inches	0.23 inches
Toe	2.22 inches	0.21 inches
Heel vs. toe: t = 4.74	Significant (at $p < 0.005$)	n = 30
t = 2.74	Significant (at $p < 0.025$)	N = 10

Table 15-5. t-test analysis of balance at foot strike in heel versus toe landing patterns

As Table 15-5 illustrates, a significant difference has finally been found involving landing patterns. Although still not as strong as most of the other effects that have been observed thus far, the heel group shows a significant advantage with balance at foot strike, compared to the toe group. The significance holds using the subject sample size of N = 10, although the strength of significance falls below the level of $p < 0.005$. The value for balance at foot strike represents the distance that the head (COMH) is off-center of the COMB. If a pitcher leans backward or forward, left or right, the balance measure will tell us how far off the pitcher is from being perfectly balanced (0.00 inches) at foot strike.

What's most telling about the results for balance is not that a significant difference exists, but rather that the stats support the suspicion that "land on the ball of your foot" might actually do more harm than good for many pitchers.

The strength of the effect is such that more research is definitely necessary to confirm the theory that landing heel-first into foot strike is an advantage for balance. Such research might show that the causal effect is in the reverse direction. In other words, landing on the heel is the likely result of strong balance into foot strike, while landing on the toe is the consequence of poor balance.

Based on observations from working with pitchers, it's likely that the style of landing is a result of balance, rather than the other way around. A pitcher has another couple of ways that he can alter his balance on the way into foot strike. The most common method is to "lead with the head," where the COMH is much closer to the plate than the COMB is during stride and momentum. Pitchers with this approach will have a weight imbalance with the head leading out in front, which creates a bit of tilt with the upper body. Such posture could potentially make it difficult for the player to land on his heel. Pitchers who land on their heel will get to a flat-foot position almost immediately, since their body is tracking forward. As such, their momentum makes it very natural for a pitcher to go heel-to-toe with a balanced delivery. Meanwhile, a pitcher who has his head out ahead of the front foot will find that it is more difficult to avoid a toe-first contact at foot strike.

Our analysis of the "land on the ball of your foot" conventional wisdom has yielded some very exciting results, which violate just about everyone's expectations. In this instance, the conventional wisdom simply did not hold water, based on the evidence provided by our motion-analysis data and our evaluation of photographs of MLB pitchers. Frankly, as researchers, the results also surprised us. We set out to challenge the conventional wisdom, expecting to find that no difference existed between these types of pitchers. The difference that did surface indicates that we may have stumbled upon a previously undiscovered relationship between the method of foot contact and balance. Best of all, the door has been opened up for more research, leading to new questions, based on the results of biomechanical analysis.

Tom's Wrap-Up

From a coaching "tool-kit" perspective, how a pitcher's landing foot contacts the ground is a biomechanical inevitability, a non-teach if he is positioned properly with balance and posture, lift and thrust, stride and momentum, opposite and equal are all timed, sequenced, and biomechanically sound. Let it happen!

16

"Stride Short"

"Shorten your stride"

Our findings, to this point, have supported the idea that achieving a long stride is a key aspect of efficient pitching mechanics. This concept, however, has many detractors who prefer the precept of "shorten your stride" as a general rule. This teach goes hand-in-hand with a previously discussed conventional wisdom, "stay tall" throughout the delivery. The underlying premise is that a relatively short stride will help a pitcher to stay tall and thereby create a higher release point. The perceived benefits of this "downward plane" are addressed in the next chapter.

As previously has been pointed out, a long stride is associated with a stronger energy angle, as well as with an increased level of momentum as the pitcher gets into foot strike. The images of the five aces that have been presented in this book have shown that many of the best pitchers in the game take advantage of all of these elements to create a mechanically efficient delivery. The motion-analysis stats further support the idea that a longer stride is beneficial. The next step is to determine if the same concept holds true when stride-length efficiency is measured directly.

All pitchers	91.63%, +/- 0.65%	n = 99, N = 33
Pro	92.50%, +/- 0.83%	n = 27, N = 9
College	92.51%, +/- 1.02%	n = 54, N = 18
High school	87.69%, +/- 1.05%	n = 18, N = 6

Table 16-1. Average stride-length efficiency

As Table 16-1 shows, the average pitcher in the sample produced a stride 91.63% the length of his height. The players at the college and professional levels were nearly identical in this category, while the high school players fell behind.

Pro-college	t = 0.04	Insignificant
College-HS	t = 5.45	Significant at p<0.005
Pro-HS	t = 5.47	Significant at p<0.005

Table 16-2. Unpaired t-test analysis of stride-length efficiency

Table 16-2 reveals that the difference between the professional and college groups were insignificant, while significant differences were found between the high school group and both of the other groups. The average between-group difference of five percent stride-length efficiency equates to about three and a half inches of distance for a pitcher who stands six-feet tall. The pitchers in the sample ranged from a low of 71.5% stride-length efficiency to a high of 106%. Using the example of a six-foot tall pitcher, the difference between these two extreme values is almost 25 inches of distance at foot strike.

Figure 16-1. Tim Lincecum of the San Francisco Giants gains such a long stride that he is almost landing on flat ground

Stride length is directly related to release-point distance, while other variables, such as trunk-rotation timing, balance and posture, and glove position, also have an impact on how far in front of the rubber the pitcher releases the baseball. In our motion analysis of players, a strong correlation was found between stride length and release-point distance, with a value of $r^2 = +0.560$.

There are many examples of MLB pitchers who gain an exceptional stride, particularly with respect to their height. Nolan Ryan recorded the best stride-length efficiency in our entire NPA database, at close to 115% for a 6'1" pitcher. Active big leaguers, such as Roy Oswalt and Tim Lincecum, take advantage of a huge energy angle and great momentum to stride more than a foot closer to

the plate than the average pitcher of their height. At approximately 5'11",
Oswalt and Lincecum are taller than the average human, but shorter than the
average Major League pitcher. Despite their relatively small stature, each of
these players compensates by striding further than other professional pitchers
who are half a foot taller.

The key advantage of a long stride is the associated release-point distance.
Any energy that is generated from extra momentum is an additional positive.
Releasing the baseball closer to home plate makes life much tougher on opposing
hitters, a factor that is obvious when watching pitchers who get extremely close,
such as Nolan Ryan, Roy Oswalt, Tim Lincecum, and Randy Johnson.

Figures 16-2. Roy Oswalt and Tim Lincecum (right) are two of a kind—while both
pitchers are less than six-foot tall, they stride closer to home plate than pitchers who
are half-a-foot taller, adding to the deception of every pitch they make.

The closer a pitcher releases the ball to the plate, the less time a hitter will
have to read, react, and make contact. In this sense, a batter will feel like the
pitcher is throwing harder than the radar-gun readings indicate, since the
perceived velocity of the pitch increases as the pitcher gets further from the
rubber at release point. In fact, pitchers can gain up to two-to-three mph of
perceived velocity for a foot of additional release-point distance, depending on
the player's real or true velocity on the radar gun.

Releasing the baseball closer to home plate also results in later movement
for curveballs, sliders, split-finger fastballs, changeups, sinkers, cutters, and
everything else that strays from a straight-fastball trajectory. Such a factor can
be a huge advantage, since a hitter must make his swing decision within a split-
second from ball release. In fact, it can get increasingly more difficult to read
pitches, depending on how close they get to the batter before the break. This
aspect explains why a hitter is often seen swinging at a curveball in the dirt. The
pitch most likely came from the same ball-release "tunnel" or trajectory as the
pitcher's fastball, and broke late enough such that the hitter had to decide to
swing before he had enough information to properly identify what pitch was
actually coming.

The benefits of greater perceived velocity and later break for non-fastballs add to the "deception" of a pitcher's delivery, and help to fool the hitter into making incorrect guesses. If a pitcher gets a long stride and releases the ball close to the plate, thereby increasing the perceived velocity of the pitch, a hitter might notice that the pitches are "sneaky fast." Greg Maddux is a great example of a pitcher whose fastball sneaks up on hitters as a result of his proximity to home plate. Maddux has also learned to utilize the concept of effective velocity to help make his pitches feel "sneaky" fast to hitters. Effective velocity is covered in more detail later in the book.

Randy Johnson's slider serves as a prime example of how a long stride and late break can give hitters fits. Opposing managers have been known to rest their best left-handed hitters on days when Johnson toes the rubber, because his slider is nearly impossible for a lefty hitter to identify in due time, especially given the fact that the hitter must also be prepared for the 97 mph heater. Managers felt they were better off taking their chances with a lineup full of right-handed hitters against Johnson, especially at his peak. His frighteningly close release point was a key culprit in their attitude. On the other hand, Johnson's slider is equally hard on right-handed batters, because it breaks so late. In fact, he has traditionally hit a lot of right-handed hitters in their back leg with his slider. When asked, he will tell you that while velocity is a blessing, command of his slider is a necessity.

Randy Johnson is the perfect example of another fundamental concept—a pitcher's height, leg length, and stride length can provide a greater benefit through release-point distance than release-point height. (This theory is addressed in the next chapter). It's easy to see how Johnson's 6'11" frame and long limbs are conducive to a release point that is relatively close to home plate. Surprisingly, his low 3/4 delivery doesn't factor in with his natural height advantage. Randy Johnson is one of the tallest players in Major League history, and one of the most dominant pitchers of our generation, but his success was influenced more by how close he got to the plate than by how high he released the baseball. His key advantage was that his long stride provided a release point closer to the target.

In addition, a physics benefit is derived from releasing the ball closer to the hitter, since air drag will have a bit less time and distance to slow down the baseball. The drag effect is actually pretty significant. Calculations conducted by MLB Pitch f/x have shown that a 90 mph fastball can actually lose about seven-to-eight mph by the time it crosses the plate, due to this drag force. The air-drag benefit from a closer release, while small (since the distance and time involved are on the order of one foot and about 0.04 seconds, respectively), does, in fact, add a fraction of a tick to perceived velocity.

Tom's Wrap-Up

This chapter has provided science-based numbers involving the benefits of achieving a longer stride length. Anytime a coach teaches "shorten your stride," he is instructing a pitcher to alter his timing and kinematic sequencing; decrease his momentum; and give the hitter a longer look at the ball. From a common-sense perspective, none of these three factors are going to help a pitcher compete and/or stay healthy. As such, in our opinion, you should avoid putting "shorten your stride" in your tool kit. One final point: Randy Johnson's statistics in his injured-back years with the Yankees were not as dominant. Why? He could not leg lift as high, torque as much, and/or stride as far.

RELEASE-POINT EFFICIENCY

Section 5

17

Breaking Down Foot Strike to Release Point

Coaches' Conventional Wisdom, Foot Strike to Release Point

- "Stay tall:"
  - ✓ "Get on top to create angle."
  - ✓ "Pull the glove to the hip."
- "Don't throw sidearm:
  - ✓ "Don't throw across your body."
  - ✓ "Don't short-arm."

Breakdown: Foot Strike to Release Point

The final stages of the kinetic chain are the most complicated, in terms of evaluation and coaching. A pitcher has about 0.30 seconds between foot strike and ball release, during which more critical events are occurring in less time than with any other part of the pitching delivery. An efficient pitcher will achieve opposite and equal just as he gets into foot strike. He then has less than one-third of a second to cover the kinematic sequencing of maximum hip-shoulder separation and delayed trunk rotation, low-back hyperextension to stack and track the upper-body toward the target, while swiveling and stabilizing the glove over front foot, reaching maximum external rotation of the throwing arm (MER) before going into low-back flexion and internal rotation of the forearm into release point and follow-through. All of these coordinated events occur in an extremely narrow timeframe, and cannot be quantified without motion analysis.

After ball release, the back foot stops dragging and lifts off of the ground during the follow-through. The throwing arm delivers the ball and pronates on every pitch, rotating the palm outward. In general, follow-through is a non-teach for coaches, because it is the inevitable consequence of all the other links in the sequence of the kinetic chain. However, the follow-through can serve as an indicator of what has occurred earlier in the delivery. Value exists in paying attention to the pitcher after ball release. The back leg of the pitcher should be checked out. In an efficient delivery, his back leg will pop up at the same angle as his throwing forearm.

Mechanical consistency has been emphasized throughout our analysis of pitching. The true benefits of this factor manifest themselves during the phase from foot strike to ball release. With regard to mechanical consistency, the primary goal is to find the same release-point position in the same amount of time on every pitch. The key to achieving this objective is to repeat the same mechanics, timing, and sequencing for the kinetic chain before foot strike, so that the multitude of events that occur after foot strike can be coordinated properly.

18

"Stay Tall"

"Stay tall."
"Get on top to create angle."

☞ **Doug:** At every level of competition, ballplayers are handpicked by coaches to take the mound, based primarily on two factors: fastball velocity and physical height. Pitchers who are tall and who throw hard garner the most attention during tryouts and showcases, because many coaches consider these attributes to be the most reliable indicators of potential ability. In the evaluation of developing players, being tall equates to having a "projectable frame." In other words, such a player can be expected to gain velocity as he matures, and to fill out the physique of a prototypical Major League caliber pitcher.

The perceived benefits of tall pitchers have little to do with the extended release point for players such as Randy Johnson. In fact, many pitching coaches prefer that a tall pitcher sacrifices release-point distance by shortening his stride, in order to release the ball from a higher position. These players are told to "stay tall" throughout the delivery, particularly from foot strike to ball release, so that they can achieve the highest possible release point. The purported objective is to create a lot of "downward plane," or increase the downward angle of the pitch from release point to hitter contact. Pitchers are told to "get on top to create angle," as conventional wisdom claims that a steep downward plane should result in a higher percentage of groundballs, and minimize extra-base hits in the process.

A natural tradeoff exists between release-point height and release-point distance, such as the connection between shortening the stride and staying tall. The slope of the mound also creates an environment where the pitcher is throwing from a lower position, relative to the ground, as he gets further from the rubber. The mound's slope drops one inch vertically for each foot of horizontal distance. While this effect isn't extreme, it amounts to a one-to-two inch height difference between the long- and short-stride players in our data set.

The concept of "get on top" is often specifically applied to the curveball, given that many coaches like to see a classic "12-to-6" break on the curve. Pitchers are asked to deliver the ball from a tall-release point that is "over the top," with the throwing arm extended near 12 o'clock. In fact, many of the pitchers in our motion-analysis database display a trend of throwing from a higher-release point on their curveball, but from a shorter distance, when compared to their fastball.

As Table 18-1 shows, this effect can be seen by looking at the within-subject correlations for release-point height and release-point distance, which gives an indication of how the relative change applies to individual players. The average within-player correlation for release-point distance and release-point height was $r^2 = -0.421$ (N = 33), which indicates that the tradeoff shows an inverse relationship between the two factors. The breakdown of the 33 motion-analysis pitchers is presented in Table 18-1.

1 player at	+0.95	→	+1.00
2 players at	+0.80	→	+0.94
3 players at	+0.45	→	+0.79
2 players at	0.00	→	+0.44
3 players at	−0.44	→	0.00
7 players from	−0.79	→	-0.45
10 players from	-0.94	→	-0.80
5 players from	−1.00	→	-0.95

Summary:
8 players positive (2 weak, 3 medium, 2 strong, 1 very strong)
25 players negative (3 weak, 7 medium, 10 strong, 5 very strong)

Table 18-1. Within-subject correlation, release-point height to release-point distance

While the whole group correlation was interesting, the breakdown of within-player values is more telling. In this analysis, eight of the 33 players (24%) showed a positive correlation, with just three of those subjects strong enough to be considered sufficiently relevant to have a positive correlation between the three types of pitches. In addition, two of the three strong positive correlations were the result of data points that were very tightly wound (i.e., very little deviation) for release-point height. For these two players, all three of the pitch types (fastball, breaking ball, off-speed) fell within one inch of one another, while the average pitcher in our data set has a range closer to five inches from the tallest pitch to the shortest. This effect helps to demonstrate the limitations of using within-player correlations with just three data points, since small changes in one variable can strongly correlate with large changes in the other.

The other 25 players displayed a negative correlation, 15 of whom (45% of the total population) were considered strong inverse relationships. Of these 15 strong negative correlations, three showed a range of values for release-point height of less than two inches (one player was within one inch). As such, their values should be taken with the same grain of salt as with the two strong positives with the same problem. When analyzing the individual data points overall, a tendency exists for particular pitchers to sacrifice release-point distance by getting on top of the ball or staying tall.

Previously, many of the benefits of a longer stride and closer release point were discussed. These benefits include increased perceived velocity and later break on pitches, relative to the hitter. The cost of engaging in a longer stride is release-point height, the effect of which is to inhibit downward plane and groundball rates, according to conventional wisdom. Testing conventional wisdom, in this instance, requires an analytical look at the functional tradeoff between release-point height and distance. In this regard, the first step is to take a look at our motion-analysis group for their release-point efficiency, which is measured as distance from the rubber to the throwing hand at ball release, divided by the pitcher's height.

All pitchers	99.04%, +/- 0.87%	n = 99, N = 33
Pro	101.46%, +/- 1.33%	n = 27, N = 9
College	98.34%, +/- 1.18%	n = 54, N = 18
High school	97.51%, +/- 1.14%	n = 18, N = 6

Table 18-2. Average release-point efficiency (distance)

Pro vs. college	t = 10.75	Significant at p<0.005
College vs. high school	t = 0.82	Insignificant
Pro vs. high school	t = 3.26	Significant at p<0.005

Table 18-3. Unpaired t-tests of the average release-point efficiency of the NPA/RDRBI data-set of groups

As Table 18-2 shows, the professional pitchers had the longest release-point efficiency, on average, followed by the collegians and the high school players. The difference between the college and high school pitchers was insignificant. Overall, however, this finding should provide us with a good understanding of the typical values. The range in values for our data set was a low of 84.3% to a high of 120% of body height for release-point distance. For a six-foot tall pitcher, this factor would amount to a range of 25.7 inches of distance at release point. Most of the players fell within the 90% to 110% range, which represented a spread of over 14 inches for a six-foot tall player. Only 16 out of the 99 data points fell outside this range. As such, it should approximate a realistic range of adjustment for the majority of pitchers.

It is also interesting to note that most players release the baseball out in front of the landing foot by almost 10% of their height compared to previously presented stride-length efficiency data. Some pitchers, however, release the ball from behind the front foot. For example, pitcher #3 in our motion-analysis group has an above-average stride-length efficiency of 96.5% on his fastball, however, he also registers just 93.7% release-point efficiency. For this particular pitcher, that discrepancy amounts to throwing the ball from more than two inches behind his front foot.

The next step is to determine how the aforementioned numbers compare to those for release-point height efficiency, which is height of the pitcher's hand at release point, divided by the player's height. In our motion analysis of players, ball-release height was measured from the zero point (0,0,0), which is set at the height of the rubber. As a result, the data presented in Tables 18-4 and 18-5 don't represent the height percentage, as measured from the ground or the position on the slope at ball release, but rather from the zero point of the rubber. For our purposes, the most important factor to consider is the relative range in values, which enables us to understand the level of potential adjustment within standard physical limits.

All pitchers	78.12%, +/- 0.64%	$n = 99, N = 33$
Pro	78.89%, +/- 0.60%	$n = 27, N = 9$
College	76.07%, +/- 0.99%	$n = 54, N = 18$
High school	83.11%, +/- 0.87%	$n = 18, N = 6$

Table 18-4. Release-point height efficiency

Pro vs. college	$t = 13.58$	Significant at $p < 0.005$
College vs. high school	$t = 26.88$	Significant at $p < 0.005$
Pro vs. high school	$t = 19.29$	Significant at $p < 0.005$

Table 18-5. Unpaired t-tests of release-point height efficiency of the NPA/RDRBI data-set groups

Surprisingly, the high school players were by far the best group, with respect to release-point height efficiency. The college players, on the other hand, had the lowest average values. While this finding could be explained somewhat by the observed tradeoff between height and distance, doing so fails to account for the fact that the college players had the lowest release-point height efficiency by a wide margin. Such a result brings into question whether a higher-release point is an advantage at all. It could also be evidence in favor of the argument that release-point distance should be emphasized as the more integral component, especially considering the tradeoff.

The range in values for release-point height efficiency fell between 58.1% and 89.8%, which equates to 22.8 inches of spread for a six-foot tall pitcher. Of the 99 players in the sample, 83 of them fell between 72% and 86%

release-point height efficiency, which is the exact same number of pitchers who were within the 90-to-110% range for release-point distance efficiency. The 72-to-86% spread represents a range of 10 inches of height at release point for a six-foot tall pitcher.

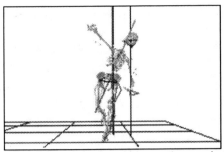

Figure 18-1. This image shows how it looks within motion analysis when a pitcher "gets on top of the ball to create angle" near release point. The thicker vertical line runs through the COMB, while the thinner line runs vertically through the COMH.

The breakdown of motion-analysis data reveals that most pitchers fall within a particular range, with respect to both height and distance of the pitching hand at release point. The average height for these pitchers was 73.8 inches, with a standard deviation +/- 0.4 inches. In other words, the six-foot tall pitcher, whom we used as an example, was a bit on the short side. Applying the same logic to a pitcher who is 73.8 inches tall yields the ranges of typical values that are shown in Table 18-6.

Measure	% pitcher height	Typical range spread	
Release-point height	72%–86%	53.1"–63.5"	10.4"
Release-point distance	90%–110%	66.4"–81.2"	14.8"

Table 18-6. Range of values for release-point height and distance

These spreads represent a range of adjustment, since most pitchers of similar height can work to adjust their mechanics and timing to achieve the extreme ends of these ranges. What needs to be asked, however, is whether it is worth it for a coach to help a pitcher make an adjustment within this range to alter the tradeoff of distance and height. In other words, for a pitcher who is about 6'2", with 79% height efficiency and 100% release-point distance efficiency (all about average), do we want to help him gain a stride closer to 110%, at the risk of losing height? On the other hand, do we want to strive for a height of 86%, with a drop in distance? While it's possible to make adjustments that extend outside these ranges, doing so is rare and should be considered unexpected. In all likelihood, the ideal results for any individual pitcher will lie somewhere between the extremes. As such, coaching to the extremes could be inefficient. In general, the basic issue is to weigh the value of 14.8" of distance against 10.4" of height at ball release. Addressing this point can help us better understand the possible options, as we work with a pitcher to determine his ideal delivery.

The previous chapter included a discussion about the fact that the perceived velocity of a pitch increases by two to three mph for every foot of distance that the pitcher gets closer to the plate. The physics behind this factor are relatively complicated, given that the drag force, which represents an important factor in the equation, is different in every environment. On the other hand, if this issue is treated like a high school physics class, those pesky issues, such as friction and drag force, can be avoided. At a minimum, doing so would at least provide a ballpark figure that could be used for our 73.8"-tall mystery pitcher.

To keep things simple, we'll ignore the complications of drag force and just concentrate on the percentages. If our average-height mystery pitcher releases the ball from the low end of 66.4 inches (5.53 feet) from the rubber, it will travel 55.0 feet before contact, assuming contact at the front of the plate. A pitch thrown from the upper range of 81.2 inches (6.77 feet) will travel 53.7 feet from ball release to hitter contact, a decrease of 2.4% of the total distance. As such, if we ignore the drag force and assume a constant pitch velocity, the ball will take 2.4% less time to travel the required distance, when thrown from the position closer to the plate. If our pitcher throws 90 mph, the hitter will feel as if the ball is thrown 2.4% faster from the 81.2" distance when compared to 66.4", which equates to over 92 mph (1.024 x 90 = 92.17 mph). Given these numbers, a relatively safe assumption is that our 73.8-inch example pitcher has about two mph of leeway, with respect to perceived velocity, based on how close he gets to the plate at release point.

Having determined a cost/benefit margin for release-point distance, the next step is to find the same for release-point height. In that regard, the high and low values within the range for release-point height can be compared. In turn, the impact of release-point height on downward plane can be studied by looking at the angle of pitch trajectory at release point. Then, physics can be utilized to see if this factor has an impact on groundball rates. It should be noted that we are measuring an indirect effect, since groundball rates are influenced by the angle of ball trajectory at the point of contact, as well as the angle of the hitter's swing plane. Therefore, it's likely that the downward angle produced by breaking balls has a larger influence on groundball rates, although gravity also plays a role. However, it should be possible to get an idea of how a higher-release point can create a steeper baseline trajectory, and subsequently, theorize how whether doing so might have a ripple effect on trajectory down the line, prior to contact.

In order to approximate the downhill trajectory of a pitch at contact, a point of contact has to be established. The strike zone is a good starting point. As such, contact can be generated toward the midpoint, near the hitter's belt buckle, at the front of the plate. Typically, this point will be about three feet off the ground, assuming some knee bend in the hitter's stance. Accordingly, for our purposes, we will assume a contact point at 36" from the ground. The release-point heights, relative to the ground, can also be measured, a step that requires adding 10" to each of our player's measurements. Doing so accounts for the zero point being fixed at the rubber. An assumption is made concerning the same release-point distance for our full range of release-height values, despite the typical tradeoff, in order to help isolate the effect with our fictional pitcher. The study utilizes the average release-point distance of 100% of player height, or 73.8 inches of distance for our pitcher. This step results in a total distance of 54.4 feet (652.8") from release point to contact. To find the angle of downward trajectory, the equation of angle = tan^{-1} [(release-point height − contact height)/(release-point distance to contact)] is used. In Figure 18-2, the equation that is utilized is angle = tan^{-1} (X/Z).

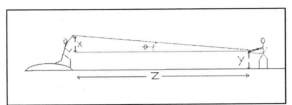

Figure 18-2. Calculating downward trajectory

Tall Release Point vs. Short Release Point to Contact	
Pitcher release-point distance:	73.8"
Distance to plate:	54.4 feet (652.8")
Hitter's reference height:	36"
Short pitcher release-point height:	63.1" (to ground)
Trajectory angle:	2.38 degrees, relative to the middle of the strike zone
Tall pitcher release-point height:	73.5" (to ground)
Trajectory angle:	3.29 degrees, relative to the middle of the strike zone

Table 18-7. Angles involved in calculating downward plane

According to the data in Table 18-7, the spread in typical values for release-point height spanned 10.4 inches, resulting in a 0.91-degree difference in downward trajectory. In general, about one degree of trajectory exists for every foot of height at ball release. The tall extreme has a 38% higher baseline trajectory than the short end of the adjustable range, despite the small size in volume overall, and based on the theoretical height of 36" at contact. The key point to take from all of this number-crunching, however, is the 0.91 degrees of leeway, with respect to downward plane at release point, given the typical range for release-point height.

Having gained a grasp of the degree of influence that a pitcher can have on downward plane at release point, the next step is to figure out how that 0.91 degrees translates to groundball percentages. Then, these findings can be compared to the two mph of perceived velocity that can be gained through adjustment of release-point distance. However, this issue goes a bit beyond high school physics. As a result, we recruited a fellow UCSD alumnus, Doug Bird, to help stare down this problem. Not to be confused with the former MLB pitcher, Doug Bird is a physicist and baseball enthusiast. Rather than paraphrase him, his full response is provided in order to give the issue the proper justice:

"Honestly, you could write a Ph.D. thesis on just this question to solve it completely. For this reason, I would make some simple calculations and argue it from a conceptual standpoint. We are assuming a perfectly elastic collision in two dimensions, where we take the cross-section of the bat and ball (both circles) and only consider whether the result will produce a groundball or flyball. As such, we make the following assumptions:

1. *The collision is perfectly elastic, i.e., no energy loss due to heating, friction, or deformation of anything (the bat doesn't crack).*
2. *Any change in the angle of the swing after making contact with the ball or the bat speed is negligible.*
3. *The ball and bat are perfectly curved, so that their cross-sections are circles.*
4. *Any change in the speed of the baseball the instant before and after contact is negligible.*
5. *The angular rotation isn't considered, for the moment. Accordingly, the ball is not spinning, and the bat is not turning. It's like two circles hitting each other, and neither circle is rotating.*

Calculations:
- *sin (angle of the ball just after contact) / sin (angle of the ball just before contact) = speed of pitch before contact / speed of pitch after contact*
- *If the speeds are the same, or very close, as we assume: sin (angle of the ball just after contact) / sin (angle of the ball just before contact) = 1*
- *Or the angle of the ball just after contact = angle of the ball just before contact*

In this way, a higher arm slot will result in a greater chance of getting a groundball, because a higher arm slot corresponds to a larger downward angle at the batter. You can extend this to determine the probability that you will get a groundball for pitches hit at various points near the top or bottom of the bat (you can't hit the back half of the bat). If the ball is moving, with no downward trajectory and no rotation, half of the places it could hit on the bat would result in a groundball. If the ball is moving at a downward angle of five degrees, 52.8% of the places on the bat would give a groundball. This comes from any contact that is five degrees above horizontal on the bat giving a groundball also. You can calculate the chance to get a groundball as follows:

- *(90 + downward angle of the ball just before contact) / 180 = % of places on the bat that will give a groundball."*

At this point, the approximate effect that downward trajectory has on groundball rates can be calculated, thanks to the equations provided by Doug Bird. It's necessary to make some assumptions in order to break down these calculations into something both manageable and within the budget of this project. Plugging in the numbers that were found for release-point trajectory, ranging from 2.38 degrees at the low to 3.29 degrees at the higher-release point, the following expected groundball rates were found:

(90 + 3.29 degrees) / 180 = 51.83%
(90 + 2.38 degrees) / 180 = 51.32 %
Difference: 0.51%

Table 18-8. Expected groundball rates

Based on Doug Bird's equations with our 73.8-inch tall sample pitcher, Table 18-8 shows the typical range of groundball percentages is 51.32% to 51.83%. Since it would be expected that approximately 50% of the groundballs would have a straight-line trajectory of 0 degrees (or 180 degrees), the higher downward angle produced by the pitcher at his release point increased the likelihood of groundballs by 1.32 to 1.83%, given all of the assumptions. The factors that are ignored through the assumptions will undoubtedly impact the raw values that we are measuring. On the other hand, because the critical measurement is taken at hitter contact, the downward angle generated by the pitcher just produces the baseline trajectory. The other factors build off of that baseline. As a result, the relative effect, based on release point, should maintain much of its value, even if an effort was undertaken to account for all of the other factors.

While getting on top of the ball to create angle helps to increase groundballs, the relative impact on groundball rates is just 0.51%. This finding is an astonishingly low number, even given the initial level of skepticism concerning the impact of downward plane. The 0.51% represents the expected "adjustment range" for our population of pitchers. On the other hand, even extreme adjustments that increase a pitcher's release-point height by two feet will only increase baseline groundball rates by about one percent.

Groundball rates are particularly interesting for pitchers, since they tend to be relatively stable on an individual level from season to season. The values also tend to vary within a fairly wide range for the player population as a whole, with most groundball rates falling anywhere between 35 and 65%. Barry Zito is a notorious flyball pitcher, whose rates for 2005-07 were 42, 40, and 41%, respectively. Groundball-machine Derek Lowe, on the other hand, used his sinking fastball to generate groundball-ratios of 64, 68, and 66% over the same time span. (Goldman and Kahrl, 2008) These numbers demonstrate that groundball rates are highly influenced by the individual pitcher, and that the 0.5% difference that can be attributed to typical ranges of downward plane is almost negligible, relative to the range in values across the entire population.

The aforementioned findings provide a comparative basis on which to weigh the relative tradeoff of release-point height and distance. Adjusting a pitcher's mechanics within the typical range to alter his release-point distance can have an impact of about two mph on perceived velocity, while doing the same for release-point height at ball release can influence groundball rates by about 0.5%. Given a choice between just those values, most players and coaches would likely prefer to maximize release-point distance and perceived velocity over downward plane, a decision reached even before considering the added bonus of achieving a later relative break on all pitches with movement.

The value of having a later break should not be underestimated. Randy Johnson's slider, for example, shows how a pitch with a very late and sharp break can make it nearly impossible for a hitter to properly identify it in time to initiate his swing. The effect is maximized by the perceived velocity of Johnson's fastball, particularly when it is combined with his true 95+ mph-pitch speed. A hitter has so little time to react to his fastball from such a close release point, it creates a sense of urgency to rush the swing decision, which makes his late-breaking slider all that much tougher to read. In this sense, release-point distance involves compounding benefits for the majority of pitchers.

The late break of Randy Johnson's slider brings up another point. An opposing hitter will often misjudge the amount of break in Johnson's slider in the relatively short amount of time he has to identify the pitch before starting his swing. As a consequence, his sliders will generate a lot of bad swings, as hitters attempt to make a late adjustment to correct for the pitch's movement. When a hitter succeeds in making contact, he's more likely to "top" the ball if he underestimates the break, which results in a grounder. We also know that the angle of trajectory produced by the break on Johnson's ball is larger than two to three degrees, as well as the fact that angle of trajectory has a greater effect on groundball rates than release-point angle, since the critical component in the equation of groundball ratios is the angle just before contact. All other factors being equal, pitchers with a long release point and a late break may generate a higher ratio of groundballs than those pitchers who create a lot of downward plane. In effect, such a situation could very well counteract some of the benefit gained from a taller-release point.

The conventional wisdom of "stay tall and get on top" is intended to help pitchers to generate downward plane, thereby altering the trajectory of the ball to make life tougher on hitters. If all of this sounds familiar, then you've been paying good attention, because it's very similar to the logic behind the conventional wisdom of "left-hander to the left side of the rubber, right-hander to the right side." Coaches will often encourage their pitchers to do anything they can to manipulate the incoming trajectory of the ball from the hitter's standpoint. Just as with "lefty to the left side," these strict pieces of advice can get in the way of what a pitcher does naturally, thereby potentially creating more of an obstacle for the player than a benefit. Another aspect these conventional ideas have in common is that they are flawed functionally, as well as mechanically. The "lefty to the left side" rule actually helps opposite-sided hitters and can produce overrotation of the trunk. In a similar vein, the "get on top" rule doesn't help groundball rates as much as perceived, while costing the pitcher critical distance at release point.

Another factor that these two conventions share is that they lead to a higher risk of injury for those pitchers who follow them. While the topic will be addressed in greater detail in subsequent parts of this book, overrotation is a major risk factor. A late change of posture is another. Many of the pitchers who attempt to get on top of the ball will bring their throwing arm through as high of a slot as possible, thereby sacrificing their posture in the process. In essence, the pitcher has to move his head out of the way (by tilting the spine) in order to bring his arm through over the top. This approach is biomechanically inefficient, and increases the stress (load force) that is put on certain parts of the body.

Regrettably, many coaches favor a high-arm slot on a pitcher, because of its influence on the pitch's downward plane. Younger players have a particular problem with this situation. Their lack of functional strength and flexibility will often result in poor and inconsistent posture at release point. As a rule, pitchers tend to struggle with their balance and posture as they mature, regardless of the instruction they receive. Telling these players to get on top further compounds the risk of injury to a developing arm. Although examples exist of pitchers in the Major Leagues with poor posture and a high-release point, the best players in the league are strong at maintaining their balance and posture throughout the delivery. As such, from a coaching standpoint, it is essential to help every pitcher achieve ideal balance and posture through release point, and to let the arm slot happen more naturally.

Tom's Wrap-Up

Baseball's Hall of Fame only has three Major League pitchers who are 6'5" or taller. This exclusive list includes Don Drysdale, Fergie Jenkins, and Eppa Rixey. While the tendency in the world of baseball is to draft taller pitchers, the effort is more about getting closer to home plate with real, perceived, and effective velocity and movement.

"Stay tall" isn't necessarily about height; rather, it's about having an upright head and spine as a pitcher's shoulders square up to the target. This positioning is referred to as "stack and track," because the last 20% of a pitcher's real velocity comes from the low back/torso going from hyperextension into flexion, just before the throwing forearm goes from external rotation into internal rotation, and the baseball is released. The longer a pitcher can stay upright, and the longer his total body tracks, the more efficiently will his torso deliver his throwing arm. In turn, his release point will be closer to home plate, and his perceived velocity will be higher.

A pitcher's body height at the start of his delivery is significantly less at release point. This circumstance is a function of how far he strides; how far he tracks into his front leg; and how much his front knee flexes before it firms up, thereby sending energy up the kinetic chain and out into the ball. A paradox exists in this situation, because no matter how "tall" a pitcher is in his setup, his posting knee will find whatever angle of flexion that optimizes the balance/posture-functional strength relationship into foot strike.

Accordingly, if "stay tall" isn't the important consideration, what is? Our research indicates that it's release point, velocity, movement, location, tunnel, and spread (note: tunnel and spread are explained in detail in subsequent chapters). In other words, with regard to the discussion of the legitimacy of the conventional wisdom of "stay tall," it isn't how tall; rather, the real issue involves how far the stride, how upright the spine, how consistent the release point, and how much the perceived and effective velocity differential is between the real velocity, movement, and location of the last pitch and the real velocity, movement, and location of the next pitch.

19

"Glove to Hip"

"Pull the glove to the hip."

☛ ***Doug:*** A pitcher's glove side is an important aspect of mechanics. As such, correct glove positioning can have a positive impact on a pitcher's level of efficiency. Previously, the effects that the glove side can have on the delivery were studied, with respect to maintaining "tightrope" balance, and to achieving opposite-and-equal arm angles into foot strike. In fact, the pitcher's glove continues to influence the delivery after foot strike and into ball release, as, it can have an impact on the position of the throwing hand at release point. The weight discrepancy between the baseball and the typical pitcher's mitt is an obstacle for this stage, as well as for opposite and equal. Failure to balance out the arm angles at foot strike will often result in a "soft" glove at release point, as well.

Conventional wisdom states that a pitcher should actively pull the glove to the hip after foot strike. The underlying concept to this piece of wisdom is that doing so will aid in creating more power with upper-body rotation by invoking the glove-side shoulder to pull back as trunk rotation begins. Theoretically, this movement would apply force along the desired direction of rotation for the trunk and shoulders, since both shoulders rotate around the spine after opposite and equal. In this situation, the throwing shoulder moves along a path toward the plate, and the glove shoulder seemingly moves back away from the plate. When watching a pitcher's upper body, from foot strike into ball release, it also appears at first glance that the glove is physically pulled in towards the body and away from the plate, given that the space narrows between the glove and torso as the pitcher tracks forward.

If pulling the glove to the hip provides meaningful benefits, then we should expect to see the five aces demonstrate this technique. Whenever possible, we try to study the most successful players when learning about proper pitching mechanics, because these great athletes typically utilize the most efficient techniques for delivering the baseball, with few exceptions. The best methods that produced the best results have withstood the test of time, having been shared by baseball's greatest pitchers over several generations, often despite conventional instruction. In that regard, Figure 19-1 shows the glove position of the best pitchers of our generation. These images help to illustrate whether these athletes pull toward the hip as they get into maximum external rotation (MER) of the throwing arm.

Figure 19-1. The five aces at the point of maximum external rotation (MER).

So much for compliance from the five aces. When an examination of the glove relative to the landing foot and knee is made, all of these elite pitchers have taken their torso to their glove, not their glove to their torso. Pedro Martinez's glove is a little behind his front knee, but he still takes his chest to glove. A review of the other four elite pitchers reveals that each one stabilizes his glove over the front foot during this phase of the delivery. In the case of Johan Santana, his glove is even out in front of his knee. Randy Johnson, Greg Maddux, and Roy Oswalt all keep their gloves stable over the front foot and in front of the torso, rather than pulling the glove to the hip.

These elite pitchers clearly avoid pulling the glove to the hip. As such, they are good examples of the next-to-last link on the kinetic chain—swivel and stabilize the glove. As a pitcher achieves opposite and equal, the palm of his glove will typically be facing downward. In this regard, the term "swivel" describes turning the glove so that the palm is facing the chest. The "stabilize" portion of the kinetic chain involves positioning the glove out over the front foot, in front of the torso, without forcibly moving the glove arm in any direction. This step helps a pitcher to track his body toward the glove, rather than vice versa. This movement can also be used to generate more power and a further release-point distance. It's important to be aware of the fact that elite pitchers continue to track their torso toward home plate as their shoulders square up to the target, a process that can be thought of as direction after rotation.

Glove stabilization is not an easy task for young players, for the same reason that opposite and equal can be particularly difficult—the weight discrepancy between the baseball in one hand and the glove on the other. Many young pitchers will drop the glove down closer to the ground and back towards the hip, because they lack the functional strength to consistently support that extra pound of weight.

When working with young players on their level of functional strength and flexibility, we ask them to hold their arms out and forearms up at 90 degrees in a "goalpost" position, as part of the warm-up. The players then perform various exercises in this upper-body position, with the glove on and a ball in the other hand. Inevitably, within minutes, most of these young athletes get tired and start lowering their arms (the glove-side arm gets weak first). In almost no time at all, the elbows of these young athletes are at their sides. The paradox is obvious. On one hand, these developing pitchers lack the functional strength to hold their arms up in a static position. On the other hand, they are expected to coordinate their strength into a balanced delivery, using unbalanced objects 50 or more times per game.

While glove stabilization gets easier as pitchers physically mature and gain functional strength, it's still an obstacle for even professional athletes. As such, a poor opposite-and-equal position at foot strike or early initiation of trunk rotation will often lead to a "soft" glove position at MER and release point, a factor that affects pitchers of all skill levels. Pitchers who are taught to pull the glove to the hip will also have poor stabilization, by definition, since the glove is moving (relative to the lower body) during the phase of the delivery in which it should be stable.

The objective is to achieve a strong stacked position as the upper body tracks forward into ball release. The components of a good stacked position, including strong balance and posture, as well as glove stabilization over the landing foot, can be evaluated at MER. In a proper stacked position, the chest and torso move toward the stabilized glove, as the pitcher continues to track from MER into ball release, rather than the other way around as taught by proponents of pull the glove to the hip.

 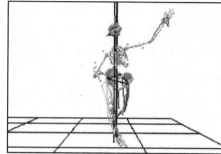

Figure 19-2. Motion analysis illustrates that this pitcher exemplifies a strong swivel and stabilize of the glove over the front foot, accompanied by a good bend in the front knee that is approaching the release point

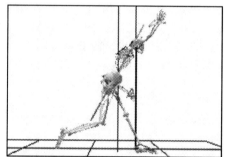 

Figure 19-3. This pitcher has a somewhat "soft" glove at release point, and appears to be actively pulling the glove toward his hip, while keeping a stiff front leg

When tracking the glove for pitchers using motion analysis, the position of the glove hand is measured, relative to the ankle of the front foot at release point. At that point, the distance between the glove hand and the front ankle is then also measured, using just the "Y" axis that runs from the rubber to home plate (parallel to the center line). If the distance is very small, it indicates that the glove is close to being directly over the landing foot. If the distance is relatively large, it means that the glove hand is closer to the hip or torso at release point. Negative values would reflect a glove position that is out in front of the landing foot. Such instances are rare, however. As such, we won't be dealing with any negative numbers when looking at group averages. Table 19-1 presents the average values for distance between the pitcher's glove and front foot at release point, separated by skill level (note: data was missing for three of our set of motion-analysis pitchers).

The pros have the smallest value for glove to foot distance by a significant margin, while no detectable difference existed between the college and high school pitchers. Even more striking is that, as a whole, the population of

All pitchers	2.14 inches, +/- 0.15 inches	n = 90, N = 30
Pro	1.88 inches, +/- 0.29 inches	n = 21, N = 7
College	2.25 inches, +/- 0.22 inches	n = 51, N = 17
High school	2.15 inches, +/- 0.30 inches	n = 18, N = 6

Table 19-1. Average distance, glove to front foot

Pro vs. college	t = 5.90	Significant at p<0.005
College vs. high school	t = 0.47	Insignificant
Pro vs. high school	t = 2.86	Significant at p<0.010

Table 19-2. Unpaired t-tests for between-group average distance, glove to front foot

pitchers averaged a distance of just over two inches from the glove to the front foot. These results strongly suggest that most pitchers finish with their mitts closer to the glove-side knee than the same-side hip, and that it is advantageous to do so. The results from the motion-analysis pitchers and the images of the five aces indicate that the "pull the glove to the hip" conventional wisdom is a less-than-optimal strategy, when compared to that of swivel and stabilize.

The data was further examined by creating groups based on glove position, just as was done previously with energy angle. This endeavor employed the same rules as the energy-angle study. The effort involved using eight pitchers per group (n = 24, N = 8), separated on the basis of their glove position, relative to the front foot at release point. As such, there were individual groups of eight players for each sub-entity—glove over foot, glove to hip, and baseline. The glove-over-foot group was comprised of the eight pitchers with the smallest average values for glove distance to front foot. The glove-to-hip group, on the other hand, was made up of the eight largest average values. The baseline group had eight pitchers who were randomly selected from the remaining set of 14 players (note: three pitchers had missing data points for glove position), just as was done with the energy-angle study. As before, the composition of the groups turned out to be nearly identical. A ratio of 2:4:2 for pro/college/high school players existed in both the glove-to-hip and baseline groups, while the glove-over-foot group had the advantage of an extra pro (at the expense of having a high school pitcher) at 3:4:1. The results of how the three groups compared on average distance, glove to front foot, are presented in Table 19-3.

Group	Average distance	SD (+/-)
Glove over foot	1.05 inches	0.16 inches
Glove to hip	3.73 inches	0.21 inches
Baseline	2.01 inches	0.22 inches

Table 19-3. Average distance, glove to front foot

The question arises concerning what is advantageous about keeping the glove stable over the pitcher's front foot? Theoretically, doing so helps a pitcher to get more out of the stack-and-track phase of the delivery, by allowing him to track his upper body toward the glove, thereby gaining a longer release point. In reality, we could just measure a pitcher's release-point efficiency to study this aspect. On the other hand, if we did just that, we wouldn't be able to tell if potential differences that were found were the result of the events that occurred prior to foot strike. To account for this effect, we simply subtracted stride-length efficiency from release-point efficiency to determine how much of the release-point distance was due to the post-foot strike events of delayed trunk rotation, stack and track, and swivel and stabilize the glove.

Group	Average Release-Point Efficiency–Stride Efficiency	SD (+/-)
Glove over foot	8.64 %	1.19 %
Glove to hip	6.46 %	1.14 %
Baseline	6.31 %	1.24 %

Table 19-4. Average release-point efficiency, minus stride-length efficiency

As Table 19-4 shows, a big gap was found between the glove-over-foot group and the rest of the pitchers in the study. The analysis also found that the glove-to-hip group actually had a better score on this measure than did the baseline group, albeit by a much smaller margin.

Foot vs. hip:	$t = 6.49$ for $n = 24$	Significant ($p < 0.005$)
	$t = 3.74$ for $N = 8$	Significant ($p < 0.005$)
Foot vs. baseline:	$t = 6.66$ for $n = 24$	Significant ($p < 0.005$)
	$t = 3.83$ for $N = 8$	Significant ($p < 0.005$)
Hip vs. baseline:	$t = 0.44$ for $n = 24$	Insignificant
	$t = 0.25$ for $N = 8$	Insignificant

Table 19-5. Between-group t-tests for release-point efficiency minus stride-length efficiency

As Table 19-5 points out, the difference between the glove-to-foot group and the other two groups was indeed significant, while the difference between the glove-to-hip and the baseline groups was negligible. This result helps to validate the concept of using swivel and stabilize to aid with stack and track in order to achieve a further relative release-point distance. It's interesting to note, though, that the glove-to-hip group didn't suffer in this category, compared to the baseline group.

Another measure to approximate the ability of a pitcher to track forward can also be utilized—the distance from the pitcher's head to the front foot. Players who stabilize the glove out in front of the chest, and who have strong balance and posture, will tend to track the body and the head closer to an "invisible wall" that goes straight up from the front foot. The wall is an imaginary line that the best pitchers tend to "hit" with the glove, the front knee, and the tip of the nose at release point.

Group	Average distance	SD (+/-)
Glove over foot	4.62 inches	0.28 inches
Glove to hip	5.54 inches	0.46 inches
Baseline	4.98 inches	0.51 inches

Table 19-6. Average distance, head to foot

Table 19-6 shows that a more consistent trend exists with the glove-over-foot group getting the closest to the invisible wall, followed by the baseline group, with the glove-to-hip group being the furthest away from the wall. It is important to keep in mind when considering these numbers that the head measurement was made from the center of mass of the head (COMH). In reality, the nose is about three to four inches closer to the wall than these values indicate. It should also be noted that some pitchers with poor balance might lead with their head out in front of the COMB, thereby approaching the invisible wall through more inefficient means. Any pitchers within this sample who lose their balance with the COMH out in front could potentially have a negative impact on the reliability of the data.

Foot vs. hip:	$t = 8.39$ for $n = 24$	Significant ($p < 0.005$)
	$t = 4.83$ for $N = 8$	Significant ($p < 0.005$)
Foot vs. baseline:	$t = 3.04$ for $n = 24$	Significant ($p < 0.005$)
	$t = 1.75$ for $N = 8$	Insignificant
Hip vs. baseline:	$t = 4.00$ for $n = 24$	Significant ($p < 0.005$)
	$t = 2.31$ for $N = 8$	Significant ($p < 0.025$)

Table 19-7. Between groups t-tests for distance from COMH to the ankle of the land foot

As Table 19-7 indicates, each of the differences holds up under the tests for statistical significance, although the glove-over-foot vs. baseline comparison slips below the significance threshold when the player sample of $N = 8$ is used, rather than the sample of $n = 24$ data points. The loss of significance at $N = 8$ for the glove-over-foot group vs. the baseline group is not all that surprising, given that the baseline group had a pretty strong average rating for distance from glove to front foot. Overall, these statistics further illustrate that a positive relationship exists between stack and track and swivel and stabilize, and how these concepts relate to release-point efficiency.

The aforementioned groups can also be used to test the conventional wisdom that "pull glove to the hip" helps to generate more rotational velocity with the upper body. This factor is tracked in motion analysis by measuring the angular velocity of the axis-line that runs through the pitcher's shoulders, as it rotates around the spine. Because the software utilized in this undertaking can also measure the maximum amount of angular velocity that is created with this trunk rotation, the resultant findings will be the best indicator concerning whether this particular piece of conventional wisdom holds water.

Group	Average	SD (+/-)
Glove over foot	899.9 degrees/second	22.0 degrees/second
Glove to hip	898.3 degrees/second	20.2 degrees/second
Baseline	920.0 degrees/second	29.7 degrees/second

Table 19-8. Average maximum angular trunk velocity

As Table 19-8 shows, the values between the glove-over-foot and glove-to-hip groups on this aspect are extremely close, and obviously insignificant, given the resultant standard deviations. The baseline group actually performs the best in this category, but its advantage appears to be pretty slight.

Foot vs. hip:	t = 0.26 for n = 24	Insignificant
	t = 0.15 for N = 8	Insignificant
Foot vs. baseline:	t = 2.67 for n = 24	Significant (p < 0.025)
	t = 1.54 for N = 8	Insignificant
Hip vs. baseline:	t = 2.97 for n = 24	Significant (p < 0.005)
	t = 1.71 for N = 8	Insignificant

Table 19-9. Between groups t-tests of maximum angular velocity of the trunk and shoulders

The baseline score, as Table 19-9 illustrates, proved significant at just above the necessary thresholds for n = 24, but the effect disappears when compared to both groups, using the player sample size of N = 8. The strategy of bringing the glove closer to the body did not help the pitchers in this sample to generate higher angular velocities of the trunk and shoulders. All factors considered, however, this study wasn't a true experiment. The pitchers in the glove-to-hip group were not instructed to physically attempt to follow the conventional wisdom. As a consequence, the findings are not necessarily indicative of a direct behavioral response. At the very least, however, the results can be generalized to show that swivel and stabilize did not hinder angular trunk rotation.

In summary, the results of our study of "pull glove to the hip," revealed that the conventional wisdom does not describe how the best pitchers position their glove from foot strike into MER. The findings also showed that the best players in our motion-analysis sample tend to swivel and stabilize the glove over the front foot into release point. The breakdown of pitchers into groups, based on glove position at ball release, indicated that the glove-over-foot pitchers tracked forward more so than their counterparts after foot strike. Furthermore, they got closer to hitting the invisible wall. The breakdown also provided relevant data that failed to show the expected advantages that are theoretically associated with the conventional wisdom. Overall, the conclusion of this study seems to be pretty clear. The strategy of swivel and stabilize the glove over the front foot, in order to increase the release-point distance and achieve functional gains of increased perceived velocity and later break on pitches, is preferable to any contradictory conventional wisdom.

While coaches can help their pitchers to practice the method of swivel and stabilize, it is critical that opposite and equal is achieved first and foremost. Otherwise, it will be difficult to coordinate swivel and stabilize after foot strike. Once the pitcher has achieved opposite-and-equal arm angles at foot strike, the glove will typically already be somewhere in the proximity over the front foot (unless the player engages in a large upper-body twist). At this point, the player can then squeeze the glove to stabilize it, as he swivels it from palm-down to facing toward the pitcher's torso. The actual swivel action occurs just after trunk rotation begins, as the shoulders and chest come square to home plate. The four-image sequence of John Smoltz, presented in Figures 19-4 and 19-5, provides an effective demonstration of the concept.

Figure 19-4. John Smoltz gets a good opposite and equal at foot strike, and then squeezes the glove as he begins to swivel over the front foot

Figure 19-5. John's glove now finishes the swivel and stabilizes over the front foot, as he gets into MER

The conventional wisdom of "pull glove to your hip" is similar to many of the other conventional rules reviewed in this book, in that it makes intuitive sense, based on what we think that our eyes see. At just 32 frames per second, however, our eyes trick us by focusing in on the relative movements of very particular parts of the body, namely the throwing arm. When someone watches a pitcher from foot strike to release point, without paying attention to the static position of the landing leg, it seems as though the glove pulls in to the pitcher. In fact, the rest of the pitcher's body has to be observed in order to realize that the body moves toward the glove during this phase of the delivery. As such, this factor is difficult for the human eye to process without using high-speed cameras to slow everything down.

Tom's Wrap-Up

One common mistake that coaches who teach the method of swivel and stabilize make is to fix the glove first, before addressing the preceding phases in the delivery. A pitcher with a soft glove is easy to spot, while flaws in other elements of his delivery, such as lift and thrust, stride and momentum, and opposite and equal can be much more difficult to identify in a bullpen or practice session. A coach, however, should never lose sight of the importance of mechanical timing and sequencing. It is critical that a coach works with a player to iron out the pitcher's delivery in the proper sequence, according to the timeline of critical events. The penultimate goal is to find the unique ideal delivery for each pitcher, beginning with balance and posture and then moving on down the timeline, all the while working with the athlete's natural timing and mechanical signature.

In order to be properly informed, coaches at all competitive levels should use a real-time visual, e.g., a digital camera, a camcorder, or even a cell phone to capture where a pitcher's glove is at foot strike. Once this position has been identified, a coach should never allow his pitcher to let his glove retreat from that distance. It can swivel, it can go up or down, it can continue forward, but it should never move back from that distance. As such, body to glove should always be taught.

20

"No Sidearm"

"Don't throw sidearm."
"Don't throw across your body."
"Don't short-arm."

☛ **Doug:** Everybody is enthralled with arm slot. On the other hand, just about every coach has a different opinion on what type of arm angles he likes to see from the pitchers on his staff. As was discussed in a previous chapter, many scouts and coaches prefer a pitcher with an over-the-top delivery that creates a higher release point to increase downward plane. With this concept in mind, and given the overall emphasis in the game on generating a downward angle to increase groundball rates, it's a natural extension that pitchers are told, "don't throw sidearm," at a very young age.

As a general rule, pitchers who have a relatively low arm slot (i.e., three-quarters or lower) are typically frowned upon, because they are perceived to lack the ability to create sufficient downward plane, due to their relatively low release-point height. It is also a common belief among many coaches that sidearm pitchers have an increased risk for injury, even though no established link exists between the two factors. In contrast, the posture changes that are necessary for a pitcher to get on top of the ball actually do expose a pitcher to an increased risk of being injured.

In reality, the conventional wisdom of "don't throw sidearm," once again makes mechanical efficiency take a back seat to a specific pitch trajectory. As such, a philosophical conundrum exists for coaches who adhere to both trajectory rules of—"lefty to the left side" and "don't throw sidearm" (or get on top of the ball). Frankly, these instructions send an extremely mixed message to a pitcher. Is he supposed to concentrate on creating an angle from the side or from the top? The correct answer, based on everything that we have examined so far, is that the pitcher should concentrate on finding the release-point position that is the natural result of good timing and sequencing, as well as one that concurrently ensures strong balance and posture throughout the delivery.

Ideal balance and posture are the most critical aspects of a consistently efficient pitching delivery. Both factors rely on the basic element of keeping the head stable above the center of mass of the body (COMB). If a pitcher leans his head away from his body at any point in the delivery, he is sacrificing balance and/or posture in the process. Gaining release-point height by "staying tall" and "getting on top" can hurt a pitcher's release-point distance. Doing so prevents the player from releasing the ball far out in front of the landing foot. It also decreases the likelihood that the pitcher can find a release-point position that is repeatable, with regard to height, distance, and angle of trajectory. As such, a lack of emphasis and focus on critical factors, such as timing, sequencing, balance, and posture can make it extremely difficult for a pitcher to find his own mechanical efficiency and consistency.

Incidentally, most pitchers who throw from a three quarters-to-sidearm slot have great balance and posture at release point. Likewise, most pitchers who have outstanding posture have an arm slot between three-quarters and pure sidearm. The underlying basis for this occurrence is that a pitcher's natural arm slot is genetically predetermined. This position can be found by observing the angle from the head and spine to the throwing arm at the shoulder. Because this angle is unique for each individual player, it does not change from one pitch to another, regardless of whether the pitcher makes his arm come through over the top or from a sidearm slot. This angle is referred to as the pitcher's biological or "intrinsic" arm slot, while the term used to describe the conventional definition of arm slot is "functional." Intrinsic arm slot is a personal aspect of each player's signature, while functional arm slot is an indication of how the batter perceives the position and trajectory of the pitch at ball release.

When analyzing functional arm slot, the term "12 o'clock" is employed to refer to a release-point position that is straight over the top. In this position, the pitcher's arm is pointing right toward the sky, like the hour hands at 12 on a clock. In this scenario, six o'clock represents the ground. Imagine a clock face overlaid on top of the picture of a pitcher at release point, centered at the player's navel, and taken from the batter's point of view. From this perspective, the functional arm slot of right-handed pitchers would typically fall between 11:00 and 9:00, while the functional arm slot of lefties would range between 1:00 and 3:00. Meanwhile, the goal of "get on top of the ball" is to get as close to 12:00 as possible.

The clock overlay is set up a bit differently when it is utilized to evaluate intrinsic arm slot. The best way to understand the spine-arm relationship is to orient the clock face, such that it is centered at the navel, just as before, but with 12:00 pointing directly at the pitcher's center of his head (COMH), rather straight up to the sky. A line running from the pitcher's navel (and center of the clock-face) to the 12:00 position represents the athlete's spine at this point in the delivery. As such, intrinsic arm slot is evaluated relative to this line. When looking at the clock for the intrinsic arm slot, it is rare to find a pitcher who has a higher angle than 10:30 or 1:30 (LHP). In this case, 10:30 and 1:30 represent exactly the three-quarter arm slot that many coaches and scouts dislike so much. In fact, the majority of pitchers have a natural biological arm slot that is actually low three-quarters to sidearm.

When comparing the different clocks for the same pitcher at release point, ideal posture is achieved when the functional arm slot perfectly matches the intrinsic arm slot. Maintaining the COMH at 12:00 on the functional clock is equal to having a perfect spine-hip relationship, such that the intrinsic 12:00 points directly upward, perpendicular to the ground. If the clocks are far from matching, it is due to a change in the pitcher's posture, a factor that a pitcher

Figure 20-1. The five aces at release point

typically adjusts in order to get on top by bending his spine toward the glove side of his body. The translation from intrinsic arm slot to functional arm slot is based on the degree of posture change, as measured by the angle of pelvis-to-spine.

Given that the best pitchers tend to have the best mechanics, it is reasonable to expect that our five aces have very good posture at release point. The intrinsic and functional arm slots for these pitchers should be close to equal, with their head directly over the navel, pointing toward 12:00. If true, then most of the best pitchers would also display a functional arm slot that is between three-quarters and sidearm, a factor that is in contradiction to the conventional wisdom involving arm slot positioning.

As Figures 20-1a through 20-1e show, the five aces, as a group, do a great job of maintaining their posture into release point, particularly when compared to the average pitcher. As the images demonstrate, both Oswalt and Santana experience a slight posture change for the pitches that they are making, as illustrated by the sideways bend at the waist. These examples show relatively minor posture changes. In fact, other pitchers in the Majors have much worse spine angles than these two exceptional players, and even these elite pitchers will lose posture on occasion. Of the two pitchers, it can be seen that Santana has the much higher intrinsic arm slot, even when accounting for the posture change, while Oswalt has an intrinsic arm slot that is closer to sidearm.

Greg Maddux is another good example of an intrinsic, over-the-top delivery. When he pitches, he exhibits strong posture, combined with a relatively high arm slot. His intrinsic arm slot is above the typical range of 10:30, a level that represents the high end of the spectrum. Of particular interest, with regard to arm slot, are Randy Johnson and Pedro Martinez, each of whom appears to have ideal posture at release point, with matching intrinsic and functional clocks and arm slots that approach "true" sidearm near 9:00 (3:00 for Johnson). It is beneficial to compare the relationship of Martinez's throwing arm and spine to that of Maddux, given that these two examples provide a vivid picture of the range of functional arm slots that are possible with great posture.

Another key factor that should be observed in the images of the five aces is the glove position. Previously, the glove position for each of the five aces was evaluated at the point of MER. Having reached ball release, every one of these pitchers has his glove out in front of the torso, with the palm of the glove facing the chest. For the most part, these pitchers have stabilized the glove over the front knee, although Santana and Oswalt are both a bit off the mark. It is not a coincidence that the two pitchers with slight posture inefficiencies also display a glove position that is just off to the side of the front knee. Pitchers with larger alterations in their posture at release point will typically display associated deficiencies with glove position.

Some coaches and players associate throwing sidearm with "throwing across your body," particularly since the term does not have a standard definition. In fact, the throwing arm of low three-quarters to sidearm pitchers does cross the middle of the body during the follow-through. Players are often told, "don't throw across your body," because the term carries a very negative connotation, even though coaches can't agree on the meaning of the phrase. The section dealing with stride direction also included mention of the fact that coaches frequently assume that a pitcher who strides closed will also throw across his body. Accordingly, these coaches tell their players to stride straight at the plate in order to avoid such a fate.

Though largely misunderstood, the general consensus amongst most professional pitching coaches is that throwing across your body equates to incomplete trunk rotation at release point. The perfect example of this factor is the knee drill, which was previously discussed in connection with the velocity study that was conducted at the NPA by Eric Andrews and Ryan Sienko. When pitchers perform the knee drill with a pelvis angle that is more closed than ideal for their personal signature, the result is that the trunk and shoulders will not rotate far enough to get square to home plate at ball release. Since the torso is not yet square, but the throwing shoulder is already going from MER into internal rotation, it appears as if the last pure "throwing" part of the delivery is actually crossing the front of the upper body. In this sense, the pitcher literally looks as if he is "throwing across his body."

The negative associations given to throwing across the body are warranted, but confusion exists as to the root of the problem. While we have found a solution to this issue, it doesn't involve getting on top to "fix" a sidearm slot, or striding straight at the plate to avoid a closed stride. Our approach is to help the pitcher find his ideal mechanics, timing, and sequencing that collectively and naturally produce the proper upper-body position, from foot strike into ball release and follow-through. Trunk position at release point is impacted by setup stance and position on the rubber, balance and posture throughout the delivery, lift and thrust, stride and momentum, timing into foot strike, opposite-and-equal arm angles, hip-shoulder separation, delayed trunk rotation, stack and track, and swivel and stabilize.

Ideally, the solution is to start at the beginning of the delivery, working down the sequencing of events to understand why an over- or underrotation is occurring. The next step is to then make sure that the pitcher has ironed out the preceding links in the chain and is properly prepared to execute the final phase of the delivery—ball release and follow-through.

Our study of pitching mechanics has shown us that the actions of the throwing arm are largely the result of signature-specific pathways that have been ingrained biologically. This aspect is true, whether the discussion concerns breaking of the hands into opposite and equal, getting from that position into MER, or getting from MER into internal rotation and ball release. When working with pitchers, the best mechanical solutions involve other parts of the body, such as the glove-side arm fix for opposite and equal and ensuring postural stabilization for pitchers who bend their spine to get on top.

The final bit of conventional wisdom that will be addressed in this chapter is one that attempts to influence the aforementioned signature-specific elements from breaking of the hands into MER and ball release, since it calls for a pitcher to remember, "don't short-arm." Coaches who are proponents of this particular piece of advice use the term "short-arm" to refer to the length of the arm path, as the pitching hand travels the distance from glove break to ball release. The transition of the pitching arm from MER into internal rotation is the fastest portion of the delivery, in terms of rotational velocity and the frames/second necessary to see what is occurring with a high-speed camera. This factor is by far the most difficult piece of the kinetic chain for a pitching coach to evaluate and adjust to if using his eyes as his only assessment tool.

In fact, most "short-armers" share the same biomechanical characteristics as their long-armed counterparts. One of the most famous big league examples is Billy Wagner of the New York Mets. Wagner puzzles many of the opponents to short-arming the ball. Even though conventional wisdom states that short-arming the ball should hinder velocity, Wagner is renowned for cracking triple digits on the radar gun. Standing at 5'10", Billy Wagner also helps trump the conventional wisdom that claims that shorter guys can't bring the heat.

Figure 20-2. Billy Wagner (left and center) and Randy Johnson (right), two pitchers separated by over a foot of height and wingspan, yet connected by their ability to throw bullets

As Figure 20-2 illustrates, Wagner does an excellent job of reaching opposite-and-equal arm angles as he gets into foot strike. He doesn't reach back in the way that many coaches dictate. Instead, he has bend in his arms, like John Smoltz. He generates a considerable stride, and uses a good stack and track to get from foot strike into maximum external rotation. At MER, Wagner looks very similar to the five aces, with excellent balance and posture, and a glove that is stabilized over the front foot. Figure 20-2b (center) shows just how similar Wagner is to the five aces, even compared with 6'11" Randy Johnson (Figure 20-2c, right).

In order to wrap up the breakdown of conventional wisdom and to tie all of the ideas discussed in this book together, we can look at the progression of another elite pitcher—Walter Johnson. Johnson was the most dominant pitcher of his time, and one of the original five inductees into Baseball's Hall of Fame, along with Babe Ruth, Ty Cobb, Christy Matthewson, and Honus Wagner. Pitching from 1907–1929, "The Big Train," as Johnson was known, compiled a lifetime record of 417–299 (.599), along with his 12 AL strikeout titles, five for ERA and six for wins. His career stats featured some other eye-rubbing numbers that are tough to comprehend in today's game, including 531 complete games and 110 career shutouts. In the days before the radar gun, stories from hitters who faced Walter Johnson and tales of Johnson's fastball that was thrown too hard to pick up with human eyes, reinforce the sort of "stuff" that Johnson possessed. Figure 20-3 presents a six-picture sequence of Walter Johnson executing his delivery over 80 years ago.

Figure 20-3. Progression of Walter Johnson's delivery, from leg lift through ball release (photographs and editing courtesy of Lee Flippin)

All factors considered, it's amazing that the best pitchers in baseball have been adhering to the same basic rules of mechanics since the beginning of the 20th century. Only recently have we been able to understand why they were successful. As such, modern technology has helped isolate and identify those factors that Walter Johnson has in common with his modern-day counterparts, for example, Randy Johnson. Both players utilize a lot of upper-body load to generate hip-shoulder separation, and both finish with near-perfect posture and a true sidearm delivery. It can also be seen that Walter Johnson had very good balance throughout the pitch sequence, and he took advantage of early momentum to get a good energy angle and a long stride. He also clearly delayed trunk rotation until after foot strike, and swivels and stabilizes his glove in time for maximum external rotation. Furthermore, it is extremely unlikely that anyone ever told Walter Johnson to "get on top of the ball," or to "not throw sidearm." He pitched in the days before pitching coaches, when players were often left to fend for themselves on the mound. Walter Johnson's case reinforces the point that few limits exist to what a capable athlete can learn about the mechanics of his sport when left to his own devices.

Tom's Wrap-Up

Our research-based, scientific approach to determining proper arm slot/arm path dictates that a coach should steadfastly avoid including "don't throw side-arm," or "get on top" in his instructional tool kit. Balance and posture should be a coach's teaching priorities. Arm slot and arm path should be left to happen naturally. In reality, these factors are two more examples of unfounded conventional wisdom that should be added to the list of things that constitute inappropriate pitching instructions.

Frankly, the conventional wisdoms that coaches employ concerning what a pitcher is supposed to do from foot strike to ball release are nothing more than a basket of instructional misinformation. Remember, most of these so-called rules evolved from guesses at what they thought they saw in a pitcher's delivery. Each piece of these conventional wisdoms are without foundation.

"Stay tall" is a teach that is meant to help a pitcher "get on top" or "stay on top" into release point to create *downward plane* or *depth* on his pitches. Too few people in baseball realize that at release point, pitchers all end up at the bottom of the mound with a bent front knee and a vertical ball-release height of five-to-six feet, whether they deliver overhand, three-quarters, or side-arm. Coaches assume that their pitchers pull their gloves to their chest because most coaches don't look at where the pitcher's glove is relative to their landing foot into and at release point (on elite throwers as well as the non-elite pitchers). Chest to glove looks like glove to chest, without the perspective of the front foot.

To be honest, no one really knows the actual origin of the conventional wisdoms of "don't side-arm," "don't throw across your body," and/or "don't short arm the ball." Arm slot occurs as a function of posture. In reality, most pitchers actually throw across their body, in the sense that the throwing arm crosses the front of the body during follow-through. Furthermore, every pitcher ends up short-arming the ball, because his throwing forearm goes into external rotation, with the elbow at 90°, no matter what his arm path or arm action was. It just couldn't be seen with the naked eye.

Finally, from a coach's perspective, if one foot of release-point height only translates into one degree of downward plane on ball trajectory, and if one foot of release-point distance translates into two to three mph of perceived velocity *with* later ball movement, then it makes better sense instructing pitchers to stride as far and as fast as strength and flexibility will allow without adversely affecting efficient timing, sequencing, and mechanics. Use dragline to position them properly on the rubber, then have them do the following:

- Stride six to seven times the length of their feet in .95 to 1.05 seconds with balance and posture.
- Land naturally with opposite and equal arms.
- Generate 40 to 60 degrees of hip and shoulder separation.
- Delay throwing shoulder rotation until the head and spine reach 80% of stride length.
- Square shoulders to target; stack and track while the throwing arm goes into external rotation.
- Swivel and stabilize the glove over the landing foot.
- Snap the throwing arm into release point in 1.25 to 1.35 seconds, 8 to 12 inches in front of the landing foot.

LOOKING AHEAD

Section 6

21

The Future of Player Development

The Future of Player Development and Evaluation

☛ *Doug:* We are not close, nor will we ever be, to reaching the saturation point with the information that has been gained from using modern-day tools, such as motion analysis. In essence, we still are in the embryonic stages of the effort to take advantage of the latest technology to improve the efficiency of player evaluation. Despite recent innovations, baseball is still trailing other major sports with regard to position-specific athletic skill evaluation. The reliance on the 20-80 scouting scale for making judgments about physical tools is unique to baseball. Scouts and coaches in other sports rely much more heavily on objective measurements. This situation is due, in no small part, to the nature of learning the game of baseball, and how it differs from some other major sports. Unlike most other sports, baseball talent is affected less by physical size and strength, and is determined more by an athlete's ability to develop game-specific skills.

Player positions in football, for example, tend to have very specific size requirements, beginning in high school and continuing with an ever-increasing level of importance throughout college and the NFL. At the most competitive levels, athletes who are at least 6'2"+ and 300+ lbs. are built for the offensive line and valued for their strength, while their 270 lb. counterparts often find themselves playing on the defensive line. In turn, the lighter, faster players are assigned to the "skill positions," such as wide receiver, running back, or defensive back. Meanwhile, the athletic big guys in the middle of the size-scale tend to play positions that line up in the middle of the field, such as quarterback, linebacker, fullback, and tight end.

In basketball, the situation is similar to football. A player's height and strength determines whether the athlete is built to play inside at center or power forward, or is better suited to play along the perimeter. In general, athletes in professional football and basketball represent the big and tall end of the size spectrum. Average fans find it difficult to imagine themselves on the field with these "giants."

In baseball, on the other hand, a player's size has less effect on the positions that are available to him. As such, players of extreme height and weight don't enjoy the same natural advantages as large athletes in other sports. Athletes of relatively average height and weight can be found all over the baseball diamond, at all levels of competition. Not to say that Prince Fielder and other athletes with his body type are equally suited to play shortstop as players who are built like Omar Vizquel. The fact is, however, that there are ballplayers who can play any position on the diamond. For these athletes, size is not an obstacle. There are players, such as Craig Biggio, Chone Figgins, and Jose Oquendo, who have the ability to play just about anywhere on the field with passable defense. For those individuals who don't remember Oquendo, he was a utility fielder for the New York Mets and St. Louis Cardinals from 1983 to 1995, and is famous for playing all nine positions in a single game for the 1988 Cardinals, which included his taking the mound.

Frankly, it would be virtually impossible for an NFL player to get his way into the game at every position, including offense, defense, and special teams. Likewise, there are maybe a handful of basketball players who have the size and skill to even attempt doing this in the NBA, where there are only five positions to be covered on the court. While general athleticism is certainly an advantage in baseball, in the sense that speed, quickness, strength, and agility impact performance, learning how to actually employ these attributes on the diamond is much easier said than done.

Another clear distinction between professional baseball and either football or basketball is the Minor League system in baseball. A player drafted in the top of the first round is likely to start for his NFL or NBA team in his first professional season, and is counted on to be a franchise cornerstone for years to come. A top 10 selection in the MLB amateur player draft, however, is just hoping to reach the Major Leagues within two-to-three years. While a few of these players may eventually become superstars, some will never see the Major Leagues. Between the day he is drafted and the day he makes his Major League debut, a player is expected to further enhance his baseball skills in order to be ready to face the best ballplayers on the planet.

This helps to explain why every year NFL teams conduct seven rounds of the draft to help fill their 53-player rosters, the NBA drafts two rounds to supplement a 15-player roster, but every organization in Major League baseball selects up to 50 players per year to help fill their various Minor League affiliates. MLB's deep draft system increases the odds that some of those players will someday impact the 25- and 40-man rosters of the big league clubs.

As such, Major League organizations place a high degree of importance on the ability to evaluate talent and develop players, two skills that are absolutely essential to produce a strong team at the highest level. The financial cost of acquiring players via free agency is prohibitive, relative to dollars spent developing players from within. Not surprisingly, most of the successful baseball organizations in recent years have been very skilled at drafting and developing their own talent. These factors have made it critical for baseball organizations to customize their approach to roster construction, including establishing subjective measures of athletic ability, objective benchmarks of performance and baseball-specific skills, and styles of player development and coaching.

Each organization places trust in its scouts and coaches to identify and train the best players to fit within their system. Every club has their own strategy for selecting player personnel, and using scouting reports, performance stats, video data, medical histories, player profiles, and other relevant information. Teams also have specific methods to transition a player through the Minors, while getting him primed for "the show." Collectively, these ingredients serve as the recipe for player development at the professional level.

Conventional stats can be useful when evaluating Minor League players and, to a lesser extent, with college athletes. In that regard, some outstanding work has been done in the realm of statistical analysis to help account for factors like park effects and league context, which, to a degree, can help to provide a measure of control for outside variables in order to evaluate an athlete's performance and potential on a level playing field. As such, a player's numbers can be analyzed to reveal tendencies within his game. Such an analysis can have predictive value, with respect to the player's future level of performance. In that area, the great work of Bill James, John Dewan, Rob Neyer, Craig Wright, Keith Woolner, Nate Silver, Clay Davenport, the members of S.A.B.R., and countless others has uncovered valuable information through the study and manipulation of performance stats.

In reality, certain limitations exist to the extent that conventional stats can reveal information about a player's skill. As a record of historical events, they can't serve to measure raw athletic ability, such as the tools that are evaluated on the 20-80 scouting scale. This factor helps to explain why scouting reports and statistical profiles are best understood in unison. On one hand, performance stats provide objectivity. On the other hand, the 20-80 scale offers subjective measures of the desired athletic tools. The stats reveal if a player steals a lot of bases at a successful rate, but they don't really detail how fast the athlete is, or whether he gets good jumps and a strong lead, or if he reads pitchers and situations well. The scouting reports provide context to conventional stats, while stats help to reveal how the tools translate to performance.

Statistics are considered an objective tool for performance analysis. However, most of the numbers that are recorded in every scorebook are based on subjective judgments. For example, the opinions of umpires have a strong influence on balls, strikes, hits, and outs. The official scorer's opinion comes into play for rulings on errors, wild pitches, and passed balls. The situation is even worse when determining unearned runs, which require the scorer to "reconstruct the inning," as if the play was made, while following certain assumptions, such as "no double-plays."

In the 1989 book, *The Diamond Appraised,* Craig Wright nailed down the problem with errors in the chapter dubbed, "Baseball's Most Useless Statistic." Sometimes, it's up to the scorekeeper to decide which pitcher gets credited with the win, for example, as when the winning team took an early lead and never lost it, but the starting pitcher was removed before the fifth inning. In this situation, the official scorer must decide which non-starter was most integral to the victory. The criteria for this decision are not well-defined, therefore, it's up to the scorekeeper to decide to whom to give the magic "W."

Another limitation of conventional stats and record-keeping is that data get recorded into discrete categories, many of which were created over 100 years ago, and were used to describe a far different game than what exists today. Errors were more relevant in the game, when players thought that wearing a mitt was "unmanly." Pitchers were assigned the "win" for the whole team, largely because they were expected to pitch each game from beginning to end, with rare exception. These circumstances provide a better understanding of some of the stats from the early era of Major League baseball, like Walter Johnson's career marks for complete games and shutouts, which are quite remarkable when compared to those of modern pitchers. Some other stats, such as the "save," have literally changed the way that pitchers are used and games are played in modern baseball, largely as a by-product of tracking specific statistical events. These examples underscore the main point, which is that context matters when evaluating performance stats.

The categorization employed in baseball scorekeeping has also helped to take out the differentiation of particular events on the field. For example, all singles are given equal value in statistical analysis, whether the single is the result of a drag-bunt, a soft-hit grounder combined with a fast runner, a "groundball with eyes," a liner over the infield's head, a bloop hit between two outfielders, or a line drive shot off the Green Monster in Fenway. It is helpful to know, however, what type of single it was, and whether the hitter has tendencies to pull the ball, hit to the opposite field, or hit a lot of groundballs, compared to fly balls. Categorizing all of these hits as simply "singles" in the scorebook strips each event of its ability to give additional information about the players and events involved.

Ways exist to account for such a paucity of more in-depth information. For example, publications such as *Baseball America's* annual *Almanac,* include spray charts that show the location of a player's hits over a given sample, and breaks down outs into grounders and flies. This information is a huge step in the right direction, with statistical analysts continuing to create measures to control for the biases of traditional scorekeeping and the categorization of data.

Baseball America is one of the best in the business at combining scouting information and performance statistics to analyze ballplayers. Its annual *Scouting Notebook* has been developed over the years to reflect the advances in modern-player evaluation. The spray charts reflect the need to dissect data for balls-in-play. As such, they provide much more information than a simple record of hits and at-bats. The potential for much-needed growth in this area exists, as MLB teams acquire the technology to track these on-field events, using hi-speed cameras to measure elements such as ball-flight velocity, trajectory, and location.

While traditional stats might fail to capture some of the aspects of physically playing the game, they have predictive value to determine individual skill. The success of statistical analysis has motivated a number of other individuals to pursue new ways of taking an objective approach to player evaluation. As a result, mountains of quality research have been produced in recent years. At the NPA/RDRBI, we can further blend the objectivity of statistical analysis with the athletic evaluation of scouting reports by taking advantage of technology, such as high-speed motion capture and analysis.

The motion-analysis strategy can be used to create task-specific models for different positions as well as different sports, such as the NPA model for pitching mechanics in baseball. When taken together, the traditional stats, advanced stats, 20-80 scores, and the motion-analysis data can provide a much more detailed picture of an athlete's physical ability, specific to his individual job. Furthermore, the motion-analysis numbers and video footage can help to explain why a scouting report doesn't match up with a player's performance record. This information can also be employed to target specific areas of improvement that are consistent with the athlete's scouting report and stat profile.

In the case of the NPA/RDRBI model, motion analysis can help bridge the information gap to explain why a pitcher has success on the mound, despite being of seemingly average size and having just average stuff. The evaluation of mechanics provides the context to more fully appreciate the pitcher's skills, both on paper and in the bullpen. Technology, such as high-speed motion capture, can be used to help distinguish baseball-specific skill and athletic ability, and to help identify the strengths and weaknesses in a player's game. The combination of motion-analysis data, performance stats, and scouting reports provides a very thorough understanding of a ballplayer's overall talent and potential. In the hands of the best talent evaluators in the game, this three-headed attack of visual, numerical, and qualitative information can greatly increase the efficiency of talent evaluation and player development.

The ultimate objective when using motion analysis and other technology is to augment the system that is already in place, rather than substitute for the established methods that are already available. The key focal point is to provide coaches and scouts with better objective information, so that they can see an individual player from every possible angle and point of view. When all is said and done, however, this information is most meaningful when it is used in conjunction with the personal input of a professional evaluator of baseball talent. Modern technology and statistical research have provided some amazing tools. While anyone can be taught to use a hammer, it takes a true craftsman to combine the knowledge, tools, and experience necessary to build a house at the professional level. These evaluators are baseball's craftsmen.

Over the years, a number of people have been quoted as stating that hitting a baseball is the toughest thing to do in all of sports. In that same vein, any pitcher will tell you that it takes more than a good fastball to succeed in the Major Leagues. The development of mental skills is instrumental to a ballplayer's success everywhere on the diamond, a process that includes setting up hitters, working the count, pitch recognition, hand-eye coordination, ball tracking, reaction time, and on-field awareness. These attributes are often referred to as "intangibles." In turn, an athlete who does these things well is labeled as a "gamer." The ability to recognize these attributes in an athlete is absolutely critical in baseball. Fortunately, the sport's culture has evolved to appreciate those individuals who can identify the intangibles and know how to use that information, in addition to stats and the 20-80 scouting scale, to make astute evaluations are greatly appreciated.

In the future, the established methods for evaluating players will be combined with the tools provided by greater technology to produce a flood of objective information. Tools that measure baseball-specific abilities, such as high-speed motion analysis, will be considered (along with stat profiles and scouting reports) as indispensable resources in the file cabinet (or hard drive) of professional coaches, scouts, and performance analysts. This information will be used with the stats and the 20-80s to provide a more cohesive picture of a player's current skill-set and future potential. It will also be utilized to help guide the athlete along a personalized development path. Evaluating pitching mechanics is just the tip of the iceberg. Technology offers many other potential practical applications within the game, including the study into how to best prevent injuries, improve hitting mechanics, track the baseball, and enhance an athlete's ability to play defense.

22

Injury Prevention

☛ **Doug:** Physical health is a critical component of performance for every athlete. Not surprisingly, the physical demands placed on professional pitchers can lead to as many injuries as any other position in sports. As such, keeping their players injury-free is a major focus for every Major League organization. Managing injury risk is an extremely complicated matter, however, especially as it relates to pitching mechanics. It's no secret that many ballplayers get hurt during their pitching career, and the number of athletes who undergo surgery for a baseball-related problem is growing every year. This situation has had a huge impact on player development and drafting strategy at the professional level, particularly since a relatively high percentage of pitchers fail to reach the Majors due to injury, rather than a lack of performance.

Every year, countless pitchers throughout the country have their careers derailed by injury. At the professional level, millions of dollars are spent on pitchers who sit on the disabled list. The injury problem is further exacerbated by the fact that players are at an increased risk of being injured before they reach the age of about 24. At that time, they must deal with ever-greater workloads, while their bodies are still developing. Nate Silver and Will Carroll of *Baseball Prospectus* have substantiated this factor through their extensive research, and have dubbed this dangerous age range as the "injury nexus" for pitchers.

Professional organizations have been working to limit the risk of injury for the pitchers within their system, by monitoring both the mechanics and the workloads of these players. In addition, they have enhanced their efforts to communicate with their team's medical and training staffs to ensure that their athletes receive proper conditioning, treatment, and rehabilitation. In recent years, teams have also been instituting strict limits on pitch counts and innings pitched for a single game or season for their pitchers, especially with their minor-league players. The goal is to help their young pitchers progress safely through the "injury nexus."

The "injury nexus" is a great example of how modern, well-focused and properly conducted research can provide new clues to the mysteries inherent in injury prevention. Will Carroll and the team at *Baseball Prospectus* have been at the forefront of providing injury-related information for a baseball audience. Furthermore, they have developed metrics and terms to help further such study. One Carroll-inspired term that is especially useful is "cascade injury," which describes a situation in which a pre-existing ailment contributes to a new injury. This factor is incredibly common with pitchers, because of the impact of mechanical sequencing and the kinetic chain on the load forces placed on a pitcher's body. For example, a pitcher might come down with a sore hamstring, which, in turn, might interfere with his maintenance of dynamic balance or generation of forward momentum. This scenario could then result in a mechanical inefficiency that stresses the pitcher's arm later in the delivery.

Several ways exist in which a seemingly minor injury can increase the risk of serious damage, especially if the player attempts to play through the pain. Most athletes are encouraged to "tough it out," when something seemingly minor gets in the way. Those individuals who attempt to play, despite being hurt, are revered as gutsy heroes. This situation is why almost no pitcher will tell a coach that he is ready to be pulled from the game. As such, it is up to the manager or pitching coach to make that decision. Having a warrior-like mentality is an advantage in baseball because of the competitive nature of the sport, especially as it involves the one-on-one battle of hitter vs. pitcher. On the other hand, it is also the responsibility of coaches to encourage honest two-way communication between themselves and their athletes. Never is this aspect more critical than when dealing with potential injury. Accordingly, it is essential that pitchers and coaches, alike, are duly educated concerning the risks involved with cascade injuries and the relationship this factor has with pitching mechanics. Such knowledge can help to keep the bulldog mentality appropriately in check.

The individuals at *Baseball Prospectus* have also developed a great tool for injury analysis, one that applies specifically to pitcher workloads. The measurement tool was developed by Rany Jazayerli and Keith Woolner, who named it "pitcher abuse points" (PAP). "Pitcher abuse points" are utilized to track pitch counts for starting pitchers throughout the Major League season, using a methodology that assigns more weight of "abuse" as the single-game pitch totals increase. The system counts zero "pitcher abuse points" until a player crosses the 100-pitch threshold in a game. The PAP score increases exponentially for every pitch that is thrown beyond one hundred, with an equation of PAP = (pitch count − 100)^3. A pitcher with a 120-pitch outing will register 8000 PAP points, while a 110-pitch effort will clock in at 1000 PAP. The primary purpose of this strategic tool is to account for the effects of fatigue, with the 100-pitch barrier representing the theoretical point at which fatigue sets in. As such, as a pitcher wears down physically during a game, he's unable to harness the strength necessary for optimal mechanics, a situation that puts the whole kinetic chain in jeopardy.

The PAP system has been an outstanding contribution to injury analysis, since it is based on an objective measure of pitcher workload that accounts for fatigue. The points accumulate through the season in order to calculate the overall wear and tear on a pitcher, relative to a baseline of 100 pitches per game. The method has also shown to have a degree of reliability when it comes to assessing injury risk, since players near the top of the PAP charts display a relative tendency to get injured following such heavy abuse.

The key to the concept of PAP is the detrimental effect that fatigue has on a player's ability to pitch. A pitcher who is physically exhausted will not only increase the risk for injury, but will also have a hard time generating velocity and command on his pitches. Fatigue can wreak havoc on pitching mechanics, thereby creating a situation where the athlete's health and performance will suffer. As such, it is extremely critical for a manager or pitching coach to properly identify when the pitchers on his staff have "run out of gas."

One limitation to the PAP system is the 100-pitch threshold for abuse. In reality, the point of fatigue is different for every player, and can vary from start-to-start during the season. Jazayerli addressed this issue in the first article he wrote on the subject. In this article, he pointed out that the system was designed as a general reference, rather than specifically applicable to every pitcher. Based on research by Craig Wright in *The Diamond Appraised*, Jazayerli's guideline of 100 pitches is a good approximation when dealing with large groups of players. On the other hand, each individual pitcher has his own unique baseline for fatigue and appropriate personal limit for pitch counts. To quote Tom's response to Craig, from *The Diamond Appraised*:

> "The biggest problem with pitch limits is that they homogenize. They treat all pitchers the same because of the dictates of history. This approach will slow down the development of pitching prospects who don't have a propensity for sore arms—and there are such people, and we can identify them."

Baseball fans across the country are familiar with the struggles of Pedro Martinez, once he crosses the 100-pitch barrier, thanks to Game 7 of the 2003 ALCS. Pitching in the bottom of the eighth inning against the rival New York Yankees, Martinez had a meeting on the mound with manager Grady Little. The Red Sox had a two-run lead, Martinez had thrown 115 pitches, and the Yankees were in the midst of a rally. Prior to this moment, the telecast had been flashing numbers on the screen that gave a breakdown of Martinez's historical stats at different pitch-count levels. Up to 90 pitches, he had been utterly dominant in the past. In contrast, he was merely an above-average pitcher from 90 pitches through 110, while his performance then took a nosedive past the 110-pitch mark in previous games. Everyone at home could see that Martinez was tired when Little opted to come out of the dugout. The Red Sox had both Alan Embree and Mike Timlin ready to come into the ball game. Little had to make a difficult decision, which involved choosing between his fatigued ace pitcher and a fresh reliever out of the bullpen. The results are now infamous. Martinez stayed in the game, whereupon he gave up a two-run double to Jorge Posada that tied the game, which the Yankees eventually won on Aaron Boone's homerun in the bottom of the 11th inning.

The primary point in bringing up Martinez's game seven is not to chastise Little's decision, or to force Boston fans to relive some harsh memories. What's striking is that Grady Little received so much flack for the decision, based on the now-current conventional wisdom that Martinez was not the same pitcher after a certain pitch count. This wisdom became conventional thanks to the television broadcast, in what was a crucial postseason game set before a wide audience, that chose to flash the stats that made everyone aware of Martinez's extreme breakdown for different pitch counts. If those particular numbers had never flashed on the screen of game seven, it is not nearly as likely that Grady Little's name would include an expletive whenever he's referred by Boston fans.

Major League organizations can benefit by closely monitoring and evaluating the pitch-count breakdowns for every pitcher in their system, with the understanding that those thresholds evolve over time. Team coaches and trainers can work with the athletes to learn how to anticipate and identify the onset of fatigue, and to help pitchers to improve strength and stamina through proper conditioning. Ideally, each pitcher would have his own PAP barrier, or a baseline pitch count, that would replace the benchmark of 100 in the PAP equation. The PAP count for some pitchers would be right around 100, while other players may not exhibit signs of being physically tired until 110 pitches or more. In turn, someone like Pedro Martinez could have a breaking point pitch-count between 90 and 95. Meanwhile, relief pitchers could fall anywhere between 15 pitches to 75, depending on their specific role. Whatever pitch-count parameters are established for a player would serve as strong guidelines for how to best utilize that particular pitcher in a given situation. These values would then be adjusted as more relevant information concerning that player is subsequently obtained.

Teams that employ a fatigue-based pitch count system with their pitchers could take a completely different approach to constructing a rotation and bullpen. MLB teams currently adhere to a relatively strict format of having 11 to 13 pitchers at a time, including a five-man rotation of starting pitchers, a closer, and five-to-seven other relief pitchers to pitch the innings in-between. In the past, baseball analysts have questioned this generally accepted approach for constructing the roster, and have proposed several alternate methods that could be used to structure a pitching staff. In this vein, the use of fatigue-based PAP scores would provide a manager with a different array of options for roster construction, as well as serve as a consistent guideline for maintaining the health of his staff. The manager would know which of his starters was capable of going 110 pitches before tiring, versus those who begin to falter after 80-90 pitches, and then align his bullpen accordingly. A team's bullpen could then be aligned based to a degree on stamina, using more than just the two basic categories of short versus long relievers.

The fatigue-based approach to pitch counts is naturally reliant on a coach's ability to subjectively identify when a pitcher becomes tired. Fortunately, objective methods exist that can be used to help better address the situation. First, it is beneficial to determine a baseline pitch-count level for each individual player, so that a manager or pitching coach can know what to expect before his team takes the field. In that regard, every team could develop very thorough data, with respect to each pitcher's relative level of stamina. This information could help a manager better understand the approximate pitch-count threshold at which fatigue sets in and mechanics start to break down. While some coaches can determine this threshold just by looking at a player, such an ascertainment may not be possible until the pitcher is already beyond his breaking point.

Two other indicators for fatigue are diminished pitch control and velocity. It is often the first sign that a manager notices when looking to make a call to the bullpen. A pitcher who has lost a few ticks from his fastball and struggles to find the strike zone won't last very long on the mound, regardless of his pitch count. All of these methods can be employed to determine an individual pitcher's personal, fatigue-based PAP barrier, utilizing information from games, bullpens, and workouts from both the season and spring training.

The value of utilizing a PAP threshold can be seen in an example that involves Pedro Martinez. If Martinez has a fatigue-based, PAP threshold of 90 pitches per start, that 90 would replace 100 in the PAP calculation. When Martinez has a 100-pitch outing, it will register 1000 PAP, rather than 0 points as in the current system. Although we know that a pitcher will not have the same level of stamina in every game, it can safely be assumed that he will become fatigued at a pitch count within a certain range around that threshold. A team's coaches should also have a good idea of when each player on their team hits a pitch count "wall," at which point his skills are greatly diminished and his risk of being injured reaches more dangerous levels.

Major League teams also have the option of using advanced technology, such as motion analysis, to study pitcher-fatigue levels even further. This technology could enable them to potentially dot up all of their own pitchers, and have them pitch at full intensity under the cameras. The coaches could then match up their subjective view of when fatigue sets in with the objective data that is obtained from motion analysis, and, in the process, better understand how fatigue affects the mechanics of each individual pitcher. In that regard, for example, one player may slow down his delivery as he gets tired, while another may fail to reach opposite and equal, or might display a "soft" glove at release point. This information could then be used to help a coach identify when fatigue strikes by using unique mechanical indicators for each pitcher. The coaches would also be better prepared to know which pitchers display higher risk mechanical inefficiencies when they get tired. These players could thus be held to a more stringent pitch-count limit.

Pitch limits and fatigue can apply to single innings, as well as to games and seasons. If a pitcher has an extremely hard-worked inning of 35 to 40 or more pitches, it can have a similar physical effect as throwing over 75 pitches that are spread out over several innings. The types of adjustments that are appropriate to such situations can also play into the manager or pitching coach's decision concerning how long to leave the pitcher in the game. This situation helps to point out why subjective analysis of fatigue is so important, along with an early identification of mechanical changes or a loss in pitch velocity or command. Overall, the fatigue-based method for establishing pitch counts provides for more sophisticated usage patterns with the entire pitching staff. As such, the strategy based on pitch counts can help to keep pitchers fresh, potentially reducing injuries by having fewer pitches thrown while fatigued, and give managers more tactics to use in the chess match that they play every game.

Words such as "abuse" and "workload" tend to paint a negative image of pitching a baseball. On the other hand, throwing on a regular basis is critical to maintaining a pitcher's health. One key to building arm strength and stamina is to schedule consistent throwing sessions, using a balance of bullpens from the mound and pitching from flat ground, with the volume of throws determined by the athlete's fatigue threshold or tolerance. Most developing Little Leaguers and travel ball players would greatly benefit from playing catch on flat ground more often, and pitching less from a mound and in competition.

☛ **Tom:** As was discussed previously, the slope of the mound is an unnatural aspect of pitching. Pitching from it physically taxes a pitcher more than throwing from flat ground. The extra forces created by a mound do not affect a pitcher's accelerator muscles and connective tissue. Rather, these forces affect a pitcher's decelerator muscles and connective tissue. Quite simply, the steeper the mound, the harder a pitcher's arm can throw. On the other hand, the harder it is for him to slow his arm down. One of the reasons Japanese pitchers have traditionally been able to handle high pitch totals is because their professional-level mounds are almost flat. Furthermore, there are no mounds at all at their amateur level.

The pitching mound is an obstacle. In fact, players can build strength and stamina while throwing for longer periods of time by pitching from flat ground. Such a strategy is a great way for young players to build their arm strength and to work on their mechanics, while throwing from a lower stress environment. The fact that Little League mounds around the country are often inconsistent or poorly maintained causes a situation where a youth pitcher needs to re-adjust his delivery each time he toes the rubber. Steeper mounds generally result in a pitcher having greater momentum, and thus less time taken into foot strike and a longer stride. The raised mounds in Major League baseball from the 1960s had a similar effect of increasing momentum for pitchers. In fact, this factor could have had a greater impact on the performance of those players than the benefits associated with an increased downward plane.

☞ **Doug:** The general awareness of pitcher workloads and accompanying injury risk has increased in recent years. As such, the expectations placed on professional athletes currently playing the game are much different from those of previous generations. Up until the 1970s, pitchers were expected to finish what they started, and strive for a complete game every time they took the mound. In the early days of Major League baseball, pitchers would even pitch deep into extra innings. Occasionally, some players were even known to pitch both games of a double-header.

The strategic employment of the bullpen is a more recent development. Pitcher fatigue is now a factor in the decision of when to bring a reliever into the game. This strategy helps managers to take advantage of platoon options at crucial points in the game, as well as keep the starting pitchers from breaking down, due to overuse. The natural result of this factor has been to create rigid pitch-count limits, which are now used by coaches at all levels of competition. In fact, current rules of Little League baseball include daily and weekly pitch-count limits that are enforced by umpires and scorekeepers, in an effort to keep youth workloads under control.

The new regulations on Little League pitch counts are essential, especially considering the poor condition of many youth-league mounds. Throw in the fact that most Little League coaches are parents with great intentions, but who often lack knowledge or quality information with respect to pitching mechanics and injury risk, and a recipe for disaster exists. The limits that are set for Little Leagues across the country are based on research conducted by Dr. James Andrews and the American Sports Medical Institute (ASMI). Dr. Andrews is a leading authority on pitcher injuries. A physician who has operated on countless Major League players, he also is renowned for developing rehabilitation programs that are designed to help save the baseball careers of his patients.

ASMI, which is located in Birmingham, Alabama, has been the center for cutting-edge medical research on athletic injuries, with Dr. Andrews and biomechanist Dr. Glenn Fleisig leading the effort. In March 2007, the doors were opened for the new Andrews Institute in Gulf Breeze, Florida, a state-of-the-art establishment that is set up for medical and athletic evaluations, with fields and facilities for assessment, recovery, training, and rehabilitation. The Andrews Institute also employs high-speed motion analysis. Dr. Andrews and his staff utilize the NPA/RDRBI model when analyzing the pitchers who come in for an assessment. Dr. Andrews and Dr. Fleisig are both members of the NPA advisory board. We work in concert with them to identify the safest methods for developing athletes. Dr. Andrews and Tom have been interacting professionally for more than three decades on and off the field. In fact, Tom is a recipient of ASMI's James Andrews Achievement Award, the only professional coach to be recognized by Dr. Andrews and his ASMI staff.

Mark Prior is an exceptional case in the files of injury prevention. A number of knowledgeable people in baseball point to his reputably flawless mechanics and wonder why he has struggled with injuries over the last few years. Most any scout who watched Prior pitch at USC, or in his early years with the Chicago Cubs, can attest to his "clean, fluid" delivery and repeatable mechanics. Some scouts have gone so far as to state that Prior had the best mechanics of any pitcher they have ever scouted. Prior has worked with Tom since he was a teenager growing up in San Diego. In reality, Prior embodies the mechanics, functional strength and flexibility, mental attitude, and baseball work ethic for a successfully developing pitcher.

Unfortunately, Mark Prior has been hampered by arm injuries over the last few years, which has thrown a wrench into a very promising Major League career. Some critics have pointed to this situation as evidence that Prior's mechanics were in fact inefficient, and caused undue stress on his arm. The evidence, however, completely contradicts this claim. Neither of Prior's major arm injuries occurred while he was delivering a pitch. In fact, both involved a traumatic impact with a solid object.

The first injury occurred on July 11, 2003, against the Atlanta Braves, when Prior collided with second baseman Marcus Giles, while he was running out a groundball. Giles took a knee to the face, which sent Prior tumbling to the ground. The contact caused Prior to land directly onto his throwing shoulder, which resulted in a trip to the disabled list, rather than to the upcoming All-Star game. The second arm injury involved a fractured right elbow that occurred on May 27, 2005, courtesy of a vicious line-drive, come-backer off the bat of Colorado's Brad Hawpe. The baseball was clocked at 117 mph after contact. It didn't have much time to slow down before drilling Prior's pitching elbow. The contact was so hard, that the ball ricocheted into the glove of the Cub's third baseman Aramis Ramirez.

The 2003 season was most likely the catalyst for Prior's later arm injuries, not only because of the collision with Giles, but also as a by-product of the number of high-stress pitches he threw that year, while helping the Cubs reach the playoffs and the National League Championship Series. According to the PAP charts on the *Baseball Prospectus* web site, Prior racked up the fourth highest PAP total in the Major Leagues in 2003, despite missing at least three starts due to injuries sustained from the Giles collision (he ranked third in PAP/start). Just 22 years old at the time, Prior was by far the youngest pitcher near the top of the list. In fact, Joel Pineiro (#10 in PAP, 24 years old at the time) was the only pitcher among the top 30 who was within four years of Prior's age at the time. In contrast, Pineiro compiled less than half the total abuse points for the season as did Prior.

Prior's heaviest workload came near the end of the 2003 season, when the Cubs were fighting for a spot in the playoffs, which they would earn by winning the NL Central by a slim one-game margin. Prior had six starts heading down the stretch in September. In those games, he rang up consecutive pitch counts of 131, 129, 109, 124, 131, and 133 pitches (stats via www.baseball-reference.com). These numbers represent an extremely heavy workload for any pitcher at any time in the year. They're particularly ludicrous for a 22-year-old kid who is trying to pitch his team to the playoffs at the very end of the season. In comparison, there wasn't a single starting pitcher in the Major Leagues who registered an outing of more than 130 pitches during the entire 2007 season. In his last three starts of the 2003 regular season, Prior compiled a total of 79,552 pitcher abuse points, a total that would rank 19th on the 2003 MLB season leader board, *if they were taken alone.* In other words, he put more mileage on his arm in those last three starts than all but 18 players did for the entire season, according to the PAP system.

Prior's saga doesn't end there. He started game three of the National League Division Series, throwing another 132 pitches in the process. When that game is added to Prior's last three outings of the regular season, his 112,320 PAP total over a span of about two weeks would qualify for ninth on the overall season list. He would subsequently pitch two more games in the playoffs that year, tossing 115 and 119 pitches in Games 2 and 6 of the NLCS. Overall, Prior's playoff performance added a total of 43,002 PAP to his regular-season point total.

All of this hard work and pitching while fatigued occurred at the end of a long season, during which he had already missed time for an injury to his throwing arm. In just his second year in the big leagues, Prior pitched like a 15-year veteran in the effort to win a championship. As such, it's quite possible that his arm suffered the consequences in the long run. Regardless of his superior ability in 2003, Mark Prior was a developing young pitcher who was still climbing out of the "injury nexus." It could be reasonably argued that the Cubs truly tested his health and durability when they allowed him to take on such a heavy workload.

A frustrating spring-training injury to his Achilles tendon cost Prior the first couple months of the 2004 season. In 2005, he was thrown off track by the Brad Hawpe line drive. Though he made only 27 starts in '05, Mark piled up 102,881 pitcher abuse points for the season, a total that was third highest in all of Major League baseball. While this total was less than half of the PAP that he generated in 2003, at 24 years old, he was also still within the confines of the injury nexus. Meanwhile, his mid-season injury was such that his elbow should have been monitored closely and treated appropriately, rather than being further taxed by throwing several pitches, while he was in a state of fatigue.

Prior literally "shouldered" this heavy workload for the Cubs from 2003–2005, while fighting off traumatic injuries from batted balls and collisions on the basepaths. This situation began to cost him via pains, strains, and tendonitis in his pitching shoulder throughout the 2006 season. Unfortunately, 2007 started out the same way for him, despite an off-season of working extremely hard to get back into his old form. There was nothing mechanical involved in the injuries that Mark Prior sustained. When he's at his best, Prior is still an excellent example of mechanical efficiency. Figure 22-1 illustrates that he compares very well to the five aces, with respect to stride and momentum, opposite and equal, balance and posture, stack and track, and glove position.

Figure 22-1. Mark Prior displays several key components of a mechanically-efficient delivery

The example of Mark Prior serves to show that many potential sources for injury exist, including workloads, mechanics, and even freak occurrences on the field. In reality, several ways exist for a pitcher to potentially get hurt. As such, "playing it safe" is never as straightforward or manageable as simply limiting pitch counts or ensuring "perfect" mechanics. The best approaches to injury prevention take all of the relevant information into account, including (but not limited to) the following aspects of pitching development:

- Mechanics
- Workloads
- Functional strength and flexibility
- Stamina
- Sound nutrition
- Quality, consistency and slope of the mound
- Recovery time

There are also a number of factors that can impact the likelihood of an injury occurring that are out of human control, such as genetics, mechanical signature, line-drive come-backers, injury history, and even the weather. Mechanics are just one part of the injury-prevention puzzle. Frankly, no one knows how many injuries are the result of flawed mechanics, and how many can be attributed to other factors. In many instances, the answer is a combination of the weaknesses in all of the aforementioned categories. On the other hand, some injuries are simply the result of bad luck.

All of the confounding elements make it extremely difficult to predict injuries with any kind of reliability. The best that can be done is to study the trends and tendencies of pitchers who stay healthy and those who get hurt. In that regard, PAP can be used to identify which players have a high-risk workload. All factors considered, players with a combination of inefficient mechanics, poor functional strength, and a heavy workload can be expected to be at a significantly higher risk for injury than the average athlete. Studying the specific contributing factors to injury enables us to better understand the relevant risks and the weak links for each pitcher. Subsequently, motion-analysis data can then be used in conjunction with the pitch-count thresholds that have been established with ASMI, along with PAP scores and subjective analysis, to help ensure that injury risk is both identified and minimized.

With regard to the specific mechanical risks that lead to pitching injuries, the many available opinions on the subject tend to fall under the category of conventional wisdom. Validation of these ideas is harder to come by, due to the fact that mechanics make up just a fraction of injury risk, a factor that is particularly relevant since validation requires a high degree of reliability. Everyone would like to have one convenient equation that unequivocally states something along the lines of, "this pitcher has a 17.3% chance of experiencing an elbow injury in the future." In reality, such an equation doesn't exist. The best available option is to look at the measurable factors that might contribute to injury, and then make comparisons to the injury trends of similar players.

We have been studying injury trends at the NPA for a number of years, as well as the aspects of mechanical inefficiency that potentially involve an increased risk of damage to the throwing arm. While nothing is definitive, we have found some interesting patterns, in which pitchers with specific mechanical tendencies tend to get hurt more often than average. We refer to these aspects of mechanics as "injury precursors." As such, these factors serve as indicators for risk assessment. A couple of the mechanical precursors to injury were previously discussed during the evaluation of various conventional wisdoms. In fact, there are other potential precursors that are currently under the microscope at the NPA/RDRBI lab.

One of the injury precursors that have already been addressed in previous chapters involved the conventional wisdoms of "left-hander on the left side" and "don't rush." Pitchers who adhere to these concepts will often experience overrotation of their trunk and shoulders into MER. The resultant overrotation takes a pitcher beyond his mechanically-efficient position of being square with home plate. Too often, this habit leads to excessive stress (and as a consequence, an injury) to the throwing elbow. In this instance, the ulnar collateral ligament (UCL) is particularly vulnerable.

Overrotating results in the shoulder being excessively stressed and at risk for an increased level of injury, as well. Furthermore, some of these overrotating pitchers will also change their posture at release point. Think of it this way. These players will drag their elbow, which causes them to pull their throwing arm from behind their squared-up shoulders, so that their forearm can snap forward from external rotation into internal rotation and ball release. This movement exacerbates the stress on both their shoulder and elbow capsule, which compounds their risk of injury. Unfortunately, many of these coaches and pitchers have come to learn the realities of a torn UCL, and that the operable solution for such an occurrence is Tommy John surgery, as well as 8-to-12 months of intensive rehabilitation before returning to competition. These coaches and pitchers also become more familiar with the terms shoulder impingement, frayed labrum, and torn rotator cuff. They also become cognizant of the fact that these pitching-related conditions can be surgically repaired, rehabbed, and made ready for competition in 6-to-12 months.

Another major injury precursor is the mechanical inefficiency of poor posture at release point, where the spine bends toward the glove side of the body, relative to the pelvis. In effect, this factor shifts the head away from the center of mass. This situation can be caused by any one or all three of the following key variables: mechanics, strength, and pitching workloads. For example, earlier it was mentioned that the best pitchers in the game display posture that involves having their head directly over their navel, with a 90-degree angle from their pelvis to their spine. This positioning enables a pitcher to find his ideal arm slot, which occurs when the functional and intrinsic arm slots match up, with the center of the head lined up with 12 o'clock. A strong body not only stabilizes posture and helps with pitch command, it also enhances release-point distance, mechanical consistency, and glove position at release point as well. Pitchers with extremely poor posture at release point usually have poor core strength and a higher relative tendency to come down with arm injuries, many of which are specific to the shoulder.

Mechanically, there is a problem with the conventional wisdom that tells players to "get on top" at release point in order to create downward plane. Adhering to this dictum invariably results in an unnaturally high arm slot, since a pitcher will sacrifice posture to increase his release-point height. Despite good intentions, this particular teach can increase injury risk and cost release-point distance, both of which can adversely affect performance.

Changing posture at release point can wreak havoc on a pitcher's command and control, particularly if the action involves an inconsistent posture change. Pitchers who consistently get through the same arm slot, with pretty much the same posture for every pitch, have learned to adapt to the delivery and make every throw down the same "tunnel." Tunneling is a concept coined by Perry Husband, which describes how a hitter sees the ball out of the pitcher's hand. A pitcher who consistently throws from the same arm slot, height, and distance at release point, with the same exit trajectory, will produce the same tunnel for every pitch. This factor makes it very difficult for the hitter to identify incoming pitches, when compared to a pitcher who utilizes a different tunnel for every pitch. Tunneling is easier for pitchers with consistently strong posture. Pitchers with a consistent arm slot will not miss their target up, down, inside or outside very often, because their tunnel typically tracks a path to the strike zone. Consequently, these pitchers don't walk many hitters.

The aforementioned injury precursors strike a personal chord with me, given that I was praised by coaches throughout my young playing career for an over-the-top delivery, even when I was playing catch. While I didn't throw all that hard, I spent time on the mound simply because I was a lefty with a splitter that could throw strikes by repeating my tunnel. When I came to the NPA, Tom got one look at my poor posture and shook his head. One minor adjustment later, and I was throwing with good posture, including a natural three-quarters arm slot, and pitching felt easier and more comfortable than I had ever experienced.

Even more enlightening to me was when Tom asked if I had any history of injury. He nodded his head when I told him that I blew out my shoulder when I was 18. Apparently, those five-hour double-headers of one-on-one tennis ball-baseball took their toll on me in high school. In our make-believe world, my buddy and I would write out the fictitious lineups, and would keep score for nine innings—pitching and hitting full speed with tennis balls and metal bats, getting in fights about ghost runners, like we were Calvin and Hobbes. The first game was often followed by another game, and then another. Not surprisingly, by the end of our fun and games, my arm would be jell-o. We simply didn't worry about pitch counts or workloads. More often than not, because we were very competitive, we kept on playing until it was too dark to see the ball. My conversation with Tom that day enabled me to learn a harsh lesson, the realization of the personal costs attendant to me ignoring the key factors involved in injury prevention with a developing arm.

Overall, more remains to be learned about the factors that can contribute to pitcher injuries. In that regard, we are working with some of the leading researchers to answer additional questions. Although injury prevention in baseball is an inexact science, we are taking every possible step to correct the problem. The work of Dr. Andrews, Dr. Glenn Fleisig at ASMI, Dr. Greg Rose at TPI, and others on the NPA Advisory Board goes above and beyond the mechanical aspects that have been discussed in this book.

As such, the injury precursors have not been verified to the extent of other NPA measurement systems, such as the ideal ranges and mechanical efficiency ratings. Unfortunately, we have a long way to go before we can fully appreciate the specific relationship between biomechanics and pitcher injuries. Injury severity, frequency, and time of occurrence are all extremely difficult to predict. Obviously, a pitcher's mechanics are just one piece in a very complicated puzzle. The confounding variables of mechanical efficiency, functional strength and flexibility, pitching workloads, nutrition, genetics, and just plain old luck can all have an impact on injury risk and performance. The factors that have been studied within the NPA model represent the biomechanical and physical aspects of injury that can be identified and adjusted with proper instruction and training. A pitcher, however, needs to be educated with respect to all of the potential danger areas in order to truly minimize the risk of injury. Tom nailed the issue on the head back in 1989 in the book *The Diamond Appraised.* In reality, we are still working on solving the problem. In that regard, something that Craig Wright said in that same chapter struck me, as well:

> *"I've pointed out the relationship between superior mechanics and the more durable pitchers, but if you ask me if baseball is going to get heavily into 'biomechanical optimization,' I have to realistically say no."* (Wright and House, 1989, pg. 248)

Hopefully, the game of baseball is evolving to the point where the answer to Craig's point would realistically be "yes," and, in the process, everyone would take advantage of all research available. Accordingly, every effort must be made to understand and optimize the relationship between a pitcher's biomechanics, functional strength, endurance, and flexibility, and how those factors, in concert with a pitcher's pitch totals, pitch ratios, and pitch frequency, can be employed to improve the health and performance of every player.

Obviously, the aforementioned medical gains are wonderful. On the other hand, they represent progress in an environment that can best be described as alarming. In organized baseball, from Little Leagues to the Major Leagues, conventional wisdom still trumps science, despite the fact that objective information from sports medicine, sports science, exercise science, and coaching science is available. Enough validated research exists for parents, coaches, and players to screen (for weak links), test (for skill and talent), assess (for movement efficiencies), and, based on results, train (for health and performance). Collectively, we refer to this process as S.T.A.T. for foundation fitness. In that regard, one of our key goals is to help make people aware that the game can do better at minimizing risk of injury and/or maximizing performance capabilities.

One of the major problems in the void that is created when conventional wisdom trumps science is that while all of the critical entities involved with baseball tend to be well-intentioned, and tend to work very hard for athletes, for the most part, they operate independently from each other. Physicians and sport scientists don't speak with the same vocabulary as coaches, coaches often cannot communicate with medical or sport-science professionals, strength training doesn't always cross-specifically support biomechanical training, and athletes receiving these mixed messages with bad information and compromised instruction tend to have an increased risk of injury and/or poor performance.

The solution? Every effort must be undertaken to facilitate better integration between information resources, as well as cross-validate instructional protocols with a common vocabulary. Accomplishing this step will prehabilitate or fix pitchers before they break down and fail competitively. For example, one step that must be taken in this regard would be to combine resources and data from contemporary research centers. ASMI, *Baseball Prospectus,* and the NPA have provided recommendations individually and collectively, safe pitching workloads, safe pitch-selection ratios, and safe pitching frequencies. Frankly, a person doesn't have to be an expert pitching coach at USC to understand these guidelines. These numbers are the easiest variables to quantify for injury prevention. The best advice, when deciding what to do with regard to preventing injuries, is what Dr. James Andrews calls the common sense rule— "Always err on the side of caution." In addition, factors, such as age, mechanics, functional strength, time of season, and how pitch totals were reached should be considered. Remember, an injured pitcher has no value. The disabled list is devastating financially and competitively to both athlete and team.

Before we get into actual numbers and recommendations, it is important to be aware of the fact that NPA research and experience do not indicate that any particular pitch, if it's thrown properly, with the right frequency, ratios, and workloads, puts any more stress on the arm than any other pitch. It should be noted, with all grips, that the thumb and middle finger must cut the ball in half. A split finger fastball is the exception to this biomechanical imperative. With this pitch, the thumb and bottom of the "V" created by splitting the fingers, cut the ball in half. The wrist and forearm angle determines ball movement. Think palm-to-target for fastball, karate chop-to-target for curveball, and thumb-to-target for a change-up. A cutter is one-fourth of the angle of a curveball, a slider is one-half of the angle of a curveball, and a slurve is three-fourths of the angle of a curveball. Going the other way, a running fastball is one-third of the angle of a change-up, while a sinker is two-thirds of the angle of a change-up. The throwing forearm, wrist, and hand go into pronation after release on all pitches. Pronation is biomechanically inevitable in deceleration.

Our three-dimensional motion analysis reveals that healthy pitchers have their grip, wrist, and forearm angle set when their hands break and maintain this angle throughout their delivery into release point. Unhealthy pitchers, on the other hand, twist and manipulate their forearm and wrist angles during their deliveries. It's this twisting and untwisting that wears and tears on the elbow.

23

Prehab: Foundation Fitness

Stability – Mobility – Flexibility

Section I: Foundation Fitness Overview and Application

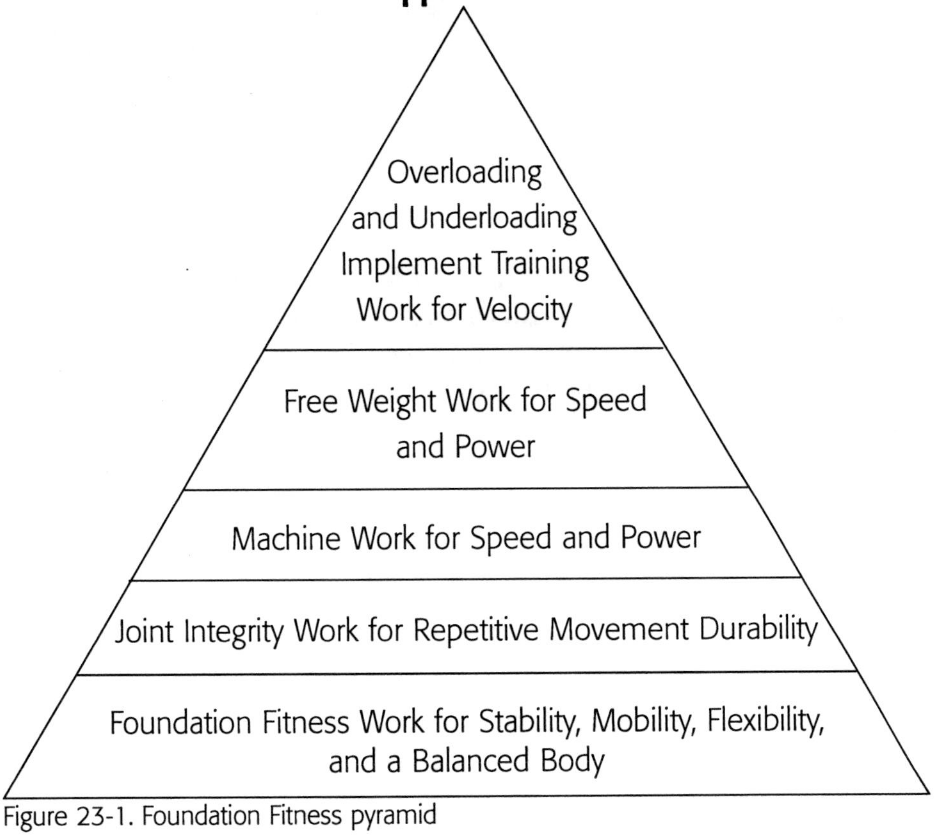

Overloading
and Underloading
Implement Training
Work for Velocity

Free Weight Work for Speed
and Power

Machine Work for Speed and Power

Joint Integrity Work for Repetitive Movement Durability

Foundation Fitness Work for Stability, Mobility, Flexibility,
and a Balanced Body

Figure 23-1. Foundation Fitness pyramid

☞ **Tom:** From infancy to old age, the physical stresses and strains of everyday working/playing environments create muscle, connective tissue, joint, and bone imbalances. These imbalances cause our bodies to inappropriately adapt and/or accommodate inefficient positions and movements, which, in turn, create weak links, premature wear and tear, pain, and injury. Most resistance-training regimens perpetuate these weak links in the body because the resultant strength gains don't balance out.

Foundation Fitness specifically addresses weak links and helps ensure relative parity in the "fitness" levels of muscles, connective tissue, joint, and bone. This approach involves training the body with body weight in functional positions and movements, including standing/lying on the floor, sitting on a chair, and pushing on a wall.

Athletes spend their lives (or career) trying to adapt/accommodate body imbalances that were created by their work/play environment. Foundation fitness is a daily work regimen that functionally retrains total-body balance. The principles behind foundation fitness progressions are based on three Pacific Rim martial-arts philosophies: 1) the body can be trained with positions and movements where, 2) resistance is created by gravity to create, 3) true balance with stability, mobility, and flexibility in extremities and core. For example, standing is the simplest method of training the nervous system to keep the body in *true* balance. The next least complex mode is isometric work to develop strength/endurance/flexibility in those particular positions required for skill-specific movement efficiency.

Concentrating on correct postural alignment and the innate proprioceptions and kinesthetic awareness of the total body *should* reinforce the positive habit of total-body balance. Most individuals, however, do not exhibit this habit in their lives because of inefficiencies created by work/play imbalances. Maintaining balance in positions/movements where weak links are requires more of an exposed effort than would otherwise be necessary, because, in those situations, nerves, muscles, and connective tissue must work harder to achieve stability, mobility, and flexibility. This phenomenon forces the body to find hypertrophic parity and true balance for function without the exacerbating impact of the imbalances that result from free-weight and machine-resistance training.

Foundation Fitness protocols feature a number of positive characteristics, including the fact they are mostly isometric, they are safe, and they can be done daily, by anybody, at any age. Foundation fitness protocols are also time-friendly, (a complete, total-body workout takes 30 minutes to an hour). Workouts can be taught one-on-one or one-on-hundreds. The only constraints are floor space, the number of chairs, or the amount of wall space. Pitchers/players can feel the results in days, not weeks. Furthermore, when used as a complement to other training regimens, these protocols can induce improvements in absolute strength gains of 10 to 15%. Because (like all people) athletes, as individuals, are only as strong as their weakest link, considerable reason exists to engage in well-designed stability, mobility, flexibility protocols. Once the body's weak links have been brought into balance, the underlying concept of Foundation Fitness, in effect, is "detrain the *too* strong, retrain the *too* weak," until the total body reaches the point of benchmarked balance. You will see a practical application of Foundation Fitness protocols in chapter 28. In this regard, the following parameters and throwing workload guidelines for training govern our effort.

Pitch Totals, Ratios, and Frequencies

- Don't overload any one pitcher. Always try to project workloads around:
  - ✓ # of games per season (or week)
  - ✓ # of innings per season (or week)
  - ✓ # of pitches per game (or week)
  - ✓ # of pitches per inning
  - ✓ 15-20 pitches = average pitches/inning
  - ✓ 35+ pitches in one inning causes as much stress as 75 pitches at 15-20 per inning.
- A start should not be more than seven innings (if the pitcher is to pitch again that week).
- If pitchers throw more than 105 pitches during a start, they should not be allowed to relieve.
- The number of total pitches per week should not exceed 120 for either starters or relievers.
- Relief pitchers should never throw more than 75-80 pitches in 72 hours (at 15-20 per inning). If a maximum of 45-50 pitches is reached in any one game, this outing should be followed by an off-day for that relief pitcher.
- Relief pitchers should stay off the mound between game outings; three "scares" (mound warm-ups in pen) = one game inning
  - ✓ 9- to 10-year-old pitchers:
    - ▪ Max = 60 pitches per game
    - ▪ 75 pitches per week, or in any seven successive days
    - ▪ 1000 pitches per season
  - ✓ 11- to 12-year-old pitchers:
    - ▪ Max = 75 pitches per game
    - ▪ 100 pitches per week, or in any seven successive days
    - ▪ 1000 pitches per season
  - ✓ 13- to 14-year-old pitchers:
    - ▪ Max = 90 pitches per game
    - ▪ 125 pitches per week, or in any seven successive days
    - ▪ 1000 pitches per season

- ✓ 15- to 18-year-old pitchers:
  - ▪ Max = 105 pitches per game
  - ▪ 130 pitches per week, or in any seven successive days
  - ▪ 1250 pitches per season
- ✓ 18- to 24-year-old pitchers:
  - ▪ Max = 120 pitches per game
  - ▪ 150 pitches per week, or in any seven successive days
  - ▪ 1800 pitches per season
- ✓ 24- to 40-year-old pitchers:
  - ▪ Max = 130 pitches per game
  - ▪ 175 pitches per week, or in any seven successive days
  - ▪ 3600 pitches per season
- Pitch Ratios for Pitch Selection per Game, Week, Month, Season:
  - ✓ 60-65% fastballs
  - ✓ 20-25% curveballs/sliders/slurves/cutters
  - ✓ 15-20% change-ups/splitters
- Options for Workload Management:
  - ✓ During the regular season, a starter's pitch totals in his first three innings are the most important of the game. High numbers early should result in him throwing fewer innings.
  - ✓ During tournament play, a coach should try to start his relievers and relieve his starters. Collectively, more pitchers should be worked for fewer innings/pitches per outing.
- Pre-Game Warm-Up by a Starter:
  - ✓ Should only throw 30-45 pitches.
  - ✓ Should only throw the last 10-15 pitches at a high level of intensity.
  - ✓ Should never max out in the bullpen.
- Pre-Game Warm-Up by a Reliever:
  - ✓ Should be able to warm-up in less than 20 pitches.
  - ✓ Should stay six pitches short of game-ready (he will get six-to-eight when entering the game).
    - ▪ Should stay loose between innings:
    - ▪ Play catch with outfielders
    - ▪ Do cord work
    - ▪ Do light dumbbell work
    - ▪ Do flexibility work
    - ▪ Do aerobic work (e.g., jog, ride a stationary bike)
    - ▪ Do anaerobic work daily (8-12 minutes)

- Pitcher/Position Player:
  - ✓ On his game day, a starting pitcher should not play a position.
  - ✓ If muscle failure is reached on the mound, a pitcher should not play any other position that day.
  - ✓ If a high number of pitches is reached, a lower number of swings should be taken.
  - ✓ If a high number of swings is reached, a lower number of pitches should be thrown.
  - ✓ If a high number of pitches is reached, less playing time on the field should be spent.
  - ✓ If there is a high amount of playing time on the field, then shorter pitch outings are a must.
- Recovery Time:
  - ✓ Muscle failure post game—ice and/or aerobics:
    - ▪ Icing max: 10 minutes for the elbow and 20 minutes for the shoulder
    - ▪ Two minutes of aerobic activity for every one minute of ice
    - ▪ Within three hours of the game
    - ▪ Given a choice between ice or aerobics, engage in aerobics
  - ✓ Average recovery time is three full days.
  - ✓ Hard thrower (i.e., throws over 90 mph):
    - ▪ Day 1 = MAX aerobic/MAX weight training
    - ▪ Day 2 = Bullpen MED aerobic/ MIN weight training
    - ▪ Day 3 = MAX aerobic/ MED weight training
    - ▪ Do anaerobic daily 8-12 minutes
  - ✓ Touch thrower (i.e., throws under 90 mph):
    - ▪ Day 1 = MAX aerobic/ MAX weight training
    - ▪ Day 2 = MAX aerobic/ MED weight training
    - ▪ Day 3 = Bullpen MED aerobic/ MIN weight training
    - ▪ Do anaerobic daily 8-12 minutes

24

Hitter-Pitcher Interface

☛ **Doug:** Motion-capture technology has greatly enhanced the evaluation of pitching mechanics. It can also be used to study baseball hitting by taking a similar methodology to the NPA Model. By analyzing the swing mechanics of the best hitters in the Majors, the physical components that are critical to success at the plate can be identified. Similar to our study of the best pitchers in the game, motion analysis of the top hitters can be employed to gain an understanding of what these great athletes have in common mechanically. As with pitching mechanics, the conventional wisdom of hitting mechanics can be challenged. As such, a coach can test his own personal theories and ideas by using motion capture and the scientific method. All it takes is a hypothesis, the collection of data, and an analysis of the results.

The study of hitting mechanics has already begun in other circles. For example, the NPA is working along with Dr. Greg Rose and the team at Titleist Golf to evaluate the similarities in swing mechanics between a golfer and a hitter. To date, a number of commonalities between golf and pitching have already been determined.

The mechanical elements of batting appear to be similar in many ways. For example, hip-shoulder separation has been found to be an integral component of power for hitters, golfers, and pitchers alike. For hitters, this factor is referred to as "load." Hitters who generate a large load, without sacrificing timing, have the ability to generate more bat speed and hit the ball a relatively long distance.

As a teenager playing tennis ball-baseball with my buddy, I used to mimic different pros. One of my favorite hitters to imitate was Albert (Joey) Belle, for a number of reasons, including the fact that Belle had an extremely large load. Even as a kid, I noticed that using a Belle-type load helped me to create a lot more power.

For a golfer, hip-shoulder separation translates to more power and a longer distance on drives. An analysis of five-time long drive champion Jason Zuback shows that he takes advantage of an extremely large load, which helps to increase angular rotation of the trunk and shoulders. This factor translates to faster club-head speed.

Likewise, pitchers with large hip-shoulder separation typically throw with more velocity, especially when they delay shoulder rotation and stay stacked until they square up to home plate. As such, all three of these throwing/striking skills have at least three key factors in common: the timing and sequencing of the mechanical events, or links, in the kinetic chain. All three tasks involve the coordination of weight transfer, pelvis/hip rotation, and trunk/shoulder rotation to deliver the arms and implement (i.e., golf club, baseball, or bat). The weight transfer in pitching, hitting, and swinging a golf club should maximize the element of linear momentum prior to the beginning of upper-body rotation. This step involves getting from first movement into foot strike efficiently and on time. A golfer will also shift his weight forward and firm up the front foot prior to the start of his downward swing, even though he won't lift his front foot or leg off the ground (with the possible exception of Happy Gilmore).

Balance is another key ingredient attendant to a successful hit, pitch, or swing. As a general rule, athletes who compete in baseball and/or golf are told to maintain their balance by keeping their head stable, directly over the navel, throughout the kinetic sequence. In reality, few exceptions to this rule exist when it comes to players succeeding at the highest level. As such, it makes intuitive sense that proper balance is essential for any athletic task. Inappropriate head movement in any direction is detrimental to mechanical efficiency, which makes it difficult to coordinate the other links of the chain.

The mechanics of Ichiro Suzuki's swing show how hitters can track forward with the upper body after foot strike. This trait is actually common among hitters from Japan, because they learn to continue forward momentum as they start the swing and drive through the ball at contact. This tactic is taught to players, based on the observation of how well it works with pitchers. As such, Japanese coaches have recognized the benefits of stack and track and the relationship between hitting and pitching mechanics for many years. The guru of hitting in Japan is home run king, Sadaharu Oh, whose hitting mechanics when he was playing looked exactly like sound pitching mechanics—a high leg lift, a big stride with momentum, large hip and shoulder separation with bat lag or delayed shoulder rotation, and an upright (stacked) head and spine into swing and contact.

Obviously, big differences exist in the execution of a batter's swing and a pitcher's delivery. The fact that the ball is moving makes a hitter's task much different than that of a golfer. A pitcher gets to take his time to set up his delivery and execute the ideal pitch. As such, the mechanical parts of his job are not directly impacted by any outside variables. The same situation is true for a golfer, who gets to take as much time as necessary to set up each shot.

Only the weather and crowd noise are factors that can get in the way of a golfer taking a swing, save for the occasional tree.

For a hitter, on the other hand, the swing is largely reliant on the pitch that is being delivered. Pitch velocity dictates the timing of the start of the swing sequence, while pitch location and trajectory (with break) guides the eventual position of the bat at the point of contact. A hitter's job is perceptual and reactionary and highly dependent on the actions of a pitcher. The ability to see, read, and hit certain types of pitches is the greatest strength and/or weakness for all players, even at the professional level.

The concept of dealing with uncontrollable outside variables also applies when we work with NFL quarterbacks. While the mechanics for both athletes are very similar, there are setup and timing differences between throwing a football and a baseball. A quarterback, for example, has to avoid pass rushers who are coming at him from different directions, while he is simultaneously looking downfield for an open receiver. Rather than take the time to get a perfect setup, quarterbacks need to continuously shift their feet, with small hops and steps, while being able to throw to a wide range of targets. In contrast, pitchers are starting in the same position, throwing at a very precise target, and nobody is trying to tackle them halfway through their delivery.

Pitching coaches can learn a lot by analyzing hitters. As such, the education should not be limited to mechanics alone. It's also a two-way street of information, given that hitting coaches have much to gain through the study of pitching. The aforementioned Perry Husband is a hitting instructor who researches many of the finer points of swing mechanics, as well as the mental aspects of pitch recognition and timing. Perry's newest book series, titled *Downright Filthy Pitching*, focuses on a concept that he has termed "effective velocity." Regular or "real" velocity describes the speeds that are seen on a radar gun, while perceived velocity is explained as how fast a pitch feels relative to the hitter, based on release-point distance. Effective velocity is similar to perceived velocity, since it measures the speed of a pitch, based on how it feels to the hitter. It combines real velocity, radar-gun readings with the location of the pitch when it crosses the plate, relative to the batter.

If a pitch is located up and in, a hitter has less time to begin his swing in order to get the bat-head out into the optimal position to hit the ball squarely. He has more time on a pitch that is low and away. This timing difference can be translated into a new velocity value, called effective velocity, in much the same way that perceived velocity was calculated previously. Using a pitch down the middle of the strike zone as a baseline speed, the effective velocity of pitches increases as the ball moves higher in the zone and closer to the batter, while it decreases as pitch location moves further down and away.

For example, a pitch that reads 86 mph down the middle on the radar gun could have an effective velocity of 92 mph when it is thrown up and in to a hitter, and an 80 mph effective velocity when it is thrown down and away. In

Perry's research on effective velocity, he tracked over 15 million pitches from Major League games, and found a very interesting trend. Perry noticed that hitters had a much higher incremental performance on pitches that had an effective velocity within ±six mph of the preceding pitch, which he termed "at-risk pitches." Perry's results clearly showed that Major League hitters gain a tremendous advantage when these pitches were put into play. On the other hand, Major Leaguers across the board had much lower numbers when they put a "non-at-risk" pitch into play.

Husband has used effective-velocity research to help hitters learn to make more informed decisions at the plate, and to better understand the impact of pitch location and timing at contact. Perry has also applied the concept to pitchers. As such, his research has helped us to take a unique look at how to approach the chess match that exists between hitter and pitcher.

Years ago, Warren Spahn voiced the famous mantra, "Hitting is timing, and pitching is upsetting that timing." Effective velocity is a new way of understanding the impact of pitch location on upsetting hitter timing, as Husband explained in his presentation at the NPA semi-annual coaches certification workshop. Husband detailed clearly why throwing an inside breaking ball is often a bad idea following a fastball low and away, since most pitchers find themselves throwing a dangerous pitch with the breaking ball if using that sequence. Intuitively, throwing two different pitches to two different locations should upset batter timing, but the effective velocity concept changes the way that the available options are perceived, with respect to real velocity and pitch location. As such, this concept impacted our approach when instructing pitchers at the NPA.

☛ **Tom:** Several MLB pitchers have intuitively understood the concept of effective velocity before Perry Husband even conducted his research. In this regard, it has helped us to better appreciate why Greg Maddux has earned the nickname, "the smartest pitcher that ever lived." Maddux (like Trevor Hoffman, Jamie Moyer, and other soft-tossing mound magicians) has made a Hall of Fame career by throwing "lock-out" pitches. Such a pitch occurs when the effective velocity of the previous pitch and location and the current pitch and location is 18 mph or greater. It should be noted that when this "spread" is 18 mph or more, not even Barry Bonds can center the ball. The brain won't allow it.

In other words, the six-mph range of effective velocity covering at-risk pitches represents the "attention zone" of a hitter, and is constantly changing as it's affected by the effective velocity of the previous pitch. The best way for a pitcher to exploit the attention zone is to have a large difference in real velocity between pitches. He also has to be able to locate each type of pitch in any spot within the strike zone. These steps provide a pitcher with the most options when it comes to deciding the appropriate type of pitch and location for a particular situation, given a pitcher's strengths, a batter's weaknesses, and the hitter's attention zone for effective velocity.

No mistake should be made, however, throwing with a velocity in the mid 90s is very desirable. On the other hand, it's throwing and locating two other pitches (a breaking ball and an off-speed pitch) with the fastball that makes a consummate "pitcher."

The situation should be thought of this way: three pitches to two locations involve a factorial of 12 (3 x 2 x 1 x 2 x 1 = 12). In other words, a hitter has 12 choices from which to guess. Even a good hitter still fails seven out of 10 times. Pitchers who can throw three pitches to two locations and strategize for maximum spreads in their effective velocity are very difficult to hit. Pitchers who can throw three pitches to three locations or, even better, four pitches to three locations, while continuing to strategize for maximum spread on their effective velocity are a team's frontline Major League starters and (possibly) future Hall of Famers. Tables 24-1 and 24-2 illustrate two examples of pitch selection, pitch location, and optimal effective velocity, ranging from a hard thrower (Nolan Ryan) to a soft thrower (Greg Maddux).

Pitch	Result
76 mph curveball down and away	Take strike one (effective velocity = 70 mph)
94 mph fastball inside	Take strike two (effective velocity = 100 mph)
78 mph change-up down middle	Take strike three (effective velocity = 78 mph)

Table 24-1. Nolan Ryan vs. a right-handed batter—the first at bat in the game

Pitch	Result
76 mph change-up inside	Pulled foul – strike one (effective velocity = 82 mph)
76 mph change-up down and away	Take strike two (effective velocity = 70 mph)
86 mph fastball inside	Jammed, weak ground ball hit back to the mound (effective velocity = 92 mph)

Table 24-2. Greg Maddox vs. a left-handed batter—the second at bat in the game

So what happened? It was basically an unhittable first-pitch curveball, followed by two lock-out pitches that resulted in a strikeout *looking* at three pitches. The bat never left the hitter's shoulders. Statistically, Ryan was the hardest pitcher to get a hit off of in the history of the game...a sure, first-ballot Hall of Famer.

So what happened? The hitter's bat was sped up, then slowed down, and then sped up, but he was unable to catch up to the inside fastball. That's location, change of speed and effective velocity worked to perfection. Very few Major League pitchers can locate their change-up and/or have the confidence to back up a change-up with a change-up to make an average fastball above average with effective velocity. No one disputes the fact that Maddox is a future Hall of Famer.

☛ **Doug:** Quality scientific research has been conducted concerning hitting. As such, some of the available theories take a functional look at hitting the baseball. A few of the investigations have involved tracking the path of the hitter's swing in order to study how certain shapes and degrees of swing-arc can result in predictably different results at contact. This effort is similar to the study of downward plane, and how breaking balls with varying degrees of downward trajectory have a differential effect on groundball rates at the point of impact with the bat. It also helps to describe why some hitters with certain swing-paths seem to "have the number" of particular pitchers. These pitchers have incoming pitch trajectories that line up with the slight upward trajectory of the swing to produce a high likelihood of solid contact. Swing-path analysis can also help identify those hitters who exhibit an ability to keep the "sweet spot" of the bat lined up for ideal contact for a longer period of time. Teams have also been working for years to study the mental aspects of hitting, such as hand-eye coordination and pitch recognition, often attempting to incorporate technology to help facilitate the process. This undertaking includes showing hitters a fast-paced slide show that features single frames of pitchers' hands with different grips at release point, or using video clips of pitcher's deliveries that have been stored on an Ipod.

Possibly, the greatest aspect of using motion-capture technology has been the opportunity to collaborate with experts from other fields. Being able to learn from the work of others has enabled us to incorporate new information into our current understanding. One of the most interesting trends that was discovered in our research is that there seems to be a universal ideal or "signature" for the timing of weight shift in all of the rotational sports we analyzed. The time it takes for a pitcher to shift his weight from first forward movement into foot strike typically takes right around one second. The same timeframe applies to a hitter's weight shift from first movement into foot contact. A similar factor is also true for the linear weight shift timing on a golf swing, a tennis serve, a volleyball serve, a softball pitch, and a pass from a quarterback.

While coaches from different sports and areas of expertise have a lot to learn from each other, too many coaches are overly concerned with protecting their current knowledge, rather than embracing new thinking from other sources. Even objective information is ignored, when it contradicts conventional wisdom. In reality, it's the nature of the game for coaches to trust their "gut." Without outside expertise involving research and development efforts conducted by the golf industry, the NPA model would not be where it is today. Frankly, whatever success the NPA has achieved to date has emanated from our desire to seek assistance from other professionals and other fields, a search that was unencumbered by a fear of being wrong. Individuals can never be totally wrong with an idea, as long as they are willing to change their mind and reshape their understanding. All factors considered, when an idea is trusted too strongly, it turns into a belief. To quote the movie, Dogma, *"I just think it's better to have ideas. I mean you can change an idea, but changing a belief is trickier."*

Throughout our exchange of ideas and insights with coaches and players from other sports, a number of individuals have expressed an interest in validating their own ideas through motion analysis. The common goal is to collect as much data as possible to get started, and then to create a model to validate the information that has been gathered. What many individuals don't realize, however, is that creating the model is only the first step in the process. As a rule, it's relatively easy to get started on a prototype. To begin, we simply ask a coach, "What do you look for in an athlete?" After each response, we follow up with, "how would you measure that?" Once these two questions have generated as many answers as possible, the first version of the model is ready for testing. Historically, our pitchers were run through motion analysis to collect data and then analyzed, based on the measurements that were quantified in the first version of the model.

The results from the first batch of data helped identify the changes that needed to be made to model version 2.0. The process was then repeated, and as much data as possible was collected. Ultimately, the validation of any model is based on collecting enough data to find statistically reliable results. The next step was to cross check the internal consistency of the findings to ensure that the actual performance and subjective evaluation of athletes matched. It has taken over 20 years and the motion analysis of about 2,000 pitchers for us to reach our current model at the NPA/RDRBI. As such, many of the lessons that we have learned, with respect to timing, sequencing, and signature of pitchers, can be applied to hitting as well.

Motion analysis can be used to study just about any factor in sports. Frankly, an evaluation model lies in the head of every coach. True creativity comes from asking the right questions to form a hypothesis, and then identifying the measurements that can have meaningful impact when evaluating performance, mechanical efficiency, and injury risk. Motion analysis provides a means for verifying ideas, because it enables researchers to obtain the objective information necessary to make an informed decision. At this time, because the technology is relatively cost-prohibitive for the general public, not everyone can expect a positive return on their investment. On the other hand, most medical, human performance institutes, and/or professional sports teams normally have the resources to obtain a system and generate a health-and-performance model. Undertaking such a step would allow many organizations to realize a positive return on their investment, especially when considering the cost of insurance, multi-year contracts, and the cost of athletes being on the disabled list.

Tom's Wrap-Up

Some final thoughts on hitting and pitching: On one hand, it's harder to hit than to pitch, while on the other, hitting has fewer health-related issues than pitching. The researchers at the Titelist Performance Institute are convinced that swinging a bat has the same "signature" as swinging a golf club. If this perception is true, baseballs' learning, teaching curve concerning science-based hitting will grow exponentially in the next few years. In reality, what remains to be studied and quantified in this instance is a hitter's visual, perceptual, reaction activity. However, no matter how much the science on swinging a bat improves, hitting a baseball will still be the hardest skill to master in all of sport.

25

Tracking the Baseball

☛ **Doug:** A pitcher's basic job is to deliver the baseball to a target, using a particular velocity and break. Once the ball has left his hand, there's nothing that he can do. After ball release, a pitcher is left to enjoy the fruits of his labor, and watch as the hitter decides whether to take a swing at what has been offered. Mechanics are used to generate maximum pitch velocity, optimum pitch location, and even the direction and magnitude of pitch break. The goal of all mechanical analysis is to achieve ideal pitch execution, with consistent repetition and minimal risk of injury.

In order to analyze pitching performance and skill, it is necessary to study not just mechanics and statistics, but also the behavior of the baseball itself. Scouts refer to the actions of the ball as "stuff." In fact, the majority of scouting grades use stuff as the primary ingredient for evaluation. Evaluating stuff can be a challenge, since the only tool available to measure stuff has been the radar gun for pitch velocity. Other aspects of stuff, such as pitch break, are usually left for the eyes to judge.

To remedy this issue, some new technology exists that is being used to track pitches from out of the pitcher's hand at release point to the point when the ball crosses the front of home plate. Anyone who has watched a game televised on ESPN has seen ESPN's K-Zone ball-tracker, which displays pitch velocity, movement, and location relative to the strike zone. Another relatively new feature that is being used by MLB Advanced Media is called "Pitch F/X," which tracks the velocity of a pitch out of the pitcher's hand and at the plate, as well as the trajectory and break of the pitch. The data for Pitch F/X, generated from cameras that are set up at the Major League stadiums, is made available in real-time over the internet. The K-Zone and Pitch F/X systems are both good examples of how camera-based tracking systems are making new waves in game-time ball-detection technology and application.

Data from the new pitch-tracking systems can also be used to learn a lot about the methods that different MLB pitchers use to get hitters out, and to answer questions, such as "Where does Greg Maddux like to locate his fastball?" and "What pitch does he like to throw in a 2-0 count, and in what location?" Furthermore, the data can be utilized to measure the decrease in pitch velocity as the ball travels from the pitcher's hand to home plate, which occurs as a result of the drag force created by air resistance. Taking it a step further, the trajectory and pitch-break data could be used to estimate the effectiveness of certain breaking balls and off-speed pitches, with respect to groundball percentages, by employing equations like those provided by physicist Doug Bird. The numbers generated from tracking the baseball can also be used to derive precise equations for effective velocity. By taking advantage of Perry Husband's research, pitchers could utilize that information to learn their own optimal pitch sequences, based on real-game situations. The pitch-location and real-velocity data that is measured with ball-tracking could also be used by Major League teams to calculate effective velocity patterns for an opponent's pitching staff, as well as their own.

An excellent example of science proving/disproving one of baseball's recent phenomena involves Dan Fox of *Baseball Prospectus*, who has used the data from Pitch F/X to effectively break down the in-game pitches of Major League players, such as Felix Hernandez and Daisuke Matsuzaka. In the case of Matsuzaka, Fox wanted to see if he could pick up a pitch pattern that would match the mysterious "gyroball." In that regard, Fox analyzed the Pitch F/X data and found that it was unlikely that Matsuzaka actually threw a gyroball. Why? Because of the 586 pitches that were tracked, only four could not be identified as another pitch type. He did find, however, that Matsuzaka throws a combination of at least six different pitches.

As such, the gyroball has produced a very interesting phenomenon. While people appear to be drawn to its mystery and intrigue, few understand what it is or how it moves. According to an article by Jeff Passan at Yahoo! Sports, the gyroball is not supposed to move at all. The individual who is credited with discovering the pitch is pitching coach Kazushi Tezuka. Tezuka claims that the gyroball is intended to look like a slider, with rifle-like spin about an axis parallel to the center line, but behave like a fastball by staying relatively straight in trajectory. The pitch is actually based on a toy called the X-zylo, which is shaped like a cylinder and can fly incredible distances when thrown using the correct motion. Throwing sidearm is also an advantage for throwing this pitch, because it helps to produce the appropriate angles for the hand, wrist, and forearm. Tezuka confirmed the legitimacy of this observation when he stated:

> "The best way to throw the gyroball is sidearm, because the mechanics—pulling down on the ball's side, like throwing a football, to create a sideways spin—are more natural."

The analysis by Dan Fox and the descriptions provided by Tezuka cast plenty of doubt to the idea that Daisuke Matsuzaka throws a gyroball. Even more intriguing, however, were the factors cited by Tezuka—a sidearm delivery and a pitch with little movement, looking like a slider, but acting like a fastball or change-up. Submarine pitcher Chad Bradford had a pitch that Oakland A's announcer and former All-Star catcher Ray Fosse called a "Frisbee." Bradford threw this particular pitch from a low-release point right near the ground. Bradford's Frisbee pitch would run upward, seem to hover as it got near the plate, and suddenly be in the catcher's glove. Moving like a flying saucer, the pitch was a true U.F.O. Because few hitters knew what to do with the frisbee, Bradford was able to use it to post some outstanding seasons out of the A's bullpen. Another player who threw a pitch that looked somewhat like a frisbee was former Chicago White Sox reliever Shingo Takatsu, who pitched in the Major Leagues from 2004 to 2005. Like Bradford, Takatsu, who spent the first several years of his playing career in Japan, was a sidewinder who threw a pitch that first appeared to be off-speed like a change-up, but spun like a slider, and yet never broke on its way to the plate. Quite possibly, Major League baseball had actually seen a gyroball-like pitch before Daisuke Matsuzaka ever pitched an inning in the Bigs.

☛ *Tom:* Bradford and Takatsu were actually throwing a backup slider (aka, "gyroball," as described by Tezuka). This pitch has been around since sliders came into organized ball during WWII. It's actually a *mistake* pitch, because the hitter reads slider, while the ball tracks like a fastball. Art Fowler (Billy Martin's old pitching coach) used the pitch quite effectively in his 10-year playing career, but couldn't teach it as a coach, because for most pitchers, it's a *mistake* pitch, not a *mastery* pitch. The key to throwing the gyroball as a mistake or with mastery is the position of the thumb, middle finger, hand, wrist, and forearm at release point. This factor is actually true of all pitches (although a minor exception exists with the split-finger fastball).

The degree of *pronation* or *supination* of the throwing forearm, wrist, and hand is the factor that allows the thumb/middle finger to put spin/break on a pitch. The term "pronation" refers to positioning of the forearm, with the palm rotated outward from the elbow up. One way to get a feel for this positioning is to put the arms up in a 90-degree, "goalpost" position, and rotate the palms away from the body. Pronation occurs after ball release for every player on every pitch. Some types of pitches, however, are thrown with a starting hand position in pronation before ball release, including sinkers, change-ups, and screwballs. If the palms are rotated inward, facing the body, then the forearms are said to be in supination, which is necessary to throw a proper curveball, slurve, slider, or cutter. Freak pitches, like the gyroball, show up because Matsuzaka and others can alter their hand position at a different axis to facilitate freak movement.

☛ *Doug:* None of these types of pitches requires a rotation of the wrist near release point, yet many coaches teach their young players to "pull the shade" (i.e., twisting their wrist like a doorknob, and snapping the fingers with the thumb flicking upward). The functional result of this teach is a pitch that leaves the throwing hand at a slight upward trajectory, which is easily detectable by good hitters. The mechanical result of the wrist twist for a breaking ball is that the throwing arm must then untwist as it is pronating after release point and during follow-through. The throwing arm has to pronate further for pitches that begin with supination, with curveballs requiring the most angular distance of rotation for the wrist and forearm. To combine a twist of the wrist in the direction against that of pronation is adding an extremely complicating factor to the process of throwing a baseball. As such, it can put unwanted stress on the elbow. The proper method of throwing a curveball looks and feels more like a karate chop than a twisted pitch. In Figure 25-1, Roy Oswalt illustrates a great example of the "karate chop curveball," with a supinated hammer that has plenty of downward break.

Figure 25-1. Roy Oswalt throwing a curveball with supination at release point. His thumb is still under the baseball, with his palm facing inward.

At the NPA/RDRBI, pitches are defined based on how they are thrown, whether with a certain degree of pronation or supination or with a particular grip, like a split-finger fastball. In contrast, other individuals may define a pitch type, based on velocity and movement or how it looks. These individuals classify pitches by the difference in velocity from a fastball, or by the speed and trajectory of the break. In essence, it boils down to the difference between watching what the pitcher does to make his pitch, and what the ball does after release point. In addition, a small problem with semantics often exists. All factors considered, everyone can appreciate an off-speed pitch that's 12 to 15 mph slower than the fastball with a late drop, regardless if the pitcher throws it like a splitter or a change-up. A problem arises when players have their professional opportunities impacted negatively by the interpretation or definition of a pitch. Such is the case when a coach leaves a pitcher out of the rotation because his curveball doesn't break in the direction that a coach expects from a hammer, or when that coach attempts to alter a pitcher's mechanics in order to find the break that the coach wants to see. As such, this situation can be similar to the practice of valuing release-point trajectory over mechanical efficiency, such as ranking downward plane above posture at release point.

26

Evaluating Defense

☞ **Doug:** Over the last several years, defensive evaluation has widely been considered the "holy grail" of statistical analysis. In that regard, sabremetricians have taken a variety of approaches to tackle the issue. The big obstacle in pursuing the defensive grail is that the influence of teammates on the field has made it extremely difficult to statistically isolate individual defensive performance. Furthermore, only a limited number of conventional stats are available for measuring defense. As such, only putouts, assists, and errors are being recorded in the scorebook.

A number of brilliant statisticians and baseball analysts have been researching how to break down the defense of individual players. The basic objective of these efforts has been to create a defensive value into a single number. Most of the existing systems, in this regard, tend to focus more on counting the number of plays made than measuring error rates, as a means of obtaining a method for quantifying a rating of a player's fielding range. More often than not, these approaches are also based on the conventional defensive stats and scorekeeping, as well as play-by-play data. A list of a few of the metrics that currently exist that address defensive evaluation includes ESPN's zone rating, Bill James' range factor, David Pinto's probabilistic model of range, Michael Lichtman's ultimate zone rating, Pete Palmer's fielding runs, and Clay Davenport's defensive translations. This list is not inclusive. In addition, several more will ultimately be developed in the future.

Each of these different defensive-measurement systems has its advantages. Collectively, they're all adding to the information base that can be used to make evaluations. Comparing the stats from different measurement systems for the same player, can show whether a level of agreement exists that can provide more confidence in the results. For example, if four different measurements agree that Adam Everett is an elite defensive shortstop, then a reasonable level of confidence can be drawn that the conclusion is valid. By the same token, when there's a large amount of disagreement on a particular player, it becomes much more difficult to determine the athlete's true level of ability.

The conventional stats fall short of providing an accurate description of player defense, a factor that is partially the result of the scorekeeping, with so few categories of defensive stats. Many of the advanced metrics are also limited, because of their reliance on the archaic system of recording in-game defense. The influence of teammates further confounds the issue. For example, a third baseman who plays alongside an elite defensive shortstop could see a drop in his range numbers, such as putouts and assists, as a direct result of the skills of his fellow infielder. On the other hand, this same third baseman would benefit from a pitcher who generates a large percentage of groundballs, since he would have more relative opportunities to make plays. In turn, the outfielders' defensive stats will suffer when a groundball pitcher is on the mound. Other factors that can affect a player's defensive statistics are home stadium/field dimensions and/or field composition. In this regard, does a player compete 81 times per season at a park, where the ball carries or doesn't carry, has big gaps, small gaps, high fences, or low fences, big or little foul territory, real or artificial turf, high grass, low grass, a hard infield or a soft infield?

One baseball researcher who has taken a different approach to measuring defense is John Dewan, author of *The Fielding Bible*. Dewan uses a very unique method, called the "plus/minus system," which involves watching thousands of hours of game film to track the results of every ball put into play throughout the season. Dewan and his staff at Baseball Info Solutions classify each batted ball into a particular category, based on the speed, trajectory, and location of the hit. Every time the hitter puts a pitch in play, it is counted as a groundball, fly ball, or a line drive, each of which is further classified as soft, medium, or hard hit. The observer uses a computer, with a field grid on the screen, to track where the ball was hit, and whether a fielder made a play to register an out.

When it comes to specifically evaluating defense, the "plus/minus system" is superior for collecting data, since Dewan and his staff perform the work necessary to essentially rescore all of the games to fit the input for the system. Rather than categorizing hits as singles and doubles, they are recorded in more detail, such as hard-line drives that are hit to the right of the centerfielder. This methodology takes advantage of tracking real events, which allows the results to be compared for Major League players to better understand their relative ability with respect to specific defensive skills. The research conducted by Dewan and Baseball Info Solutions has been used by Major League organizations, which appreciate the value of breaking down batted balls, based on physics, rather than arbitrary designations such as "F-8" or "6-4-3."

The main output is reported as a single plus/minus value, based on the number of plays made compared to the zero point, with zero set at league average. For individual plays, the measurement is made using average data for the percent chance that a fielder makes a play on balls hit with a particular speed, trajectory, and location. If a particular type of hit is converted into an out 70% of the time, and the fielder makes the play, he will be credited with a score of +0.30 for that play (1.00 − 0.70 = +0.30). If the same player misses the ball for a hit, he will receive a score of −0.70 on the play (0.00 − 0.70 = -0.70), based on Dewan's system. On one hand, this method accords a player extra credit for making a tough play, while on the other hand, it assigns a harsher penalty for missing a relatively easy opportunity.

Looking at a specific example, the 2006 edition of *The Fielding Bible* indicates that Torii Hunter was a +5 in centerfield for the 2005 season, and +44 for the three-year period of 2003 to 2005. In other words, he made five more plays than the average centerfielder in 2005, which was a very modest total for Hunter, given that he recorded scores of +22 and +17 in 2003 and 2004, respectively. This trend may indicate that he is slowing down a bit with age, or perhaps he just had a down year in 2005. Overall, the three-year value of +44 ranked Hunter tops in the big leagues over that span. As such, he has definitely earned his reputation for outstanding range on defense, even if his best years may, in fact, be behind him.

Dewan also has developed ratings for position-specific abilities, which recognize the unique skills that are required for different spots on the diamond. One of these stats is for outfield throwing arm, which is based on the percentage of times an opposing baserunner successfully advances a base, when the opportunity strikes, on a ball hit to the outfield. Torii Hunter posted a 0.565 rating on Dewan's throwing-arm analysis, which was the twelfth-ranked score among centerfielders in the Major Leagues from 2003 to 2005. Hunter's score, in this regard, suggests that his arm is not nearly as threatening as his legs and glove. Among the position-based numbers that are evaluated at Baseball Info Solutions are direction-specific plus/minus values for infielders going to their left or right, success ratios for first and third basemen covering bunts, team breakdowns of where hits fall in the field of play (compared to league average), and success ratios for middle infielders turning double plays.

If an area for improvement exists in the plus/minus system, it could be the use of more objective information for recording data, rather than simply tracking it with the human eye. For example, the use of high-speed cameras and ball-tracking software would enable precise numerical measurements to be made of such factors as batted-ball velocity, trajectory, and location, rather than subjective labels, such as "fly ball" and hit with "medium" speed. As a result, relevant information could be gathered and analyzed with an even greater degree of accuracy.

Cameras could also be used to track the fielders themselves, to obtain relatively unique measurements that are directly indicative of a player's defensive ability. Using motion-analysis technology, for example, the players could have extremely small sensors embedded in their clothing, such as their belt buckle, to non-invasively track the athlete's location on the field during games. Such a method would enable teams to account for the starting position of the fielder at the point of contact, and to measure how long it takes the player to react and get a jump on the ball, as well as how far he needs to travel to make the play.

Tracking a sensor on the belt buckle could approximate the athlete's center of mass, which, in turn, could be used to determine an average- or peak-running speed for an outfielder as he chases down a drive to the gap. This calculation could provide an estimate of his functional speed, which could then be employed to determine his approximate range for chasing down a ball hit to the outfield. This factor could even be helpful in evaluating plays where the outfielder doesn't make the catch, but makes a full effort to run it down, to measure his functional efficiency of movement. Other defensive players who are not involved in the play could also be tracked to see how well they react on contact, relative to their position, and use that information to gauge their overall field awareness.

Tracking outfielders from contact to catch, using cameras and sensors, would help determine range calculations, as well as assist in speeding up the process of data collection. Batted balls, for example, could be categorized, based on velocity, trajectory, and location, using a super-imposed grid on the camera feed of the field to mark where the ball travels, just as with the plus/minus system. The data could then be categorized along various dimensions, such as how long a fielder has to react and make the catch. Using this timing-based method, a high fly ball hit several yards to the right of an outfielder might be in the same category as a line drive that is hit just a few feet away in the same direction. Furthermore, the trends that show up in the timing data could reveal more intriguing patterns than just location or trajectory, particularly for outfielders, since ball flight time is a critical limiting factor with making a catch.

The field grid could then be littered with small dots, each marking the plays that were made, based on the location and type of hit the outfielder is chasing. The final representation could include color-coded dots specific to the speed and trajectory of the batted ball, or the time allowed to make a play. The result would be a field layout with a dense cloud of colored dots immediately surrounding each player on the diamond, with the dots thinning out as they get further away from the fielder. Each fielder's defensive cloud would be different, and would accurately reflect his strengths and weaknesses, based on real in-game data. Each player would have an oblong-shaped cloud or blob of dots, which would reach out further in the directions of greater range. For example, the data from an outfielder might reveal that he is especially strong at charging in on soft flies and going to his left for liners, but struggles to backtrack quickly enough to make plays over his head.

A Major League team could utilize the "defensive cloud" concept to create a sort of personal field puzzle, using the strengths and weaknesses that show up in the data to maximize coverage for every area in their home ballpark.

Tracking real-game defense of opposing teams could also provide general managers and performance analysts with the information necessary to seek out certain players in trade or free agency who best that fit a particular team's specific needs in the field, based on the relative configuration of defensive clouds. For example, certain players might have skills that compliment each other, such that a centerfielder's strength going to his right might cover up the lateral weakness of his teammate in left field, while a leftfielder's ability to come in on pop-ups could help to compensate for a third baseman's lack of skill on going back on those types of hits. Managers could also use this information in combination with hitter-spray charts to arrange the puzzle pieces and optimize their team's defensive alignment, based on the clouds, as well as on batter tendencies. Using this approach would provide a revolutionary way of looking at the data, compared to those systems that attempt to break defense down to a single statistic. Considering the influence of teammates in defensive situations, the optimal solution for evaluating a player's relative defensive ability could be to solve a puzzle, rather than a math problem.

Employing cameras to track the baseball could also be used to objectively measure the in-game throwing skill of players on defense. Given that both batted balls and pitches can be tracked, real-time velocity, trajectory, and location of throws by fielders should be able to be measured. As such, the numerical and visual results would provide a better representation of throwing strength and accuracy in game situations, and could be used to reveal patterns in throwing efficiency. For example, if a player consistently misses his target to the left, has too much arc on his throws, or can't hit a cutoff man, tracking the baseball would reveal that trend. By measuring the "pop" time that it takes a fielder to get from catch to ball release on the throw, it could also be determined if a particular player compensates for having low-arm strength and throwing speed with an exceptionally quick release. Measuring arm strength, particularly throwing accuracy, would provide invaluable information about outfielders and infielders alike. As such, different thresholds or baselines could be established for each position and skill level, in order to comparatively evaluate the throwing ability of ballplayers, relative to their peers.

The specific defensive skills of running, catching, and throwing are nearly impossible to assess using conventional stats. Using ball tracking and defensive clouds would provide an objective system for scouting and judging an athlete's relevant fielding range and throwing arm by measuring that player's physical attributes in real-game situations. In turn, Major League teams can take advantage of computers and high-speed video cameras to quickly generate mountains of data by recording live feeds from individual games. That information could then be used to help construct an optimal roster and set up appropriate defensive alignments in order to maximize field coverage. Combined with the trained eye of coaches and scouts, this approach could have a dramatic impact on how defense is perceived and evaluated.

☛ **Tom:** From my perspective, there are at least three or four variables that Doug and other very smart baseball minds haven't addressed. Baseball is angles, distance, and time. Assuming for this discussion that all ballparks have been created equal and that everyone has the same book on the hitters (e.g., a batter's tendencies and weaknesses) will allow us to focus on the human elements involved with defense. In that regard, the following points are particularly relevant:

- Defense starts with pitching. Teams position players on defense, assuming that pitchers/catcher can execute strategies with called pitches/locations. For example, a right-handed pitcher who hangs a breaking ball to an inside-out hitter like Derek Jeter defeats the defensive alignment of "pitch him away, play him away," therefore shading him to the right side of the diamond.

- Individual players should defend their positions as a function of their individual skills and talents. Although Tony Gywnn didn't have a strong arm, he was quick to the ball and was accurate to the cut-off man with his throws. Bo Jackson just outran his defensive mistakes and caught up with any other lapses with a plus arm. It should be noted that the longest throw *required* of any player would be gap to cut-off man.

- Team/player defense can be equated, somewhat, to bad-debt expense at a bank. (Stay with me on this one). Believe it or not, banks and ballplayers should have a certain percent of bad debts and errors, but not too much or too many, too little or too few. Why? The answer is straightforward—because zero bad debt or zero errors would mean the decision-makers and players weren't being aggressive enough. Conversely, a 25% incidence of bad debts/team or player errors could indicate too much aggressiveness (or a horrendous lack of defensive skills).

- It is important to know what having a team leading the league in double plays really means. Is it good defense, bad defense, good pitching, bad pitching, or combination of both? Do that team's pitchers hold runners closer (i.e., at better double-play depth)? Why are there a greater number of opportunities? Is a strong- armed catcher involved in the situation?

27

Building a
Million-Dollar Arm

☛ **Tom:** OK, new chapter, new question: What can actually be done with all the great new science-based research findings that are presented in chapters 1 through 26? It's a traditional coach's conundrum, because information without instruction is useless to everybody. As luck would have it, this chapter is all about instruction and application, precipitated by a series of events that could never have been foreseen, or dealt with, before 2008. It involves the National Pitching Association (NPA), the Rod Dedeaux Research and Baseball Institute (RDRBI), and the University of Southern California (USC), a couple of very smart businessman, an enlightened sports agent, and two young men from the country of India.

Try to imagine the following scenario: You are a pitching coach, working day-to-day with your pitching staff, conducting monthly camps/clinics, and giving weekly lessons, when "poof," in walk two 18-year-old athletes from India—Dinesh, a 6′ right-hander, and Rinku, a 6′2″ left-hander. Both young men are athletically gifted, physical prospects who have thrown 89-91 MPH on the radar gun and are projected to throw 95. Even more intriguing, both young men have come to you with a common goal: to be trained and developed into prospects who can sign with a professional team. It sounds exciting doesn't it? Almost a "can't miss" project. But wait, there's a catch. They don't even know how to play catch. Dinesh and Rinku have never pitched or played in a baseball game. The long and short of it? They are a genetically talented duo with a zero-skill set—two "blank slates," who believe that your information, instruction, and inspiration, along with their willingness to work hard and learn, will build a million-dollar arm for each of them.

Well, this is exactly what happened to us in early May 2008—a unique set of circumstances that were as daunting as they were exciting. This chapter summarizes the new coaching science and medical science that we implemented on and off the field, to help Dinesh and Rinku with their dream of signing a contract to play professional baseball.

Background

The series of events leading to that May day on Dedeaux field at the University of Southern California actually started with a contest conducted in India during the fall of 2007 and the spring of 2008, called "The Million-Dollar Challenge." (Individuals who want to know more about this undertaking should go to the milliondollararm.com for the details). In this contest, a professional agent, J.B. Bernstein, and a professional scout, Ray Portivant, actually tested 30,000 Indian nationals for pure velocity.

The "buzz" and the "hook" for this nationwide event in India was if any of these athletes could throw a 95 MPH fastball, off of a pitching mound, into a standard strike zone, they would win $1,000,000. As it turned out, none of the 30,000 individuals tested were able to perform the required tasks. Rinku and Dinesh came closest with their fastballs, which were clocked at 89 and 92 MPH, respectively. As such, they were declared contest winners, received prize money and, more importantly, the financial support for a 12-month visit to the USA. While visiting America, they would work with the NPA/RDRBI at USC to develop their genetic arm speed into pitching skills. Again, the ultimate goal for everyone involved in this process was to get these two young men signed by a professional team.

The rest of chapter 27 details the coaching strategies and tactics that we employed in this situation, as well as the conditioning- and biomechanical-training progressions and protocols we have implemented over the years to solve various problems with science-based coaching solutions. It also details how critical benchmarks were used to inform, instruct, and inspire Dinesh and Rinku toward pitching mastery. All of our coaching efforts were focused on four phases: physical, biomechanical, nutritional, and mental/emotional. These phases were prioritized in this order to minimize the risk of injury and maximize performance possibilities. Here is how we did it.

Problem Identification and Solution: Preparing the Million-Dollar Arm

Common sense dictated that before Dinesh and Rinku could step on a mound to max out their velocities and back up their fastballs with breaking balls and/or off-speed pitches, they had to be functionally strong enough to support their biomechanical efficiencies, as well as their pitch totals/workloads.

Arm health was our biggest concern for both these young men. The key issue in this regard was would it be possible to keep them from injury, while they learned how to pitch? Physically, we knew that we had to identify any weak links in their overall level of body strength, endurance, and flexibility by quantifying any absolute strength/endurance imbalances that might exist and determining any joint-integrity, mobility, and stability issues. At that point, a foundation-fitness training regimen could be established to achieved a functional conditioning base that would support their arm health and biomechanical development as pitchers.

Figure 23-1, "the Foundation Fitness Pyramid," provides a template that was developed to help individuals understand the screening, testing, and assessment procedures, as well as the training processes, progressions, and protocols (S.T.A.T.) that we used with both athletes to baseline, or benchmark, their "point-in-time" level of fitness and mechanical efficiency. After conducting S.T.A.T. and reviewing the results, it became obvious to us that a rigorous, cross-specific conditioning program had to precede and complement a cross-specific throwing/pitching program if we were going to minimize their risk of injury. We also realized that retesting these young men would be necessary and that their throwing/pitching workloads could only be increased (i.e., intensified) when their weak links balanced out. It also became apparent that nutritional and mental/emotional counseling would be necessary to complement everything these young men were doing both on the field and in the weight room. Figures 27-1 through 27-9 provide an overview of four health-and-performance "pyramids" that can help you to better understand the specific screening, testing, assessing, and training applications that were implemented with Dinesh and Rinku.

Pyramid #1:

Applied Foundation Fitness*

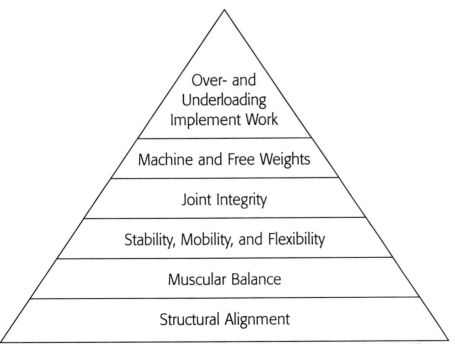

Figure 27-1. Applied foundation fitness. Note: this pyramid only addresses "fitness on the field." Appendix "B" provides a complete foundation-fitness program/protocol.

(*Special thanks to Mike Boyle, Gray Cook, and Greg Roskoff, faculty members, Titleist Performance Institute)

Progression:

- Structural alignment—optimizing posture from feet to fingertips
- Muscular balance—identifying weak links in prime movers, secondary movers, and synergists; training for total-body balance, using isometric, isokinetic, and isotonic protocols in a position, pinch, pulse, push, pull, movement progression, involving:
  - ✓ three extremity positions – straight, supinate, pronate
  - ✓ three extremity movements – linear, circular, angular
  - ✓ three torso planes – frontal, sagital, transverse
- Stability, mobility, and flexibility—training mobility without stability = vulnerability; training stability without flexibility = inefficiency
- Joint integrity—training with light dumbbells, elastic cords/grips, or plyoballs to develop durability to support stability, mobility, and flexibility
- Machines and free weights—cross-specific conditioning with position-movement resistance to tolerance, involving:
  - ✓ three extremity positions – straight, supinate, pronate
  - ✓ three extremity movements – linear, circular, angular
  - ✓ three torso planes – frontal, sagital, transverse
  - ✓ sequencing – position, pinch, pulse, push, pull movement
- Over- and underloading implement work—training with 20% heavier (a six-oz. baseball) and/or 20% lighter (a four-oz. baseball) to work on arm speed and ball velocity

Pyramid #2:

Applied Motion Analysis*

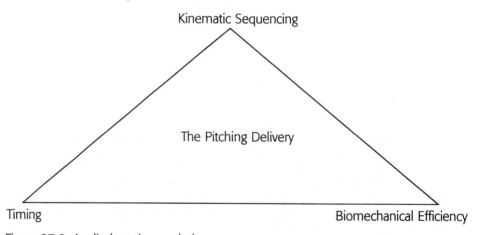

Figure 27-2. Applied motion analysis

(*Special thanks to Dr. Greg Rose, director, Titleist Performance Institute)

The following factors help clarify the key points in pyramid #2:

- Identifying genetic "signature" and instructing the pitching delivery to be on time, at the right place, with the right sequence of events for optimal biomechanical efficiency and effectiveness.
- Effectiveness without efficiency = greater risk of injury, lack of consistency in performance
- Efficiency and effectiveness = minimizes health problems and maximizes performance potential

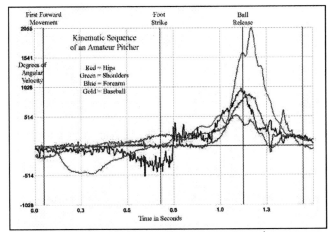

Figure 27-3. Dinesh's kinematic sequence graph

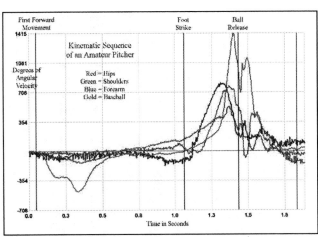

Figure 27-4. Rinku's kinematic sequence graph

Figure 27-5. Dinesh's pitching delivery animation

Figure 27-6. Rinku's pitching delivery animation

Pyramid #3:

Applied Nutrition

Figure 27-7. Optimal nutrition for the prepare, compete, repair/recover process

It should be noted that the base of the pyramid is comprised of water or hydration properties, followed by quality whole foods and microsupplementation, and capped off with special needs. These four tiers are discussed in greater detail in Appendix B. Rinku and Dinesh kept food/nutrition logs. Their off-the-field environment was quite structured (including both their sleeping and eating, which were monitored). Subtle changes, however, were made in their nutritional intake and supplementation. For example, in this regard, several factors were increased, including their level of protein consumption, their level of Omega 3 supplementation, and the amount of their joint-recovery formulas to compensate for the volume increases in their conditioning/throwing workloads.

Pyramids #4A and #4B:

Applied Mental/Emotional Mind-Body Management

Figure 27-8. Three mental/emotional issues that can cause performance problems

From a coaching perspective, pyramids #4A (Figure 27-8) and #4B (Figure 27-9) were not a problem for Rinku and Dinesh. They obviously cared a lot, but none of us knew if it was too much. Also, they were totally supported by people who had their best interests in mind. As such, no reason existed to doubt or care about what people were thinking. Finally, all they had was "the process" to work on, because they had never played the game. As such, the "results" of competitions in which they engaged didn't affect them negatively. (It was all too new and too much fun)!

Figure 27-9. Every person is three people

A disconnect between levels of the pyramid can cause a number of performance-related problems, including:

- Disconnects will cause double-binds (i.e., the body is not able to accomplish the vision of the mind).
- If you think you can or you think you can't, you are right on both counts.
- You may become cocky or confident (cocky is acting like you are prepared, while confident is knowing you are fully prepared by the process).

Rinku and Dinesh were islands unto themselves with this mental/emotional pyramid. Their sense of self was very strong, a factor we saw in them every day. As such, they had an intrapersonal/interpersonal consensus on what they wanted to be.

Hopefully, future athletes from India (or other non-baseball countries) have the same mental/emotional make-up and we can create the same learning environment for them. Our efforts with Rinku and Dinesh illustrate how we were able to integrate both science and our research into a workable coaching/athlete interaction.

The four pyramids should be kept in mind as you read the rest of this chapter. The upcoming sections provide an overview of the following: the four-phase S.T.A.T. that was administered to these two athletes, as well as the results of these procedures; the applied foundation-fitness conditioning program that was developed for and implemented with these two young men; and the instruction that they received with cross-specific throwing, pitching skill drills. As was discussed previously, it was no surprise that both Rinku and Dinesh failed many of their initial weak-link screens. Furthermore, while both young men had a remedial skill set, they were off the charts with their genetic talent potential. We were also pleasantly surprised at their capacity for motor learning. After just two months, their biomechanical-movement assessment began to look very efficient...in fact, Major League efficient.

Obviously, their ability to learn new movements, combined with a solid work ethic, sped up the development of their functional strength, endurance, mobility, and flexibility, as well as their aerobic and anaerobic capacity. Finally, it cannot be overstated that their unabated enthusiasm for the daily grind of strength work, skill-drill work, and off-the-field homework, combined with no fear of failure and an ability to laugh at themselves during the process, made for a smoother road toward their physical and biomechanical mastery of the pitching motion.

The next three sections present an overview of the weak-link screening, the baseball skill-talent testing, and the biomechanical-movement assessment that we administered to Rinku and Dinesh to benchmark their fitness and biomechanical skill levels. Finally, the foundation-fitness training regimen and the cross-specific skill drill progression that were employed with these two athletes are detailed. Both were researched and designed by the RDRBI/NPA to facilitate the development of Rinku and Dinesh into healthy pitchers who could perform on an elite level.

Phase #1:

Weak-Link Screen

- Screen 1: Sub-scapular finger probe (measures sub-scapular muscle density)
  1/2" or less: Pass _____   More than 1/2": Fail _____
  Notes:

- Screen 2: Scapular pinch (measures scapular stability, flexibility)
  Total touch: Pass _____   Less than total touch: Fail _____
  Notes:

- Screen 3: Biceps/triceps volume (measures functional balance of accelerators/ decelerators for elbow strength and flexibility)
  Scale: Volume same: Pass _____ Volume different: Fail _____
  Notes:

- Screen 4: Anterior/posterior palm presses (measures isometric, concentric shoulder strength, endurance, balance, and flexibility)
  Anterior: 60 seconds + = pass; less than 60 seconds = fail
  Palms together: Pass _____   Fail _____
  Palms out: Pass _____   Fail _____
  Palms in: Pass _____   Fail _____
  Notes:
  Posterior: 60 seconds + = pass; less than 60 seconds = fail
  Fingertips: Pass _____   Fail _____
  Palms: Pass _____   Fail _____
  Heels of hands: Pass _____   Fail _____
  Notes:

- Screen 5: Anterior/posterior palm out, up, down pulls (measures isometric, eccentric shoulder strength, endurance, balance, and flexibility)
  Anterior: 60 seconds + = pass; less than 60 seconds = fail
  Throwing hand fingers away: Pass _____   Fail _____
  Throwing hand fingers in: Pass _____   Fail _____
  Posterior: 60 seconds + = Pass; less than 60 seconds = fail
  Throwing hand palm-up finger pulls: Pass _____ Fail _____
  Throwing hand palm-down finger pulls: Pass _____ Fail _____

- Screen 6: Cobra position thigh lift (measures back extension ROM)
  Pass _____   Fail _____
  Notes:

- Screen 7: Static plank hold (measures frontal core and shoulder strength and endurance)
  Time scale (3 min): Pass _____   Fail _____
  Notes:

- Screen 8: Table tops (measures frontal strength and endurance of the legs, core, and shoulder)
  Time scale: Pass _____   Fail _____
      Hands (1 min)—straight, pronation, supination
      Forearms (2 min) _____
      Elbows (1 min)   _____
  Notes:

- Screen 9: Right and left forearm side planks (measures sagital strength and endurance)
  Time scale: Pass _____   Fail _____
  Right (3 min) ___
  Left (3 min) ___
  Notes:

- Screen 10: Side-to-side stack and track (measures transverse leg, core, and shoulder strength and flexibility)
  ✓ Posture stabilization (approximate number of inches the head moves off the target line, right and left, into foot strike)—1″ off = pass; any more than 1″ = fail
  ✓ Percentage of stride (when the shoulders square up):
    80% = pass; any less = fail
  ✓ Vertical spine (stacked during track, the number of inches off perpendicular to flat ground)—5″ or less = pass; more than 5″ = fail
  Notes:

- Screen 11: Fingernail color/clarity (purple/blue to pink/white indicates efficiency of O2 distribution)
  Pink/white/clear = Pass _____
  Purple/blue/mottled = Fail _____
  Notes:

Problem:

Both Rinku and Dinesh had total-body accelerator/decelerator imbalances and weak links for throwing/pitching. The most glaring imbalances, however, were found in their core and in their upper-body decelerators, especially their low-back extensors, scapulars, backside shoulder, and triceps.

Solution:

Cross-specific exercises were used to train their core and upper-body decelerators, which involves approximately one-third more work than for their core and upper-body accelerators. Cross-specific exercises were also utilized to train their lower-body decelerators 25 percent more than their lower-body accelerators.

Phase #2:

Baseball Skill – Talent Testing
- Sprint forward 60 yards.
- Sprint backward 45 yards.
- Standing broad jump in feet, with the inches expressed as a percentage of 12" x 10.5 x 72" baseline ÷ body height in inches = potential genetic arm/bat velocity in mph. Note: The baseline is figured with a six-foot pitcher (or 72 inches).
  - ✓ For example, with a 6' pitcher:
    - ■ 8'6"* = 8.5 x 10.5 x 72 ÷ 72 = 89.25 mph
    - ■ 8'8"* = 8.67 x 10.5 x 72 ÷ 72 = 91.04 mph
    - ■ 8'9"* = 8.75 x 10.5 x 72 ÷ 72 = 93.45 mph
  - ✓ For example, with a 6'2" pitcher:
    - ■ 8'6"* = 8.5 x 10.5 x 72 ÷ 74 = 86.97 mph
    - ■ 8'8"* = 8.67 x 10.5 x 72 ÷ 74 = 88.31 mph
    - ■ 8'9"* = 8.75 x 10.5 x 72 ÷ 74 = 90.65 mph
    - ■ * = standing broad jump performance
- Batting tee with both a light and a heavy bat for:
  - ✓ Bat speed
  - ✓ Ball-exit speed
    - ■ * ± 10% = power transfer ratio spread between light, heavy bat.
- Knee drill at 45 feet with a five-ounce baseball for:
  - ✓ Actual ball velocity. Determines the optimal position and angle of hip/shoulder separation. This number should equal 80% of velocity on a flat-ground mound. If not, it is a sequencing/mechanics and/or functional strength and flexibility problem.

- Long toss knee drill with a five-ounce baseball for:
  - ✓ Maximum distance. The hardest throwers should have the longest throws. If not, it is a sequencing/mechanics and/or functional strength and flexibility problem.
- Run-and-gun flat ground, crow-hop drill at 60 feet with four-, five- and six-ounce baseball for:
  - ✓ Actual ball velocity. Determines the percent of velocity on flat ground vs. mound, with current timing, sequencing, mechanics, and functional strength and flexibility.
- Pitch on mound at 60 feet with a four-, five- and six-ounce baseball for:
  - ✓ Actual ball velocity. Determines genetic velocity that can be achieved with current timing, sequencing, mechanics, and functional strength and flexibility.
- Run-and-gun mound, crow-hop drill at 60 feet with four-, five- and six-ounce baseball for:
  - ✓ Actual ball velocity. Determines genetic velocity that can be achieved with current timing, sequencing, mechanics, and functional strength and flexibility.
- Visual test convergent/divergent:
  - ✓ Must see to feel to do pitching, hitting, and fielding.

Problem:

With Dinesh, a disparity existed between acquired skill/strength development and genetic talent. The projected velocity from his legs was greater than the projected velocity from his core, upper body, and arms. As such, the broad jump indicated 95 mph, while the knee drill indicated 91 mph.

Solution:

More core, upper-body and arm stability, mobility, flexibility, and conditioning work. More wall drill, knee drill, and rocker drill skill work.

Problem:

With Rinku, a disparity existed between acquired skill/strength development and genetic talent. His legs and upper body/arms projected more velocity than his core. In this regard, his broad jump indicated 91 mph, the knee drill indicated 91 mph, and the long-toss knee drill indicated 85 mph.

Solution:

More core strength and flexibility training, more long toss, wall drill, and knee drill skill work.

Phase #3:

Biomechanical Movement Assessment

A three-dimensional motion-analysis synopsis of an ideal delivery model vs. a client-delivery benchmark for timing, kinematic sequencing, and mechanical efficiency:

- Ideal timing from first forward movement into foot strike = .95–1.05 seconds
- Ideal timing from foot strike to release point = .25–.35 seconds
- Ideal timing from ball release to arm deceleration is one-third–one-half the time it takes to accelerate the arm
- Ideal kinematic sequence—the hips rotate and slow down to deliver the shoulders. The shoulders rotate and slow down to deliver the throwing forearm. The throwing forearm initially rotates externally and then internally to deliver the baseball.
- Ideal core, lumbar spine, thoracic spine sequence—the low back and spine stay hyperextended and upright until the shoulders square to the target. They then go into flexion just before the throwing arm snaps straight into release. The core, upper torso, and spine lean forward toward the target immediately after ball release while the throwing forearm/hand pronate during arm deceleration.
- Ideal mechanics require:
  - ✓ Balance and posture – refers to optimal balance with postural stability that is achieved by keeping the head over the belly button between the balls of the feet throughout the delivery into foot strike, while finding an efficient posture (head/spine/hip relationship) and maintaining it. For every one inch of inappropriate head movement during a delivery (up/down, right/left), a pitcher will lose two inches of his ideal release point.
  - ✓ Leg lift and body thrust – refers to initiating forward body movement during initial leg lift, and keeping the head and spine behind an extended pelvis/butt into foot strike. A pitcher's butt should be a distance at least two times the length of a pitcher's foot in front of the rubber when total body starts forward.
  - ✓ Stride and momentum – refers to striding as far (a distance at least six-to-seven times the length of a pitcher's foot from the front of the rubber to the big toe of the landing foot) and as fast (.95–1.05 seconds into foot strike) as possible.
  - ✓ Opposite and equal arms – refers to the fact that the glove arm should be a mirror image of the throwing arm at foot strike. The forearm-and-elbow angle of the glove arm should equal the forearm-and-elbow angle of the throwing arm.
  - ✓ Hip/shoulder separation and delayed shoulder rotation – refers to the fact that a pitcher's front hip and back shoulder should get a maximum 40°–60° of separation, and his throwing shoulder should not initiate forward rotation until his head and spine have tracked to 80% of stride length.

✓ Stack and track – refers to the fact that a pitcher's low back should remain in hyperextension, with a vertical, upright spine, as his shoulders square up perpendicular to the target. The chest/torso should then track to the target, while the throwing forearm lays back into maximum-external rotation.

✓ Swivel and stabilize glove – refers to the fact that a pitcher's glove should firm up over the landing foot, in front of the chest/torso, as the low back changes from hyperextension into flexion, taking the chest/shoulders to the glove/target.

✓ Release point and follow-through – refers to the fact that as the low back flexes, a pitcher's throwing forearm snaps straight from external rotation to internal rotation and then into a release point 8-12" in front of the landing foot. The longer a pitcher's back foot drags into release point (ideally, a distance of twice the length of his foot, finishing on the center line between the middle of the rubber and the middle of home plate), the greater the release-point distance and the more efficient the deceleration and follow-through will be.

Problem:

Dinesh's timing from first forward movement into foot strike was .7 seconds. In other words, the timing of his stride and momentum was .25 seconds too fast and approximately five feet long or one foot too short. His ideal range is .95–1.05 seconds, and a distance approximately the length of six-to-seven times of his feet.

Dinesh's timing from foot strike to release point was .45 seconds. In other words, his timing was .10 seconds too slow. His ideal range is .25–.35 seconds.

The combination of these two issues results in less energy being generated at foot strike, because the shorter stride takes less time. As such, his body must work harder to generate energy, which takes more time and strength after foot strike to release the ball at the target.

Dinesh's hip-shoulder-forearm-baseball kinematic sequencing was very efficient. The problem was that he had to maximize his physical effort to achieve the sequencing.

Solution:

Every drill, every day.

Problem:

Rinku's timing from first forward movement into foot strike was 1.10 seconds. As such, the timing of his stride and momentum was .05 seconds too slow, even with a 6'3" stride. This situation occurred because his body moved away from the target at leg lift, rather than toward the target.

Rinku's timing from foot strike to release point at .35 seconds was in the acceptable range (.25– 3.5). The problem was his total body took too long (by .05 sec.) to get the ball delivered. As a result, Rinku's hip-shoulder-forearm-baseball kinematic sequencing had an inefficiency between the hips and shoulders. His hips and shoulders overrotated together in the air, instead of separating at footstrike, which causeed him to drag his throwing arm into release point. It also accounts for the late posture change that involved his head pulling to the right, as his forearm snaps from external rotation to internal rotation and launch. This factor can be seen in the 3-D animation pictures. This late posture change is the accommodation he must make in his delivery to catch his arm up into the release point.

At this point, if you are asking yourself how so much information can be learned from Rinku and Dinesh's kinematic-sequence, motion-analysis graph, you should review Figure 3-1 "Timeline of Critical Events." This figure illustrates that there are timing benchmarks that fit with the kinematic sequence and the mechanics of a perfect delivery. Figure 3-1 is a template that matches up coaching science with medical and exercise science.

Phase #4:

TRAINING
Foundation Fitness on the Field
(stability, mobility, flexibility, weak-link work)
  • Core warm-up work:
    ✓ Jog forward/backward, with the bent knees and no head movement.

Figure 27-10   Figure 27-11

✓ Perform flex "T" kariokas right and left. With big hip and shoulder separation, look over the right shoulder going out and the left shoulder coming back; keep the elbows at shoulder height.

Figure 27-12

✓ Perform posture skips forward/ backward, with no head movement.

Figure 27-13

• Leg work:
  ✓ Perform flex "T" lunges forward/ backward. Perform three-to-five reps of right leg lift, lunge forward, track forward, arch low back, squat, and hold three-to-five seconds. Repeat the left leg, and then do the same backwards.

Figure 27-14

Figure 27-15

Figure 27-16

✓ Perform flex "T" lunges, with a torque twist forward/backward; similar to the previous exercise, do three-to-five torso twists right and left, after a squat.

Figure 27-17

Figure 27-18

✓ Push in/out, squeeze and flex the knees. Keep the hands on the outside of the knees, bend 15-20", push in with the hands, resist with the knees, move in a variety of directions—right and left, circles right and left, figure-8 right and left. Repeat, pushing out with the knees, while resisting with the hands. Repeat with a double-fist between the knees, while squeezing with the knees.

Figure 27-19

Figure 27-20

Figure 27-21

✓ Assume a sumo position initially and then accordion into a downhill-racer position. Find the sumo position, with the elbows between the knees, and the palms together. Move the heel and toe (accordion) in against resistance, to tolerance, until reaching a downhill-racer position, and hold 20-60 seconds. Then, move the heel and toe out, back to the original (starting) position.

Figure 27-22

Figure 27-23

Figure 27-24

- Arm work:
  ✓ Saws—palm straight, supinate, pronate. Stand in an athletic position, with the elbows bent to 90° and touching the rib cage. Start palms in, and then saw forward/backward, 5-15 times. Repeat, with the palms up/palms down.

Figure 27-25

Figure 27-26

Figure 27-27

✓ Scissors—palms up/down. Stand in an athletic position, with the forearms and elbows touching, with the elbows on the rib cage. Start with the palms up and "scissor" left over right/right over left, 5-15 times. Repeat with the palms down.

Figure 27-28

Figure 27-29

Figure 27-30

Figure 27-31

✓ "Why-me's" arm extensions—thumbs down to up and up to down. Stand in an athletic position, with the hands at the side. Extend the elbows forward and up, and then forearms, hands, thumb down to thumbs up, 5-15 times. Start with the hands in front of the face, and the thumbs up, and then extend the forearms. Next, perform thumbs down to full extension. Reverse and repeat, 5-15 times.

Figure 27-32

Figure 27-33

Figure 27-34

Figure 27-35

Figure 27-36

✓ Perform flex "T" finger push/pulls. Stand in an athletic position, with the throwing hand and thumb down in front of the chin. Pull out for 5-15 seconds, and then push in for 5-15 seconds. Pull out—then move right/left, circle forward, circle backward, swim forward, and swim backward. Push in and repeat the same movement sequence.

Figure 27-37

✓ Perform anterior palm/forearm presses. Stand in an athletic position, with the elbows at 90° with the palms and forearms pressing together in front of the eyes. Press the palms straight for 20-60 seconds, the thumbs out 20-60 seconds, and then the thumbs in 20-60 seconds.

Figure 27-38

Figure 27-39

Figure 27-40

✓ Perform anterior backhand/finger pulls. Stand in an athletic position, with the elbows at 90°, the back of the hands/fingers together, and the throwing hand/fingers toward the face. Pull out for 20-60 seconds. Reverse the hands with the throwing hand/fingers away from the face. Pull out for 20-60 seconds.

Figure 27-41

Figure 27-42

✓ Perform posterior finger/palm/heel of hand presses. Stand in an athletic position, with the eyes up, the shoulder blades pinched, and the hands behind the back with the fingertips touching. Press for 20-60 seconds. Same body position, with the hands behind the back, and the palms touching. Press for 20-60 seconds. Same body position, with the hands behind the back, and the heels of the hands touching. Press for 20-60 seconds.

Figure 27-43   Figure 27-44   Figure 27-45

✓ Perform posterior palm up/palm down finger pulls. Same body position as the previous exercise with the hands behind the back and the throwing hand palm up. Hook the fingers, and pull out for 20-60 seconds. Turn the throwing palm down, hook the fingers, and pull out for 20-60 seconds.

Figure 27-46   Figure 27-47

✓ Butt ups—palms straight, supinate, pronate. Sit cross-legged, with the palms on the ground and the fingers facing forward. Pinch the shoulder blades and lift the butt off the ground 5-15 times. Repeat with the palms/fingers in, and then the palms/fingers out.

Figure 27-48

Figure 27-49

Figure 27-50

✓ Flex "T"—pushups palms straight, supinate, pronate. Assume the push-up position, with the palms straight, and the elbows at 90°, and then do 5-15 push-ups. Repeat the exercise with the palms in/palms out.

Figure 27-51

Figure 27-52

Figure 27-53

- Core work:
  ✓ Belly-down planks. Assume the forearm plank position and hold for one-to-three minutes.

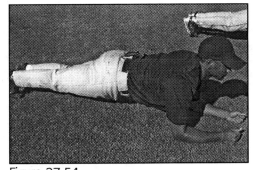

Figure 27-54

✓ Side planks. Assume the right-forearm, side-plank position, and hold for 30-90 seconds. Then, switch to the left-forearm side-plank position, and hold for 30-90 seconds.

Figure 27-55

✓ Belly-up planks on the hands, forearms, and elbows. Assume the belly-up plank position on the feet/hands, with the palms straight. Hold for 60 seconds. Repeat with the palms in for 60 seconds, and then with the palms out for 60 seconds. Assume the belly-up plank position on the feet/forearms, and hold for two minutes. Assume the belly-up plank position on the feet/elbows, and hold for one minute.

Figure 27-56

Figure 27-57

Figure 27-58

Figure 27-59

Figure 27-60

✓ Ball-in-glove abdominals. Sit on the ground, with the hands flat on the ground behind the butt. Hold the ball and glove between the knees. Lift the legs and knees to the chest—move right/left, circle right/left, figure-8s right/left. Extend the knees halfway out, and then repeat the movements. Fully extend the legs, and then repeat the movements. Repeat the exercise and movements, with the forearms on the ground. Repeat the exercise and movements while lying down. Do three-to-five reps per position and movement.

Figure 27-61

Figure 27-62

Figure 27-63

- Transition work:
  - ✓ Arm circles—small, medium, large—forward/backward, palms straight, supinate, pronate

Figure 27-64

  - ✓ Ball-in-glove throwing arm circles—fast forward/backward

Figure 27-65

The latter training protocol, "transition work," is a throwing-arm simulation that physically bridges the gap to our second training progression: "working on the biomechanics of their deliveries with cross-specific drills for pitching skills." It should be noted that this progression just involves foundation fitness, on-the-field work. Appendix "B" presents a complete foundation-fitness training regimen.

After six weeks of Phase #3 (foundation-fitness training and cross-specific skill drills training), a third protocol was added—"overloading and underloading implement training work for velocity." At that point, Dinesh and Rinku started throwing/pitching with four-, five-, and six-ounce baseballs in a nine-step progression once a week. All of the drills are easily recognizable, except "run and gun," which involves making an accelerated maximum effort, stepping behind, and throwing a ball into either a wall (on flat ground) or a catch net (on the mound).
- Overloading and underloading implement work for velocity:
  - ✓ Dynamic warm-up
  - ✓ Long-toss with five-ounce baseballs:

    5 short   15 medium   15 long

✓ Flat-ground towel drill:

    5 with 6-oz. ball   5 with 5-oz. ball   5 with 4-oz. ball

✓ Knee drill at 45 feet:

    5 with 6-oz. ball   5 with 5-oz. ball   5 with 4-oz. ball

✓ Flat ground run-and-gun into wall drill with 45 feet:

    5 with 6-oz. ball   5 with 5-oz. ball   5 with 4-oz. ball

✓ Mound towel drill:

    5 with 6-oz. ball   5 with 5-oz. ball   5 with 4-oz. ball

✓ Mound run-and-gun into screen drill:

    5 with 6-oz. ball   5 with 5-oz. ball   5 with 4-oz. ball

✓ Mound pitch into screen drill:

    5 with 6-oz. ball   5 with 5-oz. ball   5 with 4-oz. ball

✓ Pitch to a catcher drill:

    5 with 6-oz. ball   5 with 5-oz. ball   5 with 4-oz. ball

• Cross-specific drills for training pitching skills:

✓ Play catch:

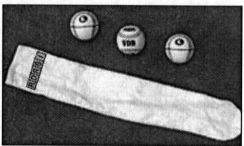

Figure 27-66. Note: sock towels can be purchased at www.nationalpitching.net or www.rdrbi.com

✓ Step-behinds. Turn sideways, step behind with the post foot, lift, and throw (distance to tolerance), 5-15 tosses.

Figure 27-67   Figure 27-68   Figure 27-69

✓ Cross-overs. Turn sideways, cross the lifting foot over the post foot, lift, and throw (distance to tolerance), 5-15 tosses.

Figure 27-70

✓ Narrow stance. Turn sideways, with the big toe of the post foot in the arch of the lift foot, lift, and throw (distance to tolerance), 5-15 tosses.

Figure 27-71

✓ Hershiser drill. Assume a cross-over foot position two feet from the wall. Bend the knees two-to-three inches (more than comfortable). Pre-set the butt/hip, with the hands in the normal position. Lift the leg, and aggressively "plant" the butt/hip on the wall, and hold for three-to-five seconds. Do 5-15 reps.

Figure 27-72

Figure 27-73

✓ Wall drill. Place the landing foot at the base of the wall, spread the legs comfortably, and bend the knees to 90°, with the arms opposite and equal. The eyes are on an imaginary target. Rock back and forth, and then push the knee into the wall for three-to-five seconds; then release the back foot, rotate the hips, and hold the shoulder separation for three-to-five seconds; then square the shoulders to the wall, the knee on the wall, the glove on the wall, the fastball on the wall, the breaking ball on the wall, and the off-speed on the wall for three-to-five seconds each; and finally, arch the low back and keep the spine upright and try to push the wall over for three-to-five seconds.

Figure 27-74

Figure 27-75

Figure 27-76

Figure 27-77

✓ Knee drill. Get on both knees, 30-45 feet from the target/partner. Find the angle with the knees/hips such that when the shoulders torque and rotate the arms to an opposite and equal, the head and spine stay upright, and the glove swivels and stabilizes in front, as the torso rotates to deliver the baseball. Do three-to-five fastballs, three-to-five breaking balls, and three-to-five off-speed pitches.

Figure 27-78

Figure 27-79

✓ Rocker drill. Find the same body position as the starting position in the wall drill. Rock back and forth into the delivery of the baseball. Keep the back foot on the ground during the release and deceleration of the arm for three-to-five fastballs, three-to-five breaking balls, and three-to-five off-speed pitches.

Figure 27-80

Figure 27-81

Figure 27-82

✓ Towel drill. From a cross-over position, hold the ball in a sock towel, then go through and complete the delivery on either flat ground or the mound. Mark off five feet from the big toe of the landing foot. Have the partner hold his glove as a target, chest-high over the five-foot mark. Make sure the drag line finishes on an imaginary center line between the center of the rubber and the center of home plate.

Figure 27-83

Figure 27-84

Figure 27-85

✓ "X" drill: Line up, 30-45 feet from a wall/fence, with an "X" for the strike zone. Start in a cross-over stance and pitch to the "X". Do 5-15 fastballs, 5-15 breaking balls, and 5-15 off-speed.

Figure 27-86

Figure 27-87

Figure 27-88

✓ Hat drill: Line up with a partner, 90-180 feet apart. Put a hat half the distance between you and your partner to use as a target. From a step behind, try to hit the hat 15-30 times.

Figure 27-89

Figure 27-90

Figure 27-91

✓ Bullpen drill: Perform skill work with 10-15 fastballs, 10-15 breaking balls, and 10-15 off-speed pitches, from a cross-over position, with a narrow stance, a regular stance, or a wind-up.

Figure 27-92

Figure 27-93

Figure 27-94

Figure 27-95

That's it for Chapter 27. Now, you know how to "build a million-dollar arm"...(HA!) Our foremost wish is that everyone who reads this text could someday be a part of a similar once-in-a-lifetime experience. It was special for all of us at the RDRBI and the NPA.

28

The Final Pitch

Applications for Coaching and Player Development

☛ **Doug:** "There is no such thing as a pitching prospect" is a phrase that was coined by Gary Huckabay in the late 1990s. Since then, it has become something of a mantra for the stat-minded crowd. Many individuals interpret this phrase (TINSTAAPP, for short) as a reflection of the high-injury risk that young pitchers face as they climb the Minor-League ladder. The relative difficulty of evaluating pitching prospects, compared to position players, is an extension of this influence, and an underlying subtext to the interpretation of TINSTAAPP. This understanding, however, fails to describe the full concept of Huckabay's idea, by neglecting an integral piece of the TINSTAAPP puzzle. Like many of the conventional wisdoms that have been challenged in the previous chapters, the repeated use of this definition has created some confusion, since it ignores certain aspects that are critical to understanding the term. To help clear things up, Huckabay offered the following explanation in a Baseball Prospectus article from March 2007:

> "When I first wrote that 'There's no such thing as a pitching prospect,' it meant two things, one of which has kind of become lost over time. Yes, it means that pitchers get hurt at approximately the same rate that methheads swipe identities and lose teeth. That's what all pitchers do, not just prospects. But it also had another meaning—that guys who are totally blowing people away in the Minors, like they're so many hot-dog pretenders before Kobayashi, are absolutely not pitching prospects—they're already pitchers, and more time in the Minors only means time off the living, pulsating clocks that are their labrums, rotator cuffs, and elbows."

While Huckabay's second point is critical to his main concept, the overall emphasis on injury rates for young players has overshadowed the corollary: that pitchers develop much differently than hitters, and that player evaluation should be sensitive to this difference. Position players tend to follow a relatively predictable performance pattern that follows a bell curve as they age. Most hitters improve throughout their early 20s, hit a performance peak around age 25 to 29, and then decline as they progress through their 30s. Pitchers don't display any such aging pattern. In fact, countless examples exist of Major League pitchers who have peaked in their early 20s or mid-30s. To a degree, this trend is due to the effect of mileage creating wear and tear on the arm, and the difficulties of safe development, when the factors of workloads, mechanics, functional strength and flexibility, and genetics are considered.

What's interesting about the trend is that developing hitters actually have the tougher job, when it comes to the influence of outside variables and the increased difficulty as they climb the Minor League ladder. The biggest mechanical distinction between hitting and pitching, from a developmental point of view, is with the initiation of movement to start the swing or the pitch. Like a free-throw shooter in basketball, a pitcher has total control of personal timing, from setup to ball release. The only variable that increases in difficulty as a pitcher rises through the system is the quality of opposing hitters, a factor that can only have an impact on pitcher performance and development after release point. In fact, some things get easier for pitchers as they progress upward through the Minors, including the quality of defense making plays behind them. On the other hand, the performance and development of hitters are dependent upon the quality of the opposing pitching, which gets tougher as they move from the low Minors to AA, AAA, and the Majors.

Pitching prospects don't necessarily need to face better hitting in order to develop better stuff, but they are expected to spend time in the Minors to learn "how to pitch," and to make the physical adjustments necessary to improve their stuff, as well as their level of stamina. This experience includes learning to play the situational chess match with hitters and honing their mechanics, in addition to developing the ability to effectively throw different pitches. While hitters must also learn the chess match, they have the added difficulty of training in pitch recognition and hand-eye coordination before they can play the game at the highest level. This development hinges upon the quality of pitchers they face, which will expose a hitter's weakness sooner and more often.

Development requires an athlete to make adjustments. Tools, such as motion analysis, can be used to create developmental benchmarks that are position-specific, with the intention of tuning the instruction toward each player's unique strengths and weaknesses, as they apply to their functional use on the field. Rather than ask a pitcher to strive for fewer walks or a better strikeout rate, the design would be such that he has personal goals, with respect to mechanics, conditioning, strategic approach, and stuff. The improvements in these areas would lead to a higher level of consistency and efficiency, resulting in better overall performance. Professional scouts, coaches, and front-office staff could integrate all of the available information, including traditional stats, advanced metrics, scouting reports, and the visual reports and the objective scouting stats that are generated through screening for weaknesses, testing for talent/skill, assessing with motion analysis for movement efficiencies, and then training accordingly.

Many scouts like to refer to a pitcher's "ceiling," or the player's upper limit to his potential ability. The concept of a developmental ceiling is based on the assumption that pitchers with limited size and velocity lack the potential to reach elite status. This assumption, however, seems to ignore the wide variation in size and stuff among the top pro players, including the five aces of Pedro Martinez, Roy Oswalt, Greg Maddux, Randy Johnson, and Johan Santana. These elite pitchers have much more in common with respect to mechanics than physical height or pitch velocity, and each has honed his skills beyond any theoretical ceiling of performance.

The NPA three-dimensional model is designed to assess the mechanical ceiling for several different variables, in order to pinpoint areas of relative strength and weakness and to evaluate how a pitcher's mechanics stack up against his peers. The mechanical efficiency ratings and other numbers that are generated using the model can be employed to identify the pitchers who have almost reached their limit for mechanical efficiency, those who still have room for development, and even the "freaks" or statistical outliers that also go above and beyond the typical mechanical ceiling, like Nolan Ryan, for example. It should be remembered that a player's ability to improve his mechanical efficiency depends on how much work he puts into training and developing functional strength and flexibility, as well as the time he spends working on mound skills. It is also imperative that a player takes to quality instruction, is willing and able to make mechanical adjustments, and that a coach gives him compelling reasons to make changes in his delivery. Finally, in the end, a pitcher might still be limited by his genetics and signature, when it comes to achieving certain biomechanical benchmarks.

The concepts of projection and ceiling assume that a limit exists as to how much a pitcher can improve. The truth of the matter, however, is that little is known about the ability for an individual player to learn and adapt to instruction. Some pitchers never approach their ceiling, because they never straighten out their mechanics, fail to develop quality secondary pitches, or can't iron out a problem that they have with command and control. Others go far beyond their projections, because they learn and adapt to professional baseball exceptionally well. The underlying reason for this situation is that the key ingredients to pitcher projection are size, velocity, and arm slot, none of which account for a player's ability to learn and develop pitching-specific skills.

☛ **Tom:** Over the years, several validated mental/emotional testing instruments have been developed (e.g., the S.T.A.R. profile for sports total assessment report). On the other hand, most organizations don't use them appropriately or effectively, because very few coaches are sports psychologists and very few sports psychologists are coaches.

It's probably a good time to bring up some of the system biases that occur in organized baseball—biases that skewer both player scouting and player development. First, in most organizations, scouting and player development don't get along. Why? Because when players fail, scouts think it's a player development issue, while coaches think it's a scouting problem. Second, very few scouts or coaches will put their stamp (or reputation) on a skilled player who is short on tools. Why? Because with failure, it's the scouts' and/or coaches' problem. The opposite is true with a talented player who is short on skill. Why? Because when talent fails, it's the athlete's fault. Baseball is a game of failure, scouted and coached by negative people in a misinformation environment. The existing system promotes trying to keep a job, rather than doing a job.

☛ **Doug:** When a pitcher has success, while lacking size and velocity, he is often praised by analysts and scouts alike as "knowing how to pitch." In the case of players like Greg Maddux, the label is well-earned and descriptive, evidenced by his ability to utilize the advanced concept of effective velocity to disrupt batter timing, rather than raw pitch speed. Maddux, also having educated himself with respect to mechanics, takes advantage of consistency and efficiency to gain impeccable command, as well as deception. Pitchers in the mold of Greg Maddux are also considered to be highly intelligent, hence his nickname of "the smartest pitcher who ever lived." While these descriptions are spot-on in the unique case of Maddux, terms like "knows how to pitch," or "can play the game" have become somewhat cliché. As such, these terms are sometimes used as a blanket statement about shorter pitchers who don't throw especially hard, and/or players who may be somewhat lacking in tools, yet still manage to put up good numbers.

With the exception of "he knows how to pitch or how to play," the idea of intelligence on the field is not often brought up in the discussion of baseball ability. A player may get tabbed as a "smart guy," because he went to an Ivy League school, but announcers rarely talk about the intelligence of making a particular play or executing an optimal pitch, unless Derek Jeter is involved. This situation isn't the case in soccer, for example, where an announcer will utter the word "brilliant" dozens of times throughout a typical English Premier League match. This effect is even more obvious in Japan, where intelligence on the field is considered one of the most important attributes for a baseball player and as indicative of potential for improvement. Mike Plugh, a writer for Baseball Prospectus who specializes in the Japanese game, used the following portrayal to describe one professional pitcher:

> *"His ability to think on the mound gives him a great deal*
> *of NPB potential, although he only tops out at 89 mph, with*
> *an average speed more usually down around 84."*

In reality, a player doesn't have to go to Harvard to have baseball intelligence, with regard to having instincts on the field, or being physically, mentally, and strategically prepared. Nolan Ryan, for example, was probably the most "country smart" pitcher with whom Tom ever worked, and it had nothing to do with Nolan's level of formal education. Nolan knew his mechanics, and that making adjustments would have certain predictable results, above and beyond what any pitching coach understood at the time. Nolan was gifted with a 100-mph arm, but he was also the most prepared pitcher on the field every day. Players like Jamie Moyer are successful, despite their size and stuff, because they put more time and effort into preparation with their tools. They have to work harder and smarter than everyone else just to keep up. They use determination and the unrelenting goal to improve and succeed with their skill, when most other pitchers with their attributes would fail.

The primary lesson to be learned from pitchers, like Greg Maddux and Nolan Ryan, is that certain key skills are teachable, and are not just the product of a high IQ. For example, any pitcher can learn how to optimize his mechanics in order to get the most out of his delivery, while maximizing the command and effectiveness of his pitches. Every player can learn to condition himself toward the specific task of hitting or pitching a baseball, and to utilize his functional strength and flexibility to aid in the development of mechanics. All pitchers can be trained in the mental and emotional aspects of pitching competitively, and the preparation necessary to succeed in that environment. The barriers that exist to gaining these skills include:

- The knowledge, awareness, and teaching ability of coaches
- The time, hard work, and determination necessary for athletes to learn the mental and physical aspects of development
- An athlete's ability to understand, adapt, and integrate what he has learned into game situations and to improvise accordingly

Major League organizations can break down these skills, based on what is teachable mechanically, mentally, and physically. Because some pitchers will respond differently to training, teams need to determine those aspects that are most integral to success on the mound, and which methods are most difficult for players to understand. It is also important to know which type of players tend to succeed with a certain system, and which ones respond well to making adjustments. These are very important questions for a front office to ask, and would go a long way toward learning more about how successful pitchers are created and developed within the organization. This approach could be further applied to the amateur baseball draft, and used to sort out those pitchers who fit within a particular developmental plan. Streamlining the developmental system for pitchers could also help to overcome that less-recognized factor within TINSTAAPP, and to create a more stable and predictable pattern of pitcher development.

The ultimate goal is to put players in more control of their own pitching career, from their mechanical delivery to their physical training and mental approach to the game. Even Little Leaguers have been known to have the capacity to learn the advanced concepts of pitching mechanics, once they understand and appreciate how it helps them to play better baseball. Every player should become his own best pitching coach, because no other person can possibly understand exactly what he sees, thinks, or feels with every pitch. Players who are encouraged to look at themselves from the lens of a coach can take a proactive approach to their development, rather than waiting for someone else to tell them how to succeed.

Young pitchers are faced with a difficult challenge, as they develop and move up through various levels of competition, and attempt to follow the particular instructions of numerous pitching coaches. From Little League to travel ball, high school, college, and on into the professional ranks, pitchers are expected to follow the explicit instructions of every coach, lest they risk falling out of favor and losing playing time. Those instructions change every season, as the player moves on to a new team, with a different coach who has his own opinions with regard to proper technique and training.

Many coaches have their own secret recipe for mechanics or drills, a formula that is often based on the methods that were used in their own playing careers. Other coaches, on the other hand, adhere strictly to conventional wisdom. As has been discussed, conventional wisdom is typically unproven, and is often misunderstood and misapplied from a coaching standpoint. Some coaches are less educated, with respect to the impact of workloads and mechanics, and are unknowingly putting their pitchers at risk. All of these factors contribute to the gauntlet that a pitcher must pass through before he can don a Major League uniform. All factors considered, the process favors the player who can be his own best pitching coach.

The role of pitching coach is similar to that of a schoolteacher, helping developing students to learn the skills necessary to succeed in their careers. At the high-school level, a student might still be developing the fundamentals that are necessary to create a solid base of understanding, a scenario that applies to math, science, and history as much as it does to pitching mechanics and conditioning. Regardless of their area of concern, once individuals have achieved a solid grasp of the basics, they can build on it with further knowledge.

When a student pitcher has reached college, he should be encouraged to think for himself on the mound, as well as in the classroom, while at the same time taking more control over his own mental and physical maintenance and preparation. To a degree, the professional ranks are the equivalent of grad school, given that students or athletes at that level are completely focused on maximizing their career potential by choosing a specialization, and learning all of the in-depth details to prepare themselves to compete at the elite level of their chosen industry.

The aforementioned approach represents a more ideal method to player development, because it takes advantage of natural human growth patterns, both mental and physical. Reality, however, reflects a much different atmosphere, one in which athletes are sometimes treated like soldiers by their drill sergeant coaches, and are often discouraged from asking questions. It's hard to imagine a schoolteacher who tells a student to run laps every time he asks a question in class, yet that's the consequence for a lot of inquisitive athletes. Since most baseball coaches are in a powerful position, they are always expected to be the most knowledgeable guys in the room when it comes to baseball. Because this situation can create quite an ego, a player who asks questions is sometimes treated as a challenge to that ego. Even though those questions represent opportunities to help the players understand the methodology of a drill, or how mechanics can add to their abilities, some coaches feel that questioning their methods is the same as not trusting their instruction, or doubting their baseball knowledge.

It is the responsibility of coaches to observe a pitcher's delivery, and then make recommendations based on what is seen. This process is much easier if a coach makes a conscious effort to communicate proper methodology with his pitchers, to explain what he sees with each player's motion, and to state why he thinks there might be weak links in the chain. A pitcher can then match up what he felt on a pitch with what the coach saw, and learn to make the adjustment when he feels a "soft glove" at release point, or early trunk rotation prior to foot strike. This step encourages self-maintenance and provides the confidence for a pitcher to make appropriate in-game adjustments.

Figures 28-1. Josh Beckett has developed his skills throughout his career, including his functional strength and flexibility, pitching approach, and mechanics. These images illustrate how his posture improved over the four years between October 2003 and October 2007.

Bridging the gap between what a coach sees and what the pitcher feels is probably the biggest obstacle in instruction. In that regard, a player's development is often determined by a coach's ability to communicate effectively. This change in the way that coaches and players interact goes hand-in-hand with the concept of working with a pitcher's personal signature, rather than against it. Coaches and players can work in concert toward the common goal of optimal development, while understanding that the determinants of success are unique to each pitcher and that instruction should be individually customized. Taking advantage of what a pitcher does naturally by working with his signature provides a personalized approach to development, rather than trying to put all players into the same mold, with the same looking delivery for every pitcher on the staff. The strategy of using strong communication and a personalized approach applies to mechanics, conditioning, and the mental/emotional aspects of playing baseball, all of which help a player learn to become his own best pitching coach.

Using communication to close the information gap, a coach can give a pitcher a set of tools for self-maintenance and preparation. These tools could be in the form of mechanical tips, strategic approaches in certain pitch counts, drills for mechanics and conditioning, or psychological strategies for handling adversity in game situations. With proper communication, training, and motivation, a pitcher can learn to self-diagnose problem areas, and then reach into his personal toolbox to find a solution.

Learning to be their own best pitching coach is a huge advantage for players as they develop and are exposed to the influence of dozens of pitching coaches on their way through college and the pros. If a player can gain a firm understanding of his craft, he will be better able to work in conjunction with future coaches and to integrate new information with knowledge already gained. From a coaching perspective, this factor requires a degree of open-mindedness, with respect to what a pitcher has learned from previous instructors. Many coaches will never ask their new pitchers about what they have been previously taught, and will apply their own methods, without gaining an understanding of the instruction that produced a player's existing delivery. As such, players can learn much more about pitching if a coach takes the time to explain differences in methodology, and makes an effort to appreciate the knowledge that a pitcher brings into a particular situation. Taking this a step further, a pitcher is more likely to respond to instruction if there is parity in his relationship with the coach, with mutual respect between the two.

The ability for a player to become his own best pitching coach is largely dependent on his motivation to learn. All factors considered, motivation usually sparks soon after a pitcher sees the impact that education has on his performance. When a coach is working in the bullpen with a pitcher, if a piece of instruction helps to increase a player's hip-shoulder separation, that player will get pumped up on the resulting velocity kick. If the coach has done a good job of answering this player's questions and explaining why hip-shoulder separation helps to generate velocity, the physical results will drive the point home. Once a pitcher has figured out how to use his mechanics to improve the effectiveness and comfort level of his pitches, his competitive drive will compel him to learn more. In reality, the best students tend to become their own best personal pitching coaches. Some of these pitchers will actually spread and test their knowledge by example.

A time once existed when kids commonly did this learning for themselves, and developed their baseball skills without the aid of coaches. Generations of players grew up playing ball with neighborhood kids at the local diamond, sandlot, grass field, or with makeshift bases in the street. The great pitchers of the early 20th century learned to play the game this way. The individuals who naturally figured out the best techniques, such as Walter Johnson, found the most success. That trend has faded with time. Just 10-to-15 years ago, we encountered relatively little competition for the local Little League fields, when we set up for tennis ball-baseball on an almost daily basis, despite living in a suburban neighborhood with plenty of kids. As such, many young players are missing out on the opportunity to learn the game for themselves, in a scenario where they play for fun, instead of trophies.

The current reality is such that most young ballplayers don't have time for disorganized play, because they spend so much time playing travel ball, Little League, fall ball, winter ball, and so on. Rather than playing two games a week during the spring, some youth ballplayers are now competing year-round, traveling to different cities to play 50-to-100 games in a year. Given that parents spend great amounts of money to fund the leagues, lessons, and equipment, they take youth sports very seriously. As a consequence, players are told to "pay attention, and do what the coach says," while keeping quiet, to get the most out of practice time. This approach detracts from the learning benefit that comes from encouraging kids to just have fun, ask questions, and figure things out for themselves. While organized baseball is crucial to player development, disorganized play has advantages that get lost when Mom and Dad are in the bleachers, and a coach is calling all the signs.

Coaching is truly an art. The best instructors use a combination of knowledge, awareness, evaluation, communication, and motivation to develop players with confidence in their abilities. Utilizing the experience of expert coaches, along with revolutionary technology, such as motion analysis, we have attempted to tackle difficult questions in the book, *The Art & Science of Pitching*. The use of objective measures of baseball-specific ability, when combined with communication among open-minded coaches and enlightened players, has the potential to change the landscape of player development.

Baseball is very unique among competitive team sports, from the playing field configurations down to the nature of the competition itself. The majority of team sports consist of a perfectly symmetrical playing area, with each team defending some sort of goal on their side of the field, while attacking the opponent's goal on the other end. A game clock determines the length of each contest. All of the major sports in America follow this type of configuration, including professional football, basketball, soccer, and ice hockey. On the other hand, baseball is closer to a one-on-one tennis match contained within a defensive team sport, with no set time limit and a primary focus on the interaction between the hitter and pitcher. Each team occupies the same turf when playing defense. Furthermore, the non-standard field configurations help determine the outcome of batted balls.

The battle between hitters and pitchers is at the core of the athletic competition that defines a baseball game. As such, the individual performances of these players make up the majority of action on the diamond. This isolation of player performance also lends itself very well to statistical analysis, particularly for hitters at the professional level. The lack of influence by teammates makes the performance data much more reliable for predicting a specific player's ability. Furthermore, the relatively large sample sizes that are collected in the Major Leagues contribute to the power of baseball stats, as well. Statistics provide the basics for keeping track of the events on the field, both through 162 games a year and over a century of Major League play.

In his foreword to *The Diamond Appraised*, baseball analyst Bill James remarked that, *"Sabermetrics is the field of knowledge which is drawn from attempts to figure out whether or not those things people say [about baseball] are true."* Not only does this statement capture the essence of statistical analysis, it also reflects our goals as we challenge conventional wisdom and test the theories of pitching mechanics. Motion analysis falls under the same category as Sabremetrics in this regard. We can only hope that our research will have the same type of positive impact on baseball, as has the work of Bill James and others.

The renowned astrophyscist Carl Sagan once said, *"Science is a way of thinking much more than it is a body of knowledge."* His words reflect the true power and motivation of science as an approach and the value of utilizing a strategy that seeks to answer questions with hard evidence. Most people are very concerned about what they know, and want to possess as much knowledge in their field as possible. In contradiction, however, many of these same people either use an inefficient process to procure their knowledge or base their decisions and beliefs on very limited information.

The main focus of science as a process and a way of thinking is to constantly ask new questions, to devise new ways of collecting information, and to consistently challenge a person's own perception of the right answer. An individual can never truly be wrong when following the scientific process. Because one key goal of this process is to continually evolve the existing model, a scientist must be willing to adjust or even abandon a long-held belief in the face of compelling evidence. In baseball, the challenge of science is to permeate the layers of conventional wisdom, and to change the way that many people approach the evaluation of players on the field. The willingness and eagerness to be proven wrong is what separates good science from pseudo science, and the progressive coaches of tomorrow from the stubborn coaches of yesterday.

A scientific approach to problem-solving in baseball is important to consider from a business perspective, as well. Because the multi-billion dollar industry of Major League baseball is constantly evolving, the organizations that anticipate this evolution have a huge advantage in the competition for fans, dollars, and victories on the field. One of the key tenets of business and baseball is the distinction between process and outcome. As such, Major League teams must apply this factor to talent evaluation, player development, and profit generation. When Paul DePodesta spoke with my fellow sports MBA students at SDSU, he emphasized the importance of process versus outcome, when evaluating a team's success on the field and at the gate. We later discussed this factor in more detail, and were in agreement that motion analysis and pitching mechanics could very well provide the next breakthrough in the processes of evaluating and developing talent in baseball. Collectively, the resultant videos, pictures, numbers, charts, graphs, and gadgets all add to the research and development of the final product on the field, which has the strongest effect on the bottom line, especially when it comes to the upper echelon of the postseason.

For the business of Major League baseball, the coaches, scouts, trainers, and statistical analysts are all part of the R & D department of each team. As such, they share the common goal of "manufacturing" the best possible product to put on the big-league diamond. Tools, such as motion analysis, can be used to increase the efficiency of this research and development effort. In this regard, the seemingly expensive startup costs of acquiring the technology are easily covered by the expected return on investment of improved player evaluation and development. Given the salary structure of athletes and the present-day value of drafting and developing players in a manner that can help ensure that those salaries are well-spent, a substantial financial advantage can be achieved by those teams that effectively utilize this technology.

The work of the late Doug Pappas provided a unique perspective on the business of baseball. Other individuals, such as Maury Brown, of the Business of Sports Network, and Gary Huckabay of *Baseball Prospectus,* continue that tradition, providing keen insight into the business aspects of operating a Major League franchise. In his recent return to writing for *Baseball Prospectus,* Huckabay shocked the audience as he boldly proclaimed that "baseball analysis is dead." He went on to qualify analysis as the *"rigorous review of player-performance data."* His point was that the big lessons from statistical analysis have mostly been learned, and the marginal gains from further study of the numbers do not necessarily offset the time and cost of doing the research. In his words, *"the utility has vanished."*

Huckabay's article was a subtle proclamation that the community of baseball analysts is ready for a new set of tools to study the game. While statistics will remain a key piece of the puzzle, the next big gains in efficiency and predictability will probably come from another source. Motion analysis could be that new source of data for baseball research. As such, the study of pitching mechanics might just provide the functional utility in today's game that is necessary to overcome the anchor imposed by conventional wisdom. It can also help to pave the way for science and technology to gain acceptance within the baseball industry, by taking advantage of the expertise of "old school" coaches and scouts to develop hypotheses and drive the research forward.

Every person, company, and baseball team spend a significant amount of time and resources trying to gain a competitive advantage in the pursuit of their personal goals, be it a job promotion, record profits, or a World Series championship. The integration of technology, adhering to a scientific approach, and the expertise of professional coaches and scouts will lead to new research that could introduce the next renaissance in baseball. As a baseball culture, we are always in a state of learning and evolution, and yet untested theories have withstood the test of time through conventional wisdom. However, we now have the tools to learn what was unattainable in the past, and to use objective assessments of position-specific athletic ability to evaluate baseball players. In that regard, an effective mix of research, experience, and communication can revolutionize the way that we approach coaching, scouting, performance analysis, and player development.

TOOL SHED

Toolbox 1.1: Breakdown of the Pitchers Involved in the Motion-Analysis Experiments

Group	# of Pitchers	Average Age	Age Range
All pitchers	33	21.5 yrs	16–33 yrs
Professional	9	26.9 yrs	21–33 yrs
College	18	20.4 yrs	19–23 yrs
High school	6	16.7 yrs	16–18 yrs

Data was collected from each pitcher for three types of pitches—fastballs, breaking balls, and off-speed pitches. As a result, our sample of 33 players includes 99 data points, at three pitch types per player. In addition, each data point represents an average value of three pitches. For example, pitcher #15's stride length on his three breaking balls has an average value of 68.80 inches from the front of the rubber to the ankle of his landing foot, with a standard deviation of +/- 0.73 inches. The standard deviations allow us to examine the player's mechanical consistency for the different types of pitches that he threw for that session. All told, our data set involves close to 300 total pitches, with three pitch types per player and three pitches per type (33 players x 3 pitch types/player x 3 pitches/pitch type = 297 total pitches).

On occasion, a few data points are missing for specific measurements, because the reflective markers that are used throughout parts of the delivery during the capture phase are sometimes missing. When this situation happens, the computer is unable to crunch the relevant numbers. For example, a pitcher might cover up the marker on his drag toe near the release point, because his foot is pointing downward close to the ground, such that the cameras cannot track it. This occurrence prevents the software from calculating certain stats, such as dragline distance.

Throughout the data analysis sections, the sample size will be noted as (n ≤ 99, N ≤ 33) for each variable that is cited, with n representing the number of data points tracked (at three per player), and N indicating the number of players in the sample. Both n and N are used to test for the significance between different groups of pitchers, in order to gauge the strength of the effect. All tests for significance utilize the t-test method for comparing populations, and assume equal variance

Toolbox 1.2: Experimental Controls for Motion-Analysis Pitchers

Specific experimental controls that were in place for every pitcher who went through a motion analysis included the following:

- All testing was conducted at the NPA Performance Lab in San Diego.
- An artificial pitching mound, built to MLB code, was utilized in both our training and testing, including a rubber at 10″ height from the ground, with a slope that drops one inch for each foot of horizontal distance to the plate.
- All pitching at a target included an outline of the strike zone, with a standard-size home plate at 60′ 6″ from the rubber.
- All pitchers wore similar attire during capture—baseball glove, athletic shoes, sliding pants, and 40 motion-analysis markers, including a head band, two arm bands, and two wrist bands.
- All pitchers used official Minor League baseballs throughout the session.
- Each pitcher threw approximately 30 pitches, including 10 fastballs, 10 breaking balls, and 10 off-speed pitches, in that order.
- Each pitcher mixed in a fastball for every three breaking and off-speed pitches, which added four to five pitches per session to the capture total.

The non-controlled variables in our experiments included how much each pitcher warmed up and played catch before the analysis began. Each player was required to go through a dynamic warm-up, including upper- and lower-body exercises, as well as playing catch until they felt comfortable to throw from the mound. It was up to each pitcher to determine when they had warmed up sufficiently. We also allowed the players to take a few throws once they got to the mound, in order to get accustomed to the slope and their pitching environment. Similar to before, it was up to the player to decide when he was ready to begin the data-capture process. Another non-controlled variable was the pitcher's mitt, which varied from one subject to another in size and weight.

Toolbox 1.3: Data Analysis—Correlation

The r^2 values for the large samples involving the full data set (n = 99, N = 33) were evaluated, using the accepted standards:

-0.09 → +0.09	No correlation
+/- 0.10 → 0.29	Weak correlation
+/- 0.30 → 0.49	Medium strength
+/- 0.50 → 0.74	Strong
+/- 0.75 → 1.00	Very strong correlation

Some of the correlations within our experiments were taken for the whole data set, and were used to look for mechanical relationships that can be generalized to the population. On the other hand, some cases existed in which a personal signature could act as a confounding variable. In those instances, we looked at within-player correlations, in addition to those for the whole group. In other words, we looked for personal player correlations for the three types of pitches—fastball, breaking ball, and off-speed—in order to attempt to control the influence of signature. It should be kept in mind, however, that for the within-player correlations to have any value, the effect had to be very strong, because of the miniscule sample size (n = 3, N = 1). As a result, we sorted the players into groups, according to the strength of the measured relationship, and based on the sample size. Only the most extreme values, however, were useful when we broke down the within-player correlations, since we were measuring the relationship between just three pitches.

FOUNDATION FITNESS

USC Baseball Strength and Conditioning 2008 Off-Season Gym Program*:

Monday/Friday—Endurance Days

■ Warm-up and integrated strength and flexibility:
- Stationary bike   10 minutes
- Foundation strength (vertical and horizontal positions):
  - ✓ Five repetitions, three positions (straight, supinate, pronate), three movements (linear, circular, angular)
  - ✓ Isometric contraction 30 seconds per position

■ Dynamic warm-up:
- Knee tuck   10 steps
- Internal hip rotation   10 steps
- External hip rotation   10 steps
- Frontal quad   10 steps
- Single-leg toe touch   10 steps
- Lunge w/rotation (f/b)   10 steps
- Side lunge   10 steps
- Stationary spider   10 steps
- Inch worm   10 steps

■ Balance:
- Single-leg toe tap on airex pad (f/l/b)   10 steps
- Single-leg airplane rotation on airex pad 15 reps
- Single-leg squat on airex pad   15 reps
- Physio-ball balance   3 min

*Jackson Crowther, Conditioning Coach, RDRBI, and USC Trojan Baseball

■ Core (isometric):

• Prone hold	2 min
• Superman hold	1 min
• Side hold (l/r)	30 sec
• Table-top hold (three positions)	1 min per position

■ Core stabilization:

• Mountain climber	20 seconds
• Physio-ball flutter kick (l/r)	10 reps
• Physio-ball walkout	10 reps
• Physio-ball scapular pinch push-up	20 reps
• Physio-ball rollout	20 reps

■ Joint integrity (upper/lower extremities):

• Elastic-tubing exercise	5 reps/3 positions
• Light-dumbbell exercise	5 reps/3 positions
• Medicine-ball wall throw (wide)	100 reps
• Medicine-ball wall throw (narrow)	100 reps
• Medicine-ball, single-arm wall throw (l/r)	100 reps
• Flex-t lunge (forward/back/side)	10 steps
• Flex-t step up (f/b in three positions w/feet)	10 steps
• Open clam w/thera band (abduction)	20 reps
• Close clam w/12′ foam roller (adduction)	15 sec hold/15 sec pulse

■ Strength circuit program (one set x 15 repetitions)

■ Lower body (five repetitions/three positions):
- • Dumbbell step-up into a back lunge (l/r)
- • Walking dumbbell lunge (f/b)
- • Dumbbell squats w/physio-ball
- • Leg press
- • Single-leg press
- • Leg curl
- • Single-leg curl
- • Calf raise
- • Single-leg calf raise

■ Upper body/torso (five repetitions/three positions):
- • Horizontal pull-up
- • Vertical pull-up

- Reverse pec deck (posterior)
- Pec deck (anterior)
- Lat pulldown (90°, 45°, 180° body planes)
- Seated pull/extension
- Seated machine press
- Seated machine row
- Alternating dumbbell press w/physio-ball
- Single leg dumbbell row
- Alternating dumbbell incline press w/physio-ball
- Cable crossover

■ Upper extremities (15 repetitions):
- Dumbbell shrug (linear/circular)
- Alernating dumbbell curl
- Alternating hammer curl
- Single-arm tricep kickback
- Dumbbell tricep extension
- Forearm curl
- Forearm reverse curl
- Forearm rotation
- Forearm dumbbell squeezer
- Raquetball squeezer (100 squeezes)

■ Aerobic training:
- 30-minutes on an elliptical machine—15 minutes forward/15 minutes backward, at level 7 resistance or greater
- 30-minutes on a treadmill—15 minutes striding forward at 7 mph or greater speed/15 minutes striding backward at 3.5 mph or less

USC Baseball Strength and Conditioning 2008 Off-Season Gym Program:

Tuesday/Thursday—Agility/Rotational Training Days

■ Warm-up and integrated strength and flexibility:
- Stationary bike   10 minutes

- Foundation strength (vertical and horizontal positions)
- Five repetitions, three positions (straight, supinate, pronate), three movements (linear, circular, angular)
- Isometric contraction, 30 seconds per position

■ Dynamic warm-up:
- Knee tuck   10 steps
- Internal hip rotation   10 steps
- External hip rotation   10 steps
- Frontal quad   10 steps
- Single-leg toe touch   10 steps
- Lunge w/rotation (f/b)   10 steps
- Side lunge   10 steps
- Stationary spider   10 steps
- Inch worm   10 steps

■ Agility:
- Single-leg hop (f/b)   10 reps
- Lateral hop (f/b)   10 reps
- Squat jump   10 reps
- Lateral-bound toe reach   10 reps
- Saggital lunge   10 reps

■ Balance:
- Penny pick-up w/airex pad (sequence 1)   10 reps
- Penny pick-up w/airex pad (sequence 2)   10 reps
- Bent-knee raise w/airex pad   15 reps

■ Rotational training of the kinetic chain:
- Medicine-ball lunges w/rotation (f/b)   10 reps
- Medicine-ball side lunges w/rotation (l/r)   10 reps
- Medicine-ball seated twist   30 sec
- Medicine-ball abdominal sequence   5 reps/3 movements
- Medicine-ball stand up chops (l/r)   15 reps
- Medicine-ball stand up twist   15 reps
- Medicine-ball stand up side scoops (l/r)   15 reps
- Medicine-ball half kneeling scoops   15 reps
- Cable staggered single-arm pulldown (l/r)   15 reps
- Cable staggered single-arm row (l/r)   15 reps
- Cable squat into rotational reach (l/r)   15 reps

■ Anaerobic training:
- Heavy jump rope (4-5 lbs)   3 sets/75 reps
- Interval bike sprint   10 each, 30 sec on/30 sec off

■ Aerobic training:
- Stationary bike   20 minutes

USC Baseball Strength and Conditioning 2008 Off-Season Gym Program

Wednesday—Strength Day

■ Warm up and integrated strength and flexibility:

- Stationary bike   10 minutes
    - ✓ Foundation strength (vertical and horizontal positions):
    - ✓ Five repetitions, three positions (straight, supinate, pronate), three movements (linear, circular, angular)
    - ✓ Isometric contraction, 30 seconds per position

■ Dynamic warm-up:

- Knee tuck   10 steps
- Internal hip rotation   10 steps
- External hip rotation   10 steps
- Frontal quad   10 steps
- Single-leg toe touch   10 steps
- Lunge w/rotation (f/b)   10 steps
- Side lunge   10 steps
- Stationary spider   10 steps
- Inch worm   10 steps

■ Balance:

- Single-leg toe tap on an airex pad (f/l/b)   10 steps
- Single-leg airplane rotation on an airex pad 15 reps
- Single-leg squat on an airex pad   15 reps
- Physio-ball balance   3 min

■ Core (isometric):

- Prone hold   2 min
- Superman hold   1 min
- Side-up hold (l/r)   30 sec
- Table-top hold (three positions)   1 min, per position

■ Core stabilization:

- Mountain climber   20 seconds
- Physio-ball flutter kick (l/r)   10 reps
- Physio-ball walkout   10 reps
- Physio-ball scapular pinch push-up   20 reps
- Physio-ball roll out   20 reps

- ■ Joint integrity (upper/lower extremities):
  - Elastic-tubing exercises — 5 reps/3 pos
  - Light dumbbell exercises — 5 reps/3 pos
  - Medicine-ball wall throw (wide) — 100 reps
  - Medicine-ball wall throw (narrow) — 100 reps
  - Medicine-ball single arm wall throw (l/r) — 100 reps
  - Flex-t lunge (forward/back/side) — 10 steps
  - Flex-t step-up (f/b in three positions w/feet) — 10 steps
  - Open clam w/thera band (abduction) — 20 reps
  - Close clam w/12' foam roller (adduction) — 15 sec hold/15 sec pulse

- ■ Strength circuit program (one set x six repetitions)

- ■ Lower body (two repetitions/three positions):
  - Dumbbell step-up into a back lunge (l/r)
  - Walking dumbbell lunge (f/b)
  - Dumbbell squats w/ physio-ball
  - Leg press
  - Single-leg press
  - Leg curl
  - Single-leg curl
  - Calf raise
  - Single-leg calf raise

- ■ Upper body/torso (two repetitions/three positions):
  - Horizontal pull-up
  - Vertical pull-up
  - Reverse pec deck (posterior)
  - Pec deck (anterior)
  - Lat pulldown (90°, 45°, 180° body planes)
  - Seated pulls/extension
  - Seated machine press
  - Seated machine row
  - Alternating dumbbell press w/physio-ball
  - Single leg dumbbell row
  - Alternating dumbbell-incline press w/physio-ball
  - Cable crossover

- ■ Upper extremities (six repetitions):
  - Dumbbell shrug (linear/circular)
  - Alternating dumbbell curl
  - Alternating hammer curl

- Single-arm tricep kickback
- Dumbbell tricep extension
- Forearm curl
- Forearm reverse curl
- Forearm dumbbell squeezer
- Racquetball squeezer (100 squeezes)

■ Aerobic training:
- 30 minutes on an elliptical machine—15 minutes forward/15 minutes backward at level 7 resistance or greater
- 30 minutes on a treadmill—15 minutes striding forward at 7 mph or greater speed/15 minutes striding forward at 3.5 mph or less

USC Baseball Strength and Conditioning 2008 Off-Season Gym Program

Saturday—Flexibility/Cardio Day

■ Warm-up and integrated strength and flexibility:
- Stationary bike   10 minutes
  - ✓ Foundation strength (vertical and horizontal positions)
  - ✓ Five repetitions, three positions (straight, supinate, pronate), three movements (linear, circular, angular)
  - ✓ Isometric contraction 30 seconds per position

■ Dynamic warm-up:
- Knee tuck   10 steps
- Internal hip rotation   10 steps
- External hip rotation   10 steps
- Frontal quad   10 steps
- Single-leg toe touch   10 steps
- Lunge w/rotation (f/b)   10 steps
- Side lunge   10 steps
- Stationary spider   10 steps
- Inch worm   10 steps

■ Aerobic training:
- 40 minutes on a treadmill—20 minutes running forward/20 minutes striding backward

■ Warm-down stretching

NUTRITION INFORMATION AND GUIDELINES TO PREPARE, COMPETE, AND REPAIR/RECOVER

Appendix C

The Rod Dedeaux Research Baseball Institute has collaborated with world renowned nutritionist Robert Yang to provide the most effective and applicable information on food intake. Essentially, our goal is to provide our athletes with a nutritional template that conforms to a lifestyle, rather than a temporary diet. In turn, our objective is to ensure that each athlete has a general understanding in the areas of hydration, food valuation, timing of food intake, quantity vs. quality, and macro/micro supplementation.

Due to the ongoing self-imposed battles concerning what foods and liquids should and should not go into our bodies, it is important that each athlete has a food template that can be understood and followed routinely. The following four-tiered food pyramid is a template that each athlete should be able to manage and maintain with enough planning and self-discipline.

■ **Tier #1:** Despite the fact that water is vital to optimal health, the majority of young athletes prefer sport drinks and sodas as their means of hydration over the course of the day. Proper daily hydration should comprise of one-half an athlete's bodyweight in ounces. A volume of 20-24 ounces should be taken first thing in the morning, followed by smaller volumes throughout the course of the day. In addition, it is recommended that an athlete choose a water source that consists of 200-300 parts per million of total dissolve solids (TDS). Artesian and spring waters (e.g., Evian, Trinity, or Fiji) are some of the best options, in that regard. On the other hand, if convenience and budget limit the use of these brands, a great way to fortify standard drinking water is to add a small pinch of unrefined gray Celtic sea salt (80+ trace minerals) to it. The following significant facts reinforce the importance of water consumption:

- Case studies have shown that one percent of dehydration significantly impairs cognitive function.
- Water is essential for the transport of nutrients and hormones, the lubrication of connective tissue and joints, the maintenance of energy levels, nerve conduction, proper digestion, and optimal muscular efficiency.
- Over the duration that an individual sleeps, the lack of hydration puts the body in a dehydrated state in the morning. As such, one-fourth of a person's total water intake should be in the morning.
- Individuals should avoid drinking large amounts of water during meals. In fact, an excessive water intake can impair the dilution of digestive enzymes and the absorption of nutrients. Less than 12 fl oz. of water with meals is recommended.

■ **Tier #2:** No one has seen processed foods grow from a tree. Then, why do people eat them? The United States has an immense problem with obesity. Ignorance and the quality guidelines set forth by the US government to sustain economies of scale have created an epidemic in this country that is affecting the preadolescence demographic group. Quality whole foods, which are completely free of additives, preservatives, hormones, etc., should comprise Tier #2. As such, it is recommended that athletes eat whole foods that are organic, natural, and uncooked (fruits and vegetables) whenever possible. Over-cooking kills food and in turn degrades the nutritional value of the food, which is why fruits and vegetables should be consumed in raw form, whenever possible. Engineered foods (e.g., protein powder/protein bars) should only be consumed whenever real food is unavailable. The functional metabolism that is essential to support an athlete's work/play environment and to help ensure optimal physiological function should meet the following parameters:

- Food combinations should be based on a 40:30:30 ratio. Forty percent should be comprised of low-glycemic carbohydrates. Thirty percent should consist of protein, and thirty percent should encompass essential fats.
- Food intake must stabilize blood-sugar levels. A blood sugar that is slightly rising will have a cascading effect on stabilizing insulin levels, which in turn will inhibit cortisol hormonal release (causation of stress). As such, starches should always be combined with protein, fiber, and fats to lessen insulin responses.
- The times and quantities of each meal should always be prioritized. A balanced breakfast (breaking the fast) is essentially the most important meal of the day, because it sets an individual's daily metabolic rate. Hydration and food selection should be the priority of the morning every day. Caloric intake should often coincide with the anticipated level of

physical activity in which the athlete will participate. Large meals should be consumed if strenuous workloads are expected, while small meals should be eaten prior to bedtime, given the anticipated level of inactivity.

- Having variety in food consumption should also be prioritized. Athletes should try not to eat the same food that is prepared the same way in a 72-hour period, which will help minimize the likelihood of food allergies and inflammation occurring. It is important to note that people are foragers as a species. The more variations of food eaten, the more variations of vitamins and minerals are ingested.

Carbohydrate intake should predominately be from organic fruits and vegetables that are prepared either raw or lightly steamed. Dark green and bright pigmented vegetables should be consumed. Because fruit contains a lot of sugar, it should be eaten in moderation daily. It is strongly suggested that athletes stay away from foods that are gluten-rich, made of grains (breads, cereals, bagels, muffins, etc.), and are high-glycemic. A glycemic index score of less than 100 should be a baseline. Information on the glycemic index and the food tables is available at www.glycemicindex.com.

The main source of protein should be derived from animals which are pasture-fed, free-range, and/or breed under stringent USDA organic guidelines (e.g., eggs that are free-range without antibiotics or hormones). Proteins are vital in sustaining lean-muscle mass. Not only is protein brain food, it also supports stimulation of neurotransmitters. As such, individuals should try to intake one gram of protein per one pound of lean-muscle mass per day (28 grams = 1 oz). In turn, they should be very careful of too much protein intake due to the formation of uric and lactic acid.

Although essential fatty acids are often misunderstood, they are vital to optimal physiological health. Conventional wisdom has minimized fat in the American diet. As such, the body needs omega 3, 6, and 9 for optimal organ function, joint health, inflammation/anti-inflammation responses, useful energy, and balanced brain and blood chemistry. Whole foods should be cooked in bacon grease, butter, or coconut oil. Olive oil should be used as a dressing for salads or foods that have already been cooked. The use of canola oil, corn oil, cotton seed oil, soybean oil, and olive oil should be discouraged when cooking. High temperatures induce trans-fats with these oils. Mixed nuts, flax seed, olives, avocados, and cold-pressed olive oil are a few examples of smart fats that should be incorporated in healthy diets.

Engineered foods are becoming increasingly popular among athletes. As such, eat protein bars that are cold-pressed and are labeled with the following: free of gluten, 100% organic, alkaline forming, and free of refined sugars and GMOs. In that regard, we recommend three bars, when natural food is not readily available: a Living Fuel product that is called the Cocochia Bar (www.livingfuel.com), which is an energy bar made of high-grade organic ingredients; an Organic Food Bar (www.organicfoodbar.com), which is a product that is a meal-replacement bar made of 100% organic ingredients that have not been altered by the cooking process; and a Cliff Balance Bar, which can serve as a centerpiece for a complete breakfast. All three products taste great and support healthy bodily function.

■ **Tier #3:** This level involves the supplementation of the athletes' macro-nutrient intake. In reality, six-to-seven servings of fruits and vegetables are virtually impossible to consume on a daily basis, which is why every athlete must take additional supplements. The FDA recommends, at the bare minimum, that a multi-vitamin be taken on a daily basis. Although food should be used as the main foundation, there should be fortification of the macro-food intake with a multi-vitamin, a mineral supplement, and a fish oil supplement that is free of PCBs and heavy metals.

■ **Tier #4:** This level caps the food pyramid. It involves anything that is added to address the special needs of the athlete. Aside from the supplements that an athlete takes in Tier #3, an individual may need more of a particular supplement to either address specific reparative properties an athlete may have or serve as a legal performance enhancement. Examples of supplements that specifically pertain to this level would include the following:

- Joint support: Glucosamine/chondroitin, SAM, MSM, and wobenzyme
- Recovery: Creatine, glutamine, NO2, and sodium bicarbonate (baking soda)

Suggested References and Recommended Reading

Callis, J., Lingo, W., and Manuel, J. (2008). (Eds.) *Baseball America Almanac 2008*. Durham, NC: Baseball America Inc.

Carroll, W. (June 5, 2003). Under the Knife: The Usual Suspects. *Baseball Prospectus*. http://www.baseballprospectus.com/article.php?articleid=1965

Dewan, J. (2006). *The Fielding Bible: Breakthrough analysis of Major League Baseball defense – by team and player*. Skokie, IL: ACTA Sports

Fox, D. (June 5, 2007). Schrodinger's Bat: Searching for the Gyroball. *Baseball Prospectus*. http://www.baseballprospectus.com/article.php?articleid=6419

Goldman, S., and Kahrl, C. (2008). (Eds.) *Baseball Prospectus 2008*. New York, NY: Plume, of Penguin Group

Goldstein, K. (Dec 18, 2006). Chat with Kevin Goldstein. *Baseball Prospectus*. http://www.baseballprospectus.com/chat/chat.php?chatId=248

Goldstein, K., and Plugh, M. (Sep 22, 2007). Future Shock: Hawaiian Winter Baseball Preview. *Baseball Prospectus*. http://www.baseballprospectus.com/article.php?articleid=6741

Gomez, C. (May 1, 2007). If It Ain't Broke. *The Hardball Times*. http://www.hardballtimes.com/main/article/if-it-aint-brokea-video-review-of-phil-hughes-mechanical-changes/

House, T., Heil, G., and Johnson, S. (2006). *The Art & Science of Pitching*. Monterey, CA: Coaches Choice Publishers

House, T. (2007). *Fastball Fitness: How to Train to Throw with Real Velocity*. Monterey, CA: Coaches Choice Publishers

Huckabay, G. (May 5, 2007). Hope and Faith: How the San Francisco Giants Can Win the World Series. *Baseball Prospectus*. http://www.baseballprospectus.com/article.php?articleid=5933

Huckabay, G. (Sep 4, 2007). 6-4-3: For What You Are About to Receive. *Baseball Prospectus*. http://www.baseballprospectus.com/article.php?articleid=6666

Husband, P. (2006). *Downright Filthy Pitching*. www.hittingisaguess.com

James, B. (2008). *The Bill James Handbook, 2008*. Skokie, IL: ACTA Sports

Jazayerli, R. (June 19, 1998). Pitcher Abuse Points: A New Way to Measure Pitcher Abuse. *Baseball Prospectus*. http://www.baseballprospectus.com/article.php?articleid=148

Passan, J. (Feb 21, 2007). Finally, the gyroball mystery solved. *Yahoo! Sports*. http://sports.yahoo.com/mlb/news?slug=jp-mlb_07_gyroball022107

Penn, N. (Sep 2006). How to Build the Perfect Batter. *GQ*. (pp. 296-305).

Silver, N., and Carroll, W. (Feb 26, 2003). The Injury Nexus: A Look at Pitcher Injuries. *Baseball Prospectus*. http://www.baseballprospectus.com/article.php?articleid=1658

Woolner, K. (May 21, 2002). Analyzing PAP (Part One): The Immediate Impact of High Pitch Counts on Pitcher Effectiveness. *Baseball Prospectus*. http://www.baseballprospectus.com/article.php?articleid=1477#hist

Wright, C., and House, T. (1989). *The Diamond Appraised*. (pp. 15, 55-58, 243, 248). New York, NY: Fireside, of Simon and Schuster, Inc.

Baseball-reference website for stats: www.baseball-reference.com

Photo Credits

Section 1	Rich Pilling/MLB Photos/Getty Images
Figure 3-2a	Lisa Blumenfeld/Getty Images
Figure 3-2b	Jed Jacobsohn/Getty Images
Section 2	Scott A. Schneider/Getty Images
Figure 6-1	Stephen Dunn/Getty Images
Figure 6-3	Mark Cunningham/MLB Photos/Getty Images
Figure 7-1	Brian Bahr/Getty Images
Section 3	Louis DeLuca/MLB Photos/Getty Images
Figure 9-2a	Al Bello/Getty Images
Figure 9-2b	Scott Boehm/Getty Images
Figure 9-2c	Jonathan Daniel/Getty Images
Figure 9-2d	Jed Jacobsohn/Getty Images
Figure 9-2e	Diamond Images/Getty Images
Section 4	Rich Pilling/MLB Photos/Getty Images
Figure 13-1a	Steve Grayson/WireImage
Figure 13-1b	Rich Pilling/MLB Photos/Getty Images
Figure 13-1c	Jonathan Daniel/Getty Images
Figure 13-2a	Ezra Shaw/Getty Images
Figure 13-2b	Lisa Blumenfeld/Getty Images
Figure 13-3a	Rich Pilling/MLB Photos/Getty Images
Figure 13-3b	Rich Pilling/MLB Photos/Getty Images
Figure 13-4	Richard Schultz/WireImage
Figure 13-5	G Fiume/Getty Images
Figure 13-7a	Ron Vesely/MLB Photos/Getty Images
Figure 13-7b	Elsa/Getty Images
Figure 13-8	Jim McIsaac/Getty Images
Figure 14-1a	Rich Pilling/MLB Photos/Getty Images
Figure 14-1b	Ezra Shaw/Getty Images
Figure 15-1a	Chris Trotman/Getty Images
Figure 15-1b	Jim McIsaac/Getty Images
Figure 15-1c	Otto Greule Jr/Getty Images
Figure 15-1d	Mark Cunningham/MLB Photos/Getty Images
Figure 15-1e	Bruce Kluckhohn/MLB Photos/Getty Images
Figure 16-1	Brian Bahr/Getty Images
Figure 16-2a	John Williamson/MLB Photos/Getty Images
Figure 16-2b	Brad Mangin/MLB Photos/Getty Images
Section 5a	Rick Stewart/Getty Images
Section 5b	Ron Vesely/MLB Photos/Getty Images
Figure 19-1a	Greg Fiume/Getty Images
Figure 19-1b	Scott Boehm/Getty Images
Figure 19-1c	Jonathan Daniel/Getty Images
Figure 19-1d	Tom Hauck/Allsport
Figure 19-1e	Michael Zagaris/MLB Photos/Getty Images

About the Authors

Tom House is considered by many to be the "father of modern pitching mechanics." He is the founder of The Rod Dedeaux Research and Baseball Institute (RDRBI) and the co-founder of the National Pitching Association (NPA). The RDRBI and NPA are renowned for their health and performance research and their development and use of three-dimensional analysis of human movement. The investigative efforts of both organizations also address the physical preparation and training necessary to support athletes in movement, including detailing the metabolic requirements of proper nutrition to fuel human activity and enhancing the abiity of athletes to engage in competition by refining their mental/emotional management skills.

Tom pitched on the professional level from 1967 to 1979 for the Atlanta Braves, Boston Red Sox, and Seattle Mariners. From 1980 to 1997, he coached for the Houston Astros, San Diego Padres, Texas Rangers, and Chiba Lotte Marines (Japan), as well as in Latin America. On the amateur level, Tom is an information and instruction coordinator for 12 baseball academies across the United States and Canada. He directly accesses 8,000-10,000 players, coaches, and parents per year in clinic settings. He travels the world as an international consultant, performance analyst, and sports psychologist. Tom is currently the pitching coach at the University of Southern California, serves as an advisor with both the American Sports Medicine Institute and the Titleist Performance Institute, and gives seminars for the American College of Sports Medicine.

Tom and his wife, Marie, live in Del Mar, California.

Doug Thorburn is an ambitious student of baseball research and player development, blending his professional experience in coaching, scouting, performance analysis, baseball operations, and sports-business management. He arrived at the National Pitching Association in 2005 as an intern from the inaugural class of the Sports M.B.A. program at San Diego State University. Since then, he has taken the lead role with high-speed motion analysis and the NPA model for pitching biomechanics. Thorburn's subjective experience in the bullpen and his thorough knowledge of the objective tools involved in motion analysis provide him with an impeccable skill set for his role at the NPA. His mastery of his craft enables him to help guide the research that is being conducted at the NPA with an eye toward identifying the optimal training methodology and achieving maximum functional results. Prior to joining the NPA and earning his M.B.A., Doug worked with the front office of the Sacramento River Cats, and earned a B.S. in cognitive neuropsychology from the University of California San Diego.